IN THE CROSSFIRE

Adventures of a
Vietnamese Revolutionary

Ngo Van

IN THE CROSSFIRE

Adventures of a
Vietnamese Revolutionary

Edited by Ken Knabb and Hélène Fleury

Translated from the French by Hélène Fleury,
Hilary Horrocks, Ken Knabb and Naomi Sager

AK PRESS

In the Crossfire is a translation of Ngo Van's *Au pays de la Cloche fêlée* (Paris: L'Insomniaque, 2000) and of excerpts from Ngo Van's *Au pays d'Héloïse* (L'Insomniaque, 2005). It has been edited by Ken Knabb and Hélène Fleury and translated by Hélène Fleury, Hilary Horrocks, Ken Knabb and Naomi Sager.

ISBN 978-1-84935-013-6
Library of Congress Control Number: 2010925754

AK Press
674-A 23rd St.
Oakland, CA 94612
www.akpress.org

AK Press
P.O. Box 12766
Edinburgh, Scotland EH8 9YE
www.akuk.com

Cover illustration: *Saigon Insurrection 1945* by Ngo Van
Cover design: Kate Khatib

The paintings following page 168 are by Ngo Van. Most of the other illustrations are from the original French editions of Ngo Van's works.

Printed in Canada

CONTENTS

INTRODUCTION / vii

NGO VAN, RELAYER OF LIVING HISTORY / xiii

MAPS / XX

I. In the Land of the Cracked Bell
   Preface / 1
   1. Arrest / 3
   2. Childhood / 17
   3. Years of Apprenticeship / 40
   4. In the Central Prison / 67
   5. From One Prison to Another /89
   6. In the Mekong Delta /103
   7. Caught in a Crossfire / 119
   8. Toward Other Shores / 140
   9. And My Friends? / 151

II. In the Land of Héloïse
   1. Worker in the Promised Land / 183
   2. New Radical Perspectives / 197

Articles
   A Factory Occupation in May 1968 / 207
   On Third World Struggles / 217
   Reflections on the Vietnam War / 219

TRANSLATORS' NOTES / 223

NOTE ON STALINISM AND TROTSKYISM / 234

CHRONOLOGY / 238

BIBLIOGRAPHY / 246

INDEX / 250

Note on the Present Edition

In the Crossfire is a translation of Ngo Van's *Au pays de la Cloche fêlée* (Paris, 2000) and of excerpts from Ngo Van's *Au pays d'Héloïse* (Paris, 2005), including three articles reprinted in the latter volume. An initial English translation of *Au pays de la Cloche fêlée* was made by Hilary Horrocks; the translation that appears in the present book is a revised version made by Hélène Fleury, Ken Knabb and Naomi Sager. Ken translated the selections from *Au pays d'Héloïse* and the three articles (revising earlier versions of the articles by Brian Pearce and Jackie Reuss). Ken and Hélène prepared the introductions and end matter. Ken then reviewed the whole project and prepared the book for publication, with technical assistance from Charles Weigl.

Hélène Fleury (Paris) collaborated with Ngo Van on his later writings. She is also the author of a study of Shelley: *La Mascarade de l'Anarchie,* and has participated in various radical publications.

Hilary Horrocks (Edinburgh) is a writer and editor. In the 1980s she also ran a radical bookshop in Glasgow. She met Ngo Van in the 1990s and has written several articles about his life and work.

Ken Knabb (Berkeley) has translated numerous works by Guy Debord and the Situationist International. His writings and translations are online at his "Bureau of Public Secrets" website: www.bopsecrets.org.

Naomi Sager (New York) has since the 1940s been associated with individuals and groups close to the workers council movement: Paul Mattick, Maximilien Rubel, Noir et Rouge, ICO, and more recently Ngo Van and Hélène Fleury.

INTRODUCTION

"History is written by the victors." With the increasing spectacular-ization of modern society, this truism has become truer than ever. The most radical revolts are not only physically crushed, they are falsified, trivialized, and buried under a constant barrage of super-ficial and ephemeral bits of "information," to the point that most people do not even know they happened.

Ngo Van's *In the Crossfire* is among the most illuminating revela-tions of this repressed and hidden history, worthy of a place along-side such works as Voline's *The Unknown Revolution* and Harold Isaacs's *The Tragedy of the Chinese Revolution*. It is also a very moving human document: dramatic political events are interwoven with intimate personal concerns, just as they always are in reality. In this respect, Van's book is perhaps more akin to Orwell's *Homage to Catalonia* or Victor Serge's *Memoirs of a Revolutionary*.

The two-stage Vietnam war against French and then American occupation (1945–1975) is still fairly well known; but almost no one knows anything about the long and complex struggles that pre-ceded it, including the fact that many of those struggles were in-spired by an indigenous Trotskyist movement that was often more popular and more influential than the rival Stalinist movement under Ho Chi Minh. While Ho's Communist Party slavishly followed the constantly shifting policy lines ordered by his masters in the Krem-lin (which often called for alliances with the native landowners and bourgeoisie in the name of "national unity," or at times even with the French colonial regime when France happened to be allied with Russia), the Vietnamese Trotskyists expressed more consistently radical perspectives. The situation was somewhat analogous to what was going on in Spain during the same period. In both cases a radi-cal popular movement was fighting against foreign and reaction-ary forces while being stabbed in the back by the Stalinists. One significant difference was that in Spain the popular movement was predominantly anarchist, whereas anarchism was virtually unknown in Vietnam.* [See Translators' Notes, beginning on p. 223.] Many Vietnamese rebels thus understandably saw the Trotskyist movement as the only alternative, the only movement fighting simultaneously against colonialism, capitalism and Stalinism.

In any case, spontaneous popular revolts often bypassed whatever ideologies were officially in play, implicitly calling in question the whole social order even when their explicit demands were much more minimal. What stands out is the readiness of ordinary people to create their own forms of action—workers forming underground unions and carrying out illegal strikes, peasants seizing land and forming "soviets," prisoners organizing resistance networks, women breaking out of their traditional roles, students and teachers putting their learning to subversive use, neighborhoods organizing themselves into "people's committees," streetcar workers creating an independent militia, and most astonishing of all, 30,000 coal miners forming a workers-council "Commune" that manages to hold out for three months before being destroyed by the Stalinists. These are not the proverbial "masses" meekly waiting for some leader or "vanguard party" to tell them what to do. They are participants in one of the most broad-based and persevering revolutionary movements of the twentieth century.

Ngo Van took part in that movement as a young man, and in his old age, half a century later, he became the preeminent chronicler of its remarkable victories and tragic defeats.

In Part I of this book Van recounts his experiences growing up in a peasant village; working as a teenager in Saigon; discovering the true nature of the colonial system; becoming aware of movements that were fighting it; cautiously seeking out other dissidents; attending clandestine meetings; establishing underground networks; disseminating radical publications; organizing strikes and protests; taking part in insurrections and partisan warfare; being jailed and tortured by the French; and facing the murderous betrayals by the Stalinists, who systematically liquidated the Trotskyists and all the other oppositional movements in the aftermath of World War II.

Constantly harassed by the French colonial police in Saigon and

risking assassination by the Stalinists if he ventured into the countryside, Van emigrated to France in 1948. As described in Part II,
he became a factory worker, struggled with tuberculosis, took up
painting, and discovered new political perspectives. His encounters with anarchists, councilists and libertarian Marxists reaffirmed
the most radical aspects of his previous experiences while verifying
his increasing suspicions that there were significant problems with
Trotskyism as well as Stalinism. From that point on, Van carried out
his activities as an independent radical more or less in the council-
communist tradition, whether in taking part in rank-and-file worker
struggles or in writing articles on East Asian politics and history.

After his retirement in 1978, Van devoted the next seventeen
years to researching and writing his monumental history, *Vietnam
1920–1945: révolution et contre-révolution sous la domination coloniale*. Following the publication of that book in 1995, he wrote a
parallel autobiographical account of the same period: *Au pays de la
Cloche fêlée* (2000). When that was done, he returned to his more
"objective" history of modern Vietnam. (I might mention here that
in addition to his works on Vietnamese history, he also authored two
studies of radical currents in ancient China and put together a collection of Vietnamese folktales. See the Bibliography for information
on these and other publications.)

After completing the second volume of his Vietnam history, *Le
Joueur de flûte et l'Oncle Hô: Vietnam 1945–2005*, Van returned
to his autobiography, envisioning a continuation that would cover
his years in France. Unfortunately he did not live long enough to
complete this latter project. He died January 2, 2005, at the age of
92. Later the same year his publishers, Insomniaque, issued a memorial volume, *Au pays d'Héloïse*, comprising the few chapters he
had completed (mostly about his life during the 1950s) along with
several articles, numerous photographs and a selection of his lovely
paintings, many of which are reproduced in the present volume.

* * *

Anticolonial movements have long been a source of political
blackmail. People who become aware of the horrors of colonialism usually know little else about the countries involved and have

often been ready to applaud any purportedly "progressive" leadership, supporting practices they would never dream of defending if they took place in a modern Western country. Radical social critique has been discouraged by the argument that criticizing even the most brutal Third World regimes is "playing into the hands of the imperialist powers." Moreover, in many cases apologists have been able to argue that despite regrettable defects, those regimes are the only possibility, there are no apparent alternatives.

But this is not always the case. Readers of *The Tragedy of the Chinese Revolution* are aware that China did not have to go Stalinist (i.e. Maoist); there were other currents and other strategies that might have led to different results. The same is true of many other countries, including Vietnam. Ho Chi Minh's Communist Party was not the only serious oppositional movement; it ultimately made itself so only by ruthlessly destroying all its rivals. Ngo Van's books bear witness that there were many other possibilities.

There is nothing eccentric or exaggerated about those books. They are scrupulously accurate and thoroughly documented, and you can find verifications of most of the material in many other reliable sources. But to do so you would have to search long and deeply, wading through the immense mass of lies and distortions that have surrounded this topic. Van has brought it all together into a coherent and comprehensive account in his two-volume historical chronicle (as yet untranslated), then narrated the same events in a briefer and more personal manner in the autobiography that we are presenting here.

* * *

I met Ngo Van in Paris in 2001, along with his friend Hélène Fleury, and during the next few weeks saw them several more times. Although I could hardly get to know Van all that well in such a short period of time, we almost immediately became very dear friends.

Those who had the pleasure of knowing him will agree that despite the horrors he had endured and his lack of illusions about the violent nature of the present social order, Van was the sweetest and most gentle person one can imagine. His rebelliousness arose not only out of a justified rage at poverty and meanness and oppression,

but out of his profound love of life. He was an all-round and wide-ranging person: a *bon vivant* at home in the lively give-and-take of Parisian bars and cafés, but also capable of quietly appreciating nature and solitude; a factory worker who was at the same time an artist and a connoisseur of classic literature; a radical agitator who was also a radical historian; a resolutely antireligious person who was nevertheless graced with an almost Buddhist stoicism and equanimity and who ultimately became a scholar of East Asian religious movements; a modest, unassuming man of the people who yet possessed a great nobility of character. It was a pleasure to know him, and it's been a pleasure to work with Hélène and the other translators in presenting his work to English-speaking readers.

KEN KNABB

Ngo Van beside the Seine in Paris (1970s)

NGO VAN,
RELAYER OF LIVING HISTORY

Ngo Van lived through almost the entire twentieth century (1912–2005) and his life and work are intimately intertwined with the revolutionary hopes and conflicts of that century.

In his writings he speaks not as an academically "neutral" historian, but as a participant actively engaged in the events he recounts; not as a "party spokesperson," but as a humble individual struggling alongside so many other anonymous, unknown persons, the "wretched of the earth" who are also the salt of the earth, fraternal, generous and inventive. With them he experiences those sublime moments when people unite to attack the sources of their exploitation and enslavement; when they break through the bounds of the "possible" and strive to create a life worthy of their deepest dreams and aspirations. With them he also experiences the merciless repression the established powers invariably resort to when they sense that their system is in danger.

After emigrating to France in 1948, Van continued that struggle as a resolutely independent individual, without label or party, in groups of councilist revolutionaries and alongside other rebellious workers in the factories.

It was a time when anticolonial movements, in the colonized countries and the West alike, were dominated by the ideology of "Third World-ism"—an ideology that obscured the real enemies while weakening or paralyzing truly radical social criticism. Faced with this situation, Van sought to transmit the real, hitherto unwritten history of Vietnam, to challenge and refute the official histories propagated by the "masters of the present"* and uncritically parroted in Europe and America by the self-proclaimed supporters of the "struggles of the Vietnamese people." Following his retirement in 1978, and with the constant support of Sophie Moen (his partner from 1952 until her death in 1994), Van devoted the next seventeen years to researching and writing *Vietnam 1920–1945: révolution et contre-révolution sous la domination coloniale* (1995). In that book he brought back to life the era of fierce class struggles that preceded the two Vietnam wars, a period when the workers and peasants believed that putting an end to colonialism was inseparable from a social revolution. In so doing he also exposed the devious maneuvers of the Communist Party as it seized control over those struggles through double-dealing, lies, intimidation and murder.

I first met Van in November 1995, and there was an immediate rapport between us—an alchemy of elective affinities and of shared dreams and convictions. Having just finished *Vietnam 1920–1945,* he was wondering whether to undertake an autobiographical account of the same period before returning to his more strictly "objective" history. I and several of his other friends convinced him to do so. It is hard to convey just how exciting it was to share in this project. Though it involved returning to the past, it was at the same time a march forward, a call for new perspectives, a defiance of time. Nine years of companionship in shared journeys, readings, writings, discoveries, friendships. . . .

Van's memoirs of his Vietnam years, which form the first part of the present volume, were published in 2000 under the title *Au pays de la Cloche fêlée*. The title alluded both to Baudelaire's poem "La Cloche Fêlée" (The Cracked Bell)* and to a subversive journal of the same title published in Vietnam in 1923–1926 by Nguyen An Ninh, a journal that influenced a whole generation of anticolonial revolutionaries. Van shared a period of detention with Nguyen An Ninh in the Saigon prison and remained permanently marked by the encounter.

Having completed *Au pays de la Cloche fêlée,* which he considered essential in perpetuating the memory of his departed comrades, Van envisaged a sequel that would recount his years in France. He did not have time to complete this project, except for a few fragmentary chapters, but he had already chosen the title. As chance would have it, during the last twenty years of his life he lived in a small apartment on the Île de la Cité, an island in the heart of the most ancient part of Paris, near the home of the medieval philosopher Peter Abelard. Led by his insatiable curiosity, Van explored the audacities and misadventures of this great spirit and of his brilliant student and secret lover, Héloïse. The story of these dissident and tragic lovers inspired the title of the second part of his autobiography—*Au pays d'Héloïse*—and their correspondence became part of his personal literary pantheon, alongside the libertine poetry of Claude Le Petit (burned at the stake in 1662), the fiery poems of Louise Michel, "Père Duchêne" sung by the implacable Ravachol as he climbed to the guillotine, Jonathan Swift, Oscar Wilde, Céline, Traven, and last but not least the classic Chinese writings populated with rebels, bandits and cantankerous hermits. Ever on the lookout for sparks of poetic freedom, he was delighted to discover connections between the anarchistic Taoists of ancient China and the enemies of capitalism the world over. His researches in this area led to the publication of an erudite study, *Divination, magie et politique dans la Chine ancienne* (1976), as well as to a smaller and more accessible book, *Utopie antique et guerre des paysans en Chine* (2004).

A chapter is missing from *Au pays d'Héloïse* that Van particularly wished to include: what he called "The Story of the Book." The reputation of *Vietnam 1920–1945* had soon spread beyond small circles of radicals to reach a much larger readership among Vietnamese people throughout the world. For many of them the book was an unhoped-for chance to reconnect with their own history. Enthusiastic responses arrived from the diaspora and from within Vietnam itself (where a number of copies or photocopies had been smuggled in). People were moved to discover their old friends and comrades mentioned in the book by name. Researchers furnished Van with precious information drawn from difficult-to-access archives. Others provided him with dissident texts, old and new, or with accounts by other survivors. Support from these diverse contacts also enabled him and his publisher friends at Insomniaque to print a Vietnamese-language edition of the book, making it much more accessible to the people most directly concerned.

These new-found contacts and collaborations also paved the way for several trips to Barcelona, London, Edinburgh, Boston and New York. Van was particularly interested in sharing experiences with

At a protest against police brutality in New York (1998)

Americans, who in their different way had also been so strongly affected by the Vietnam War, and was thrilled to hear their stories of draft refusal, demonstrations and other forms of antiwar resistance, both in the United States and among the soldiers in Vietnam; notably including the practice of "fragging," that desperate act echoing the mutinies of 1917–1918 and putting into practice the famous cry: "Let's save our bullets for our own generals!"

On the opposing side, too, not all the soldiers in the North Vietnamese army submissively marched off to slaughter. Although the exact numbers are unknown, many did indeed desert and many were executed. Van was able to hear several firsthand accounts when, after forty-nine years of exile, he finally made a trip back to his native country in 1997. He had intended to tell the story of that visit in the second part of his autobiography, but there was not enough time. He did, however, succeed in completing the second volume of his history of twentieth-century Vietnam, *Le Joueur de flûte et l'Oncle Hô: Vietnam 1945–2005,* and that book contains some references to his trip back to Vietnam, though in a less personal form.

One day as we wandered around in Hanoi, we kept running into the huge mausoleum where Ho Chi Minh's embalmed corpse is enshrined. As a fitting tribute to the despicable occupant of that temple of servile submission, Van sang Céline's "Le Règlement" [Payback] at the top of his lungs:

Mais la question qui me tracasse
En te regardant:
Est-ce que tu seras plus dégueulasse
Mort que vivant?

[But looking at you, I can't help asking myself: Will you be any more rotten dead than alive?]

One of the consequences of the American intervention was that it enabled the new "Socialist" Republic of Vietnam to conceal the destructive nature of its own system of oppression. In *Le Joueur de flûte et l'Oncle Hô,* Van shows how Ho Chi Minh rose to power, and how this master of a system of coercion and terror modeled on Stalin's succeeded in becoming "Uncle Ho," a figure admired by millions of devoted anti-imperialists around the world who either did not know anything about the Vietnamese people's actual fate or preferred to ignore it in order to avoid tarnishing the image of the charismatic leader. Ho's bloody "agrarian reform" and his repression of dissident intellectuals in the mid-1950s were every bit as vicious as the repressions in other Stalinist countries during the same period, from Mao's double-crossing of the "Hundred Flowers" movement* to the Russians' crushing of the revolutionary insurrection in Hungary. And over the decades since that time we have continued to see the same sorts of sordid manipulations at the summit of the state machine—rivalries, plots, betrayals, along with a number of "suicides" and "accidents."

Upon his return to Saigon, Van was brought close to the daily lives and working conditions of present-day Vietnamese people, thrust by the "new" economy into development projects funded by South Korean, European, American and Japanese capital. *Le Joueur de flûte et l'Oncle Hô* provides numerous firsthand accounts by workers at companies like Nike or Coca-Cola, whose foreign owners are pleased at how easily the exploited workers can be kept in line by the police-state machinery. The book also provides information on strikes and other signs of revolt against these conditions and against the current regime.

By a tragic irony of history, the heirs of the old anti-imperialist generation in Vietnam, although still professing an obligatory devotion to the memory of Uncle Ho, have turned to the country's former enemy for support, welcoming the almighty dollar while the "heroic masses" continue to struggle for survival. But this new-found complicity in Vietnam between private capitalism and state capitalism came as no surprise to Van, who had always said that those enemies were in fact blood brothers.

With Abel Paz in Barcelona (2004)

When we were in Barcelona on the occasion of the publication of the Spanish version of *Au pays de la Cloche fêlée,* someone asked him, "Why, after all this time, do you so stubbornly persist in bearing witness to this past history?" He replied, "Because the world hasn't changed."

During our Vietnam trip, Van also returned to the village of his birth. Nieces and nephews whom he had left as children told him candidly, and often with humor, about their life during the decades of war, when they had been caught in the crossfire between the Vietcong, the Binh Xuyen pirates and the South Vietnamese army, in some cases joining one to protect themselves from the others, thus becoming alternately deserters and new recruits.

Each night when we went back to our hotel we would discuss the day's events and conversations, so as to compare and then record our recollections. During one of those sessions Van described his encounter with one of his nephews:

> He urged me to come back and stay with them. "Come back and I'll build you a room. You can live with us and when the time comes for you to die, the children will be around you as you go to your final resting place." Ancestor worship is very strong. He wants me to be buried in the family graveyard. His idea is that in my final hour the children and grandchildren will surround my mortal remains. We must lie among our ancestors, that way we will always feel close to them and won't be lost in the world. But me, I'm a wanderer. I've always believed that once you're gone, you're gone, and there's nothing more to say. I couldn't care less about how I go.

Then he began softly singing this fragment from Brassens:

> *J'aimerais mieux mourir dans l'eau, dans le feu, n'importe où,*
> *Et même, à la grande rigueur, ne pas mourir du tout.*

[I would prefer to die in water, in fire, anywhere at all, or even, if it were possible, not to die at all.]*

Then he continued: "It's life, the instant of life, that is eternity. . . . I feel immortal, I feel eternal. You may die tomorrow or right now, but when you really immerse yourself in some project you're living beyond the hundred revolutions of the earth around the sun. Actually, time has nothing to do with it. When you're eternal, you're eternal."

HÉLÈNE FLEURY

Vietnam Under the French

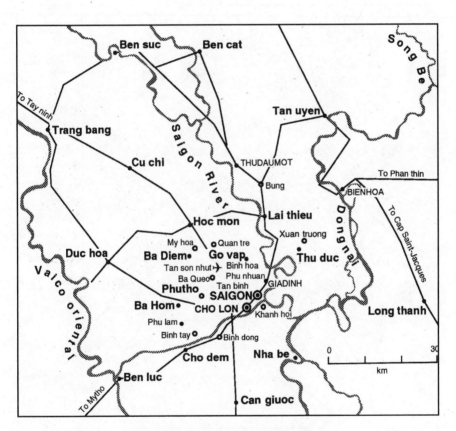

Saigon and Surrounding Area

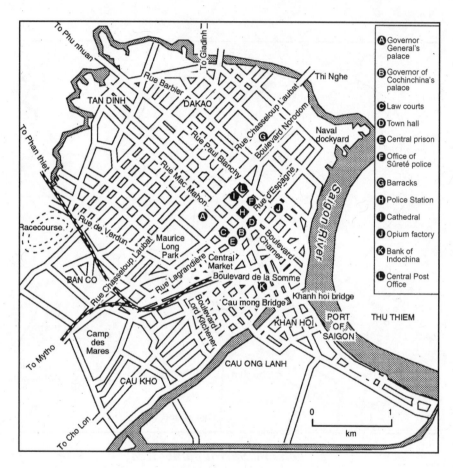

To Phu nhuan

To Giadinh

Thi Nghe

Rue Barbier

TAN DINH

DAKAO

To Phan thiet

Rue Chasseloup Laubat

Boulevard Norodom

Naval
dockyard

Rue Paul Blanchy

Rue Mac Mahon

G

Racecourse

Rue de Verdun

Rue d'Espagne

A

L

F

H

J

Saigon River

Rue Chasseloup Laubat

Maurice
Long
Park

C

E

D

B

Boulevard
Charner

BAN CO

Rue Lagrandière

Central
Market

Boulevard de la Somme

K

To Mytho

Boulevard
Lord Kitchener

Cau mong Bridge

Khanh hoi bridge

Camp
des
Mares

KHAN HOI

PORT
OF
SAIGON

THU THIEM

CAU KHO

CAU ONG LANH

To Cho Lon

0   1
km

A Governor
General's
palace

B Governor of
Cochinchina's
palace

C Law courts

D Town hall

E Central prison

F Office of
Sûreté police

G Barracks

H Police Station

I Cathedral

J Opium factory

K Bank of
Indochina

L Central Post
Office

Saigon in 1945

Part I

IN THE LAND OF THE CRACKED BELL

For Do, Oanh, Da, and Hélène

PREFACE

"The only historians I trust are those who risk getting their throats cut" (Pascal).* Considering the present "Socialist" Republic of Vietnam and its official history, which is uncritically accepted virtually everywhere, I cannot read this maxim without a strong sense of how narrowly I managed to survive.

In *Vietnam 1920–1945: révolution et contre-révolution sous la domination coloniale,* I attempted to rescue that period from oblivion—a period that was marked not only by the struggle against colonial imperialism, but also by movements striving instinctively for an internationalist social revolution, movements that refused to subordinate themselves to the dictates of Stalinist Russia. In the present text I am going to speak as a direct witness of that period. Most of the others who took part in that struggle, if they were not massacred, imprisoned or sent to the penal colonies by the French colonial regime, or forced into exile, ended up being murdered by Ho Chi Minh's "Communist" Party.

Scarcely eleven years had elapsed since the October 1917 revolution in Russia when I became fully aware of the oppressive reality of Indochinese society and fully determined to revolt against it. For me, like so many others, the Russian Revolution was a hopeful sign of possible liberation. Yet even then, during those early years of my apprenticeship in life and revolt, the rare news that reached us from Russia sometimes contained disturbing features. Oppositionist revolutionaries were being hunted down and Trotsky had just been forced into exile. Through the Third International, Stalin was imposing a totalitarian policy that seemed to us to betray the internationalism integral to every revolutionary struggle. Under these circumstances, confronted with the emergence of a regime whose full horror became glaringly evident with the Moscow Trials, it was natural that our critique of Stalinism was initially oriented around the ideas and partisans of Trotsky.

1

Since my departure from Indochina in 1948, if the hope and conviction of the necessity of overthrowing the despicable world order never left me, they were nourished by new reflections on Bolshevism and revolution. In France I found new allies in the factories and elsewhere, among French people, colonized people, and refugees from the Spanish Civil War of 1936–1939—anarchists and Poumistas who had gone through a parallel experience to ours.* In Vietnam, as in Spain, we had been engaged in a simultaneous battle on two fronts: against a reactionary power and against a Stalinist party struggling for power.

These encounters, along with rereading Marx (illuminated by the work of Maximilien Rubel), discovering the 1919 workers councils in Bavaria and the 1921 Kronstadt revolt in Russia, then seeing the resurgence of workers councils in Hungary in 1956, led me to investigate new revolutionary perspectives and permanently distanced me from Bolshevism-Leninism-Trotskyism.* I developed a total distrust of anything that might turn into a "machine." The so-called "workers' parties" (Leninist parties in particular) are embryonic forms of the state. Once in power, these parties form the nucleus of a new ruling class and bring about nothing more than a new system of exploitation. "The existence of the state is inseparable from the existence of slavery" (Marx).*

Orwell rightly noted that those who control the present control the past. When history adopts the discourse of the victors, concealing and dissolving all past struggles with a simplistic Manicheanism that obscures what was truly at stake, the present reality seems inevitable and inescapable. The future of human societies thus depends on our capacity to wrest this past from the cold grip of the present masters. Voices have been lost. We must try to bring them back to life; to rediscover the living traces of the relay of rebellion that traverses time; to restore them and to pass them on.

Chapter 1

ARREST

That afternoon, Wednesday, June 10, 1936, Lu Sanh Hanh came to my workplace on the floor above the Descours & Cabaud metal products store to discuss our call for a general strike and for forming action committees. I had hidden a red cotton banner above the shelves at the back of the store, but had not yet finished painting the slogans in white. Around five o'clock, two Frenchmen suddenly appeared. Lu Sanh Hanh recognized one of them.

"The Sûreté!"* he hissed and raced down the stairs four at a time.

"Put on your coat and follow me," one of the policemen snapped at me. "We have a warrant for your arrest."

I put on my jacket and descended the stairs, flanked by the two policemen. On the ground floor, the astonished stares of workers, salesmen and coolies* followed us to the door. In their haste, the cops hadn't noticed the mimeographed copy of *Class Struggle* from America that I had been deciphering when work slacked off, which still lay on my desk.

They pushed me into a tarp-covered truck parked about a hundred meters away on the Quai de Belgique. There I found Lu Sanh Hanh, breathless and handcuffed: an Annamite* cop had overtaken and tripped him as he ran away. They handcuffed me also and drove us to the Sûreté headquarters at the upper end of Rue Catinat. On the way, I said to myself, "From this moment on, a page has turned in your life. There's no going back."

The cops left Lu Sanh Hanh at the police station and told me to take them to my home. I lived in Xom Ga (Village of the Hens) in a northwest suburb of Saigon, but I pretended I was living with my mother, some 15 kilometers from town. Three kilometers from Thu Duc the truck stopped at the side of the road, from which there were only footpaths bordered by woods. It was getting dark, and the four

3

cops escorting me were on their guard, perhaps still haunted by the specters of the village police officials who had been murdered by peasants a few years earlier, in 1930 and 1931. Dogs barked as we passed near the straw huts, arousing the whole hamlet of Tan Lo.

The two Annamite henchmen were posted behind the hedge while the French inspectors searched the house in the presence of my mother. She was terrified, but didn't utter a sound. I was sick at heart to see her silent grief. My few books in French, carefully stored in the old cupboard, were tossed onto the camp-bed. They left Rousseau, Plato and Plutarch, but confiscated *Mustapha Kémal ou l'Orient en marche* and Georges Garros's *Forceries humaines*. After exploring the dark corners where the rice jars were kept and some clothes were hung on a line, they asked me where I kept my own clothes. I had no choice, then, but to take them to my real home in Xom Ga.

It was completely dark by the time the truck stopped in front of my lodging. Having quickly grasped what was going on, Sung, my young fellow lodger, escaped by jumping over the back hedge. Vo Van Don was less agile, and was captured by the cops. They discovered a mimeographed edition of our clandestine newsletter, *Tien Dao* (Vanguard), underneath the mat in my room, and packed my entire library in a small trunk to take away. I still remember the titles of some of the books: the *Communist Manifesto,* Trotsky's *Permanent Revolution,* Louis Roubaud's *Vietnam: la tragédie indochinoise,* John Reed's *Ten Days That Shook the World,* Riazanov's biography of Marx, and a book on Sun Yat-sen. Personal papers—including my crude attempts to translate Remarque's *All Quiet on the Western Front* and Silvio Pellico's *My Prisons*—were also confiscated.* My reading had been guided by the lists of subversive books and pamphlets seized during raids on other militants, which were naïvely published in newspapers. As for the Marxist texts, I had ordered them from Paris and they had escaped postal censorship.

At the Sûreté headquarters on Rue Catinat my comrades and I were separated. I spent the night in the guardroom, one ankle in shackles fastened by a rod to some other prisoners arrested for gambling. Thus attached, we lay crammed side by side on filthy wooden planks. The next evening, the examining magistrate charged my

friends and me with subversive activities and placed us under a committal
order. As night fell, we were taken to
the Central Prison,* where we had to
surrender our tax cards, our shoes, our
money, and anything else we had on us.
Then we were taken back to the Sûreté,
each of us flanked by an Annamite cop
to keep us from talking to each other.

I was taken alone to a room on the
top floor. Gélot, a huge mixed-race cop
with squinting pig-eyes, said he'd kill
me if I didn't "talk." Four other cops
surrounded me. Gélot ordered me to
strip. All five attacked me, punch-
ing and kicking. I collapsed and soon

Entrance of the Central Prison

lost consciousness. I came to in a pool of urine. An Annamite cop
brought in Lu Sanh Hanh to mop the floor. They had already beaten
him badly, and he looked dazed. Then Gélot pushed me out of the
room and down the hall. Stopping in front of the closed door of another room, he motioned me to look through the keyhole. To my
horror, I saw a young man my own age, completely naked with his
face battered.

"Who's that?" asked Gélot.

"I don't know."

"You know very well who it is!" he said threateningly.

The prisoner I had glimpsed through the keyhole was Ngo Chinh
Phen, a comrade whom I would later meet in prison.

I was then placed in solitary confinement, completely naked in a
concrete cell. My clothes were hung outside on the iron hinges of
the massive, double-padlocked door. My bed was a narrow inclined
plank on the concrete floor. In one corner was the latrine hole; in
another, a hole in the wall containing several liters of water. It was
very hot. The stench of urine and excrement was suffocating. From
a hole in the ceiling, three meters above the floor, a dim bulb behind
a grate cast its pallid light on my new universe. It seemed like the
antechamber of the first of the ten chambers of the Buddhist hell.

My skin was damp and sticky. I tried to get some air by standing on tiptoe and pressing my nose against the tiny holes in the iron spyhole at the top of the door. Twice a day the door would open just enough to pass in a bowl of poorly husked rice with a few scraps of dried fish, or sometimes beans and one or two strips of meat the size of a train ticket. At any other time, the sound of keys would make your heart skip a beat: it meant that you or someone in an adjoining cell would be dragged out for interrogation—in other words, to be tortured. I knew that it was usually in the evening or during the night that the Sûreté Political Police took prisoners to the top floor, into rooms with all the doors and windows closed so the screams of the tortured could not be heard out in the street.

One evening my turn came. I was brought before the squinty-eyed cop. With him was Superintendent Perroche, chief of the Political Police, who looked like a snake with spectacles. They stripped me and told me to "confess." A hefty Annamite cop and notorious torture specialist, Chin Ngoc, attached my thumb to the bared end of one long electric wire and my big toe to another. The two wires were hooked up to a huge truck generator mounted on a small table. The cop turned the crank, sending high-voltage shocks through my body. I winced, leaped up and shuddered involuntarily, then collapsed to the floor, my muscles twitching convulsively.

This went on and on . . . I don't know for how long. At one point Perroche himself seized the crank with his left hand—his right arm ended in an artificial white-gloved fist—and turned it energetically. Then Chin Ngoc removed the wires. My thumb was scorched. He forced me to lie face down on the floor, his right foot pressing down on my lower back. Crossing my arms behind my back, he raised them slowly toward my head. An atrocious pain shot through my flattened thorax, then I suddenly blacked out. An instant in the void, in a dream of infinite peace and security. Then the shock of violent blows by a rattan cane on the soles of my feet brought me round, dazed, only half-conscious, and stupefied to see all those pigs standing around me—the same dull pork-eyes, the same cobra-with-spectacles, and the infuriated mad-dog mug spitting out threats and curses at me, as if I had defiled his ancestors' tomb. This form of torture was called "gizzard twisting" (*lan me ga*).

My ravings apparently did not suffice for the required "spontaneous confession." The cop kept me on my stomach, forced a cylindrical wedge of wood between my jaws, pushed it to the back of my mouth, and tied it tightly behind my neck with a rope. He also bound my wrists to my ankles—my legs were bent behind my back. Then, as he pulled on the rope with one hand, he laid into me with the other, ferociously caning the soles of my feet. Every blow was followed by a short pause to let the pain sink in. During these pauses he would prod me in the gut with the sharp end of a stick. I tried to cry out, but could barely whimper like a dying dog. My body arched, I kicked convulsively. I felt that my skull was exploding with each snap of the cane.

The session was over. Now they forced me to jump up and down in place on my battered legs so that the contusions would be reabsorbed to bring down the swelling and bruises on the soles of my feet. These torturers were experts in bursting prisoners' lungs, crushing their guts and inflicting atrocious suffering while leaving little or no trace. I was taken back to my cell.

In the wan light, uncertain days gave way to nights of anguish for me and for my companions in the neighboring cells, whose misery I suspected was equal to my own. We had all suddenly found ourselves thrust to the other side of life, into a world apart, given over naked to bestial beings like those pictured in paintings of the Buddhist hell, with buffalo or horse heads, hawk beaks, and chicken claws. We knew the date of our capture but we had no idea when, or if, we would ever escape their clutches. The big clock on the nearby cathedral struck each quarter hour, reminding me that I was there for an indefinite time. I tried to concentrate with all my might on the aged and respected Phan Van Truong's advice when confronting our "civilizers": Make it a principle to never fear another person, *come what may*.

One afternoon I was taken to an office, where I found myself alone with a stocky Annamite man. He wore French-style clothes and had a very sincere and courteous expression. His large black briefcase was on the desk. He invited me to sit down facing him.

"My name is Le Van Kim. I'm a lawyer and I have been appointed to handle your defense."

I felt I could trust him. In a low voice, I recounted all that I had endured during the interrogations. After being cut off from the world for an eternity—a week, perhaps more—this unexpected, unhoped-for human contact meant that my link with the outside world was not entirely severed.

After the lawyer's visit, I was transferred to the Sûreté jail, alone in a gloomy, gray, narrow room without any openings except the door to the guardroom. Yellowed cartons of files were piled against the wall. At night I explored them and discovered a comprehensive handwritten lexicon of Annamite communist terminology with French translations, including words and expressions newly introduced in underground communications since 1930. By what tortures had the enemy uncovered all these secrets?

One afternoon, I was struck with anguish when I caught a fleeting glimpse of Ho Huu Tuong crossing the courtyard in handcuffs. He had been something of a secret advisor to us.

At first contact, the guard called Tay did not seem cast in the same mold as the others. He looked calm. On his leather cigarette case I noticed an unexpected motto traced in purple ink: *Chi vi thuong* ("It's because I love"). He let me out to relieve myself in the lavatories across the courtyard. One morning, though, I saw this same cop in a fit of anger violently thrashing a prisoner with a broom and shouting curses at him.

A few days later we were taken to court and brought one by one before Tran Van Ty, a rat-faced judge with a puny moustache and flashing crafty eyes behind spectacles set in a thick brown tortoise-shell frame. His role was to sign warrants and entrust the Sûreté with pretrial investigations. Prisoners brought before him who had been held by the Sûreté were invariably asked, "Do you abide by your confession?" If the accused retracted their statements, the judge returned them to the interrogators until the "spontaneous confessions" extorted in the torture chambers were confirmed before him.

The judge was Annamite, but he questioned us in French. Those of us who understood that language could respond immediately. The others, instead of being questioned in Annamite, had to rely on an interpreter. As a result, from the judge's chamber to the courtroom, anyone who didn't know French had no idea what all the magistrates, clerks, cops and lawyers were plotting among themselves. Only when their deliberations were over did the all-powerful interpreter finally inform the prisoner whether he would be thrown into hell, or freed, or shortened by a head.

The servile dispensers of justice, whatever their color and whether Annamites, Indians or Martinicans, were often more pitiless than their white masters toward poor wretches who fell into their clutches.

Ta flamme importune, on la couvre,
On la fait éteindre aux valets. (Victor Hugo)

[They have their lackeys snuff out your troublesome flame.]*

Judge Tran Van Ty questioned me about my complaint of torture. "Why would they have mistreated you if you were telling the truth?" he said. One of the witnesses, a young French cop who had taken part in beating me up, interrupted: "We never mistreated him." I felt caught in a snare as I signed the papers the Annamite clerk had scribbled down at the judge's dictation. This net, a thousand invisible knots carefully woven of words, of seemingly inconsequential sentences, of innocent-looking phrases, had you tightly bound and tied. The more you struggled, the tighter you were strangled in the meshes of their legal web. Signatures were appended "without other objection" at the bottom of these obscure documents, and the case was closed. Then the judge told the policemen to keep us squatting in the hall and had us given pastries and hot coffee bought in town by the court attendant.

Handcuffed two by two and escorted by the same Sûreté cops, we left the court by the side door opposite the Central Prison. This short crossing to the prison on the other side of the street and away from the Sûreté's torture chambers seemed to us like the antechamber to release.

Above the entrance to the *Kham Lon* (Great Prison) compound, surrounded by hideous gray walls bristling with glass shards, was a Gorgon's head with furrowed eyebrows jutting out over two black holes, a grimacing mouth and snakes framing its face. The heavy steel door opened with a muffled rumble just enough to shove us in, then banged shut behind us. Bars everywhere. The cops took off our handcuffs and the Annamite warders in their khaki uniforms searched us under the watchful eye of the Corsican Head Guard. His pot belly wobbled under the white uniform, sleeves adorned with enormous silver braids. In exchange for our civilian clothes, we were handed rush mats and clean prison uniforms. Common-law prisoners, I later learned, were given used mats and uniforms that sometimes harbored itch-mite scabies and crabs in the seams. I received a shirt of rough dark-blue cotton with wide sleeves stopping at my elbows and a front split halfway down, barely covering my navel, and some knee-length trousers.* I probably looked like one of those monkeys that animal handlers put on show in village squares. I was given a four-by-five-centimeter wood plaque (*dinh-bai*) bearing my four-digit prison number and the initials MAP (*maison d'arrêt politique:* prison for political detainees). I attached the *dinhbai* to a buttonhole by passing a piece of string through the hole on its top edge.

We passed the death-sentence cell. Next to the spyhole on the black iron door we could see the identity, offenses and date of sentencing of someone named Nay, an invisible man lying on a mat behind the door, his feet held in justice's shackles while he awaited his legal murder. A narrow staircase took us to the second floor. To the right were the cells with relatively comfortable beds reserved for French prisoners (*kham tay*); to the left, Cells 7, 6 and 5, all opening onto a narrow courtyard girded by a wall half a man's height and topped by a steel fence.

The guard put us in Cell 7. About twenty men, some naked to the waist, others in blue uniforms, gathered around us fraternally in the gloomy light. Once the iron door was shut, they helped us put our mats away. Old and new prisoners mingled, greeting each other like old friends with something approaching joy, but without asking any questions about identity or activities.

There were about twenty-five of us, with just enough room to move around without bumping into each other. We slept wrapped in our mats right on the concrete floor, packed in rows like sardines. The walls were painted black up to a man's height. In one corner was a pitcher of water, in the other a latrine hole. The back wall separating us from the outside was topped by thick steel sheets with airholes the size of a finger; these holes, too high to be reached even by one prisoner standing on another's shoulders, were our only source of daylight and air. By giving someone a leg-up, we could observe, through the narrow slit above the door, the comings and goings of new prisoners and Sûreté police.

Our fellow prisoners were peasants from Duc Hoa, arrested on May 6, 1936, by the Annamite Deputy Administrator, who had had them beaten into "talking" before handing them over to the Sûreté Political Police. Nguyen Van Sang, a hearty, well-built fellow, told us about his interrogation at the Rue Catinat police station. How, under electroshock torture, he tried in vain to keep from falling to the floor. He mimed a comical version of the scene: on one bent leg with the other leg stretched forward, the big toe as though wired up to a generator, one arm stretched in front of him, the fist closed and thumb sticking out, likewise wired up to the instrument of torture.

I met Ho Huu Tuong again. I had glimpsed him in the courtyard at the Sûreté. He had been arrested a week after Lu Sanh Hanh and me in the halls of the courthouse as he was handling some matters with lawyers for our defense. Ironically, it was only there, in that tightly closed and locked prison cell, that we were finally able to come together in a group and talk freely with each other. Outside, with the constant fear of being followed, we only met in twos or at most threes, in places we hoped were unknown to the police. Another advantage of prison was that we didn't have to worry about our daily rice. I was to experience the same exhilaration twenty years later in the sanatorium in the Pyrenees where I spent a year free from the grind of the factory. So, for the time being, there we were, a dozen companions-in-struggle with the opportunity to finally really get to know each other.

To begin with, we were filled with joy by what Ho Huu Tuong had to tell us: Two days after our arrest, during the night of June 12–13, 1936, the League* comrades who had escaped the dragnet handed out our leaflets in the city announcing that "Hundreds of thousands of workers in France have gone on strike and occupied their factories. Let's rise up in every factory, in every province and every village. We should elect worker and peasant delegates

and form action committees everywhere. . . ." Some of the leaf-
lets were pasted on the newsroom wall of the *Dépêche d'Indochine*
[Indochina Dispatch], and the newspaper published the entire text in
Annamite in its June 13 issue.

The widespread movement of strikes and factory occupations
in France* filled us with enthusiasm and convinced us to spread
the spark, with the hope of igniting the rebellious forces simmer-
ing under the surface among the workers and peasants of Indochina.
Believing that the revolution had begun in France, we felt that the
time had come for us colonized people to propagate it in our own
countries.

Every morning the door opened around 6:30 and we went out
into the courtyard. Under the watchful eye of the Annamite warder,
two Cambodian common-law prisoners clambered up the steep
stairs until they reached our floor, carrying water in a wooden barrel
hung on a pole across their shoulders. They filled our water jug and
swept the floor. Around eight o'clock the Head Guard would appear,
a veritable caricature of colonial authority in his spruce white uniform, black sunglasses half-hiding his face, and cap jammed tight
on his head. He was accompanied by a French guard clad in khaki
with a big gun at his belt, and by a barefoot "jail-boy" dressed in un-
bleached cotton, notebook and pencil in hand. We lined up on either
side of the courtyard. The Head Guard advanced slowly down the
lines without looking at anyone—at least we couldn't tell where he
was looking from behind his mask. Next he entered our empty cell,
peering into each corner. Then, at the same slow pace, the procession left the courtyard.

At around ten o'clock common-law prisoners, followed closely
by the guards assigned to prevent any communication with us "politicals," brought us our meager meal: a tub of unhusked rice and a
smaller tub of fish and boiled vegetables. Everyone was issued a tin
mug and a pair of bamboo chopsticks. Squatting on the ground in
the courtyard around the tubs, under the hot sun, we gulped down
our rations. At the end of the meal we had to return to our quarters
and the courtyard was washed down by the common-law prisoners.
We lined up inside, the old warder came to count us, and then the
heavy iron door was closed. In the afternoon at around four o'clock

La semaine de 40 heures à Saigon

Des tracts la demandent

Un peu partout en ville ce matin, on a trouvé dans les rues et collés sur les murs aux abords de certains ateliers des tracts invitant les ouvriers de Saigon à faire grève pour obtenir la semaine de travail de 40 heures.

D'autres tracts, d'un autre texte, ont été également lancés et voici le libellé de trois d'entre eux qui furent collés dans notre salle des dépêches

Anh em thợ-thuyền dân cày và binh lính Đông Dương

Cách-mạng vô sản ở Pháp đang sôi hồi dữ-dội : Mấy trăm ngàn thợ đã đình công. chìm là máy và đang dự bị tổng đình công

Chúng ta hãy đứng lên ; Trong mỗi lý máy rồi sản nghiệp, mỗi làng mỗi lính, anh em thợ-thuyền và dân-cày cử đại biểu.

Thành lập uỷ-ban hành-động khắp nơi. Liên hiệp nhau lại ; Đứng lên tổng đình-công hưởng ứng giai-cấp vô sản Pháp !

Đả đảo Đế quốc Pháp !

Đông dương hoàn toàn độc lập !

Tịch thâu ruộng đất của địa chủ giao dân-cày !

Cách mạng vô sản Pháp, Đông Dương muôn năm !

Liên Ủy thợ - thuyền liên - hiệp
Chánh-đoàn · Cộng sản Quốc tế chủ nghĩa

(phải tán thành Đệ tứ Quốc tế)

La traduction de ce tract est celle-ci :

Des centaines de mille d'ouvriers en France font la grève et ont pris possession des usines. Soulevons-nous dans nos usines et sur les propriétés, dans chaque province et dans chaque village. Que les ouvriers et les agriculteurs élisent des délégués, constituent des comités qui fassent de la propagande partout.

Faisons la grève comme les ouvriers de France! Renversons le gouvernement impérialiste d'Indochine! Que l'Indochine soit intégralement indépendante! Prenons les rizières aux propriétaires pour les remettre aux travailleurs.

Vive le communisme de France et d'Indochine!

Signé: LE COMITÉ DES OUVRIERS COMMUNISTES.

───

Il est assez curieux de constater que c'est juste au lendemain où la Sûreté opéra des perquisitions dans des cellules que des tracts ont été lancés, comme pour faire la nique aux services de recherche. Ces libelles sont rédigées en un style pas très correct et ont été imprimées avec une machine genre Roneo.

La distribution de ces tracts a dû s'effectuer ce matin à la première heure et n'est pas chose étonnante, car les communistes locaux ne font que suivre l'exemple de leurs camarades de France.

La Dépêche d'Indochine (June 13, 1936)

we were subjected to the same counting and the iron door shut again.

With our peasant friends we discussed how to organize our communal life. Sitting on the floor in a circle, we decided on a few rules and on the election of a cell delegate—preferably someone who could speak French. Since no one volunteered for the job, I was chosen "unanimously" by my comrades. I was a little nervous about exactly what was expected of me and how I would go about defending everyone, alone against the warders. *Do what must be done, come what may.*

That afternoon, when our cell door opened, I was delegated to get us an additional jug of water. The old Annamite guard, polite and diplomatic but embarrassed by our demand, took me to the Head Guard.

The blazing sun flooded the grassy courtyard. Around all sides, a verandah bordered by yellow columns screened the doors to the disciplinary cells. In the middle of the yard stood the ochre-colored watchtower. Crossing the courtyard, we headed toward Agostini, the Head Guard. All my comrades, clinging to the courtyard fence, followed us with their eyes to see what would happen.

It was unusual for a prisoner to be taken to see the Head Guard. Agostini, astounded, found it intolerable. Red with rage, he yelled, "Who allowed you to come here?"

"It was . . ."

He cut me short.

Forcing myself not to react, I waited, standing still against the wall facing his desk. He took a huge dusty book down from the shelf and slapped it furiously onto his desk.

"Here are the prison rules! I will apply them! I'll have you all disemboweled by the guards!" and he pointed a threatening forefinger at the Colonial Infantry's quarters.

I remained silent, not moving an inch. The maniac calmed down.

"What do they want?" he asked the old warder.

"Another jug of water, that's all."

"We'll see about that."

He walked toward our quarters, and we followed.

We got our extra jug of water. After that, every morning when the Head Guard and his escort came around, I listed our needs, such as aspirin or writing paper, which the jail-boy wrote down in his notebook.

* * *

The Central Prison, covering a whole block, dominated the city center. The entrance was at 69 Rue Lagrandière. It was located opposite the Hall of "Justice," while to the left it was only separated from the Cochinchina Governor's Palace by Rue Mac-Mahon. It blocked off Rue d'Espagne, a busy commercial street. The right side of the prison was separated from the Criminal Records Office laboratory by Rue Philippini, which ran parallel to Mac-Mahon. Finally, the boundaries around this singular world were marked by massive gray walls twice the height of a man, ridged with glass shards. In watchtowers on each of the three free corners, a French Colonial Infantry soldier armed with a rifle stood guard day and night. At night, every quarter hour we would hear the cry, "Sentry, watch one! Sentry, watch two!" From inside the prison, those of us on the upper floors could see the tops of the tamarind trees in the surrounding streets, whose falling leaves told us another year had passed. We calculated our remaining term of imprisonment in "tamarind seasons."

After undergoing torture at the Sûreté headquarters, our young comrade Van Van Ky began coughing up blood and losing weight before our eyes, which made us very worried. When he started hemorrhaging, he was taken to the Cho Quan hospital. Three days later he was brought back in worse condition than before. In the hospital he first received injections, but because he struggled when they shaved his head, the doctor had him put in a straitjacket for twenty-four hours. Then they handcuffed his hands behind his back, shackled his legs, and sent him back to prison without any further medical care. Taking care of him by turns, we tried to ease his pain using traditional methods of healing by rubbing and massage. From then on, we decided we would look after each other ourselves, and we taught each other how.

One morning in early July, at ten o'clock, an Annamite warder came for Ho Huu Tuong, Lu Sanh Hanh and me. As we descended the iron stairs, we wondered whether we were being taken to a session at the Sûreté headquarters. Two plainclothes policemen were waiting for us in front of the Head Guard's office. Had other comrades fallen into their hands, and were we being taken for a confrontation? We were handcuffed and led across the street to the courthouse to see Judge Tran Van Ty.

Because our lawyers had lodged complaints about the torture and bad treatment we had allegedly received while held at the Sûreté headquarters, Tran Van Ty said he was going to have the Sûreté searched to find the torture instruments mentioned in our statements (truck generator, rattan canes, gags, etc.). "Now it's the Sûreté's turn to be searched," he snarled, smiling sardonically.

Then he picked up the telephone and notified Sûreté Political Chief Perroche of the search. At that point we understood that we had been assigned the role of naïve puppets in a shabby farce! Escorted by plainclothes cops, we set out for Rue Catinat in a covered truck, preceded by Tran Van Ty and his interpreter.

My heart shrank as we mounted the stairs to the torture chamber on the top floor of that gruesome building, with which we were all too familiar. As Tran Van Ty and Perroche entered the room, they motioned for us to stay outside. Suddenly I felt someone hit me hard but discreetly in my lower back: I turned to find Gélot, our torturer. I didn't cry out. Was I afraid of retaliation? The sinister Tran Van Ty beckoned us into the room and, with a sly smile, asked us to point out the offending instruments. The cramped room was bare and unfurnished except for an old chair and a small table. The only thing left behind was the switch on the table that Gélot used to summon Chin Ngoc, the Annamite torture specialist, and in the corner to the left, the small washbasin where the interrogators washed their hands after the torture sessions. There was no trace of the huge generator. My head swirled with visions of the atrocities I had suffered; it made my flesh creep.

We could breathe again only when we had returned to the Central Prison.

Chapter 2

CHILDHOOD

Great-Lady departs,
a pair of deadly serpents accompany Her.
Great-Lady returns,
a pair of black dragons escort Her.

I think my prison companions felt the same as I did: prison life, however intense, seems to suspend time, encouraging inmates to look back at their past, at their childhood and the "apprenticeship" that marked the course of their life.

I came into the world one night in 1912, toward the end of the Year of the Rat. The village custom was to allow a lapse of time before registering a birth, so that if the infant was carried off by evil spirits the parents would be spared having to revisit the registrar to declare the death of their newborn. So I was officially born in April 1913.

Whenever a woman in the village gave birth, my mother was summoned. She helped as best she could, relying on age-old practices. When her turn came to give birth, she cut the umbilical cord herself with a strip of bamboo bark freshly cut from our hedge and as sharp as a razorblade. I was born swathed in a purple membrane—a sign of good fortune, my mother said.

When the 1914 War began, my older brother—Brother Seven— was of the age to be drafted into the infantry, i.e. to "pay his blood tax" and become either cannon-fodder or a killer of poor people. The village notables* forcibly seized young peasants and sent them to France. Those who resisted were tied up, suspended like pigs from a thick pole, and transported to the Village Hall. Elder Brother Seven escaped by lying low in the pineapple grove and then leaving for the city to hide out in the home of Sister Five.

In January 1916, 150 to 200 peasants from the adjoining region, armed with machetes and a few rifles, attacked the Village Halls where the notables were proceeding with such "voluntary enlistments." Seizing their guards' guns, the prisoners mutinied and joined the peasants. The agitation spread throughout Cochinchina, culminating in February with an attack on the Central Prison in Saigon. Around three in the morning on February 15 an armada of small boats brought in some 300 peasant rebels armed with spears, swords and machetes. In front of the Central Prison they killed the sentry and wounded other guards. The Guard Post, however, succeeded in blocking the entrance and opened fire on the assailants, who dispersed in the greatest confusion, leaving dead and wounded all along the sidewalks. More than 150 peasants were immediately tried in military courts. Thirty-eight were executed; the rest were sent to the Poulo Condore penal colony.* In the course of the year, more than a thousand rebels or suspected rebels from the countryside were charged with conspiracy and belonging to secret societies.

Haunted by the repressive atmosphere pervading the country, my father took the precaution of removing the handle from his machete, which he customarily used to prune the thick spiny bamboo hedges around the house.

I was five years old when my father, though only a small peasant, was able to put a tiled roof over our heads, very close to a pineapple grove. We gathered dead branches in the grove to cook our food. My mother pulled tendrils from the pineapple leaves to use as sewing thread. Our ancestors rested under the broad, outstretched arms of the *cay go,* a massive, century-old tree in which our Guardian Spirits dwelled. In a hollow three meters up its trunk lived a family of owls. My brothers captured the baby owls, which we cared for inside the house. For several nights we heard the mother owl moaning miserably, but our childish hearts remained pitiless! We caught frogs and toads to feed those warm little balls, so touching and so voracious.

In the shade of that tree of life my mother had a small temple set up for the worship of her Guardian Spirit, Ba (Great-Lady). Anh Tu,

Ngo Van's childhood home

the village magician and my cousin by marriage, officiated at the solemn inauguration of the temple. The aromatic smoke of incense sticks, mingled with the fragrance of burnt sandalwood, rose skyward in transparent swirls. My mother meditated alongside Anh Tu as he chanted incantations:

> *Ba di co cap ran trun,*
> *Ba ve co cap rong mun dua Ba.*

[Great-Lady departs, a pair of deadly serpents accompany her.
Great-Lady returns, a pair of black dragons escort her.]

Suddenly, to our astonishment, a turtledove swooped down from the tree's branches, flapped its wings several times and alighted on the magician's shoulder. Then the "messenger of Great-Lady" flew off again.

Later, one night when my mother saw a sparkling meteor traverse the sky and disappear at the top of the tree, she told us that it was a chariot drawn by black dragons taking Great-Lady back to her home.

My father, who was literate, belonged to the village Council of Notables and kept the registers in Annamite *nom,* composed of ideograms taken from Chinese script.

My parents, my three elder brothers—Brother Seven, Brother Ten and Brother Twelve—and I, Brother Thirteen and last, all lived under the same roof.* Brother Seven was born of a previous marriage. Three buffalos—our workforce and beasts of burden—were also part of the family.

In the evening, I would fall asleep lying beside Brother Seven as he chanted the popular epic poem *Luc Van Tien*. He was also the one who taught me the ABCs and, with a pointed strip of bamboo, showed me how to trace "a," "â," or "ê" on banana leaves.

When I was little, my task was to keep the hungry roosters and hens from eating the unhulled rice spread out on a rush mat to dry in the sun. Lying in the shade of a grapefruit tree in our courtyard, I watched the long processions of red ants climbing its trunk. They carried their prey to their globe-shaped nests that hung from the branches, globes composed of leaves that had been stuck together with perfect artistry.

Sometimes I spent whole days perched on the back of the buffalo we called *Trau Voi* (Elephant), playing a bamboo flute made for me by Brother Ten. My job was to look after the buffalos in the fields that stretched from the front of our house to the distant stream below. A thin but still visible scar on my right forearm bears witness to an adventure that haunts me even today like a bad dream.

It's almost nightfall. Huge black clouds gather dramatically on the horizon. The wind rises with increasing violence. The clumps of bamboo bend over, the tall grass flattens. In the space of a few seconds a soot-colored sky obscures the earth. Sensing the oncoming storm, the buffalos start on the return path by themselves. Suddenly great sheets of rain pour down, stirred by the wind, and the buffalos break into a gallop. Terrified, I flatten myself and cling to buffalo Elephant's back. As we approach the house our buffalos, instead of taking their usual route alongside the bamboo hedge, all of a sudden lower their heads and charge through its thickest part. These animals are not stupid: instinctively they are taking the shortest way to the stable. Plucked from my perch by the spiny branches, I fall into the

middle of the hedge, bristling with steely points. It's pitch black and the deluge continues. Unable to move, I feel all around me the menace of the thorns. Terror-stricken, I wait for an eternity until finally, from far away, comes my mother's call: *"Con oi, con o dau, con o dau?"* (Son, where are you? where are you?) Then, in the torchlight, the gleam of my mother's eyes and the happy shouts of my brother accompany my extraction from the fearsome trap.

Great Uncle, who lived a dozen kilometers away on the Plain of Cucumbers, sometimes sent a Moi slave on horseback as his messenger. He had acquired the slave back when he used to barter with Moi tribes living in the mountainous Loc Ninh and Hon Quan regions. He would load up salt and salted sardines in an ox cart and exchange his goods for resin gathered by the Moi deep in the forest.

Our affectionate nickname for that messenger was Anh Lo (Brother Lo). I loved his smooth face tanned by the sun. My brothers and I marveled at the sleek stature of the noble brown horse he rode, like a steed out of an ancient tale and so different from our familiar mount, the stocky black buffalo. When the horse whinnied and bared his teeth, it seemed to us he was laughing uproariously, and we laughed with him. But Anh Lo always had to leave at dusk. What beauty there was in the pure silhouette of the slender rider, smoothly gliding past the curtain of bamboo!

Our father, though sometimes cross, was tender-hearted and loved his offspring. One day, touched by our enthusiasm, he came home with a horse as handsome as Anh Lo's, which he had borrowed for a while from a friend. Our new friend, attached to a stake by a long rope around its neck, grazed peaceably on the sparse grass in the field next to our house, making his impressive lips vibrate with an amusing "b-r-r-r . . ." that enchanted me. In the evening we took him into the stable; the buffalos moved to the other side of the house in the open air. My brothers closed off the narrow entrance to the stable by fitting two hewn crossbars into holes on the doorposts. To hold the ends of the crossbars firm, they used a mallet to drive wooden wedges into the holes.

One morning, my brothers gave in to my entreaties and hoisted me up so that, straddling the stable entrance, I stood with one foot on either upright post and my hands holding the roof joists. The plan was for my brothers to remove the wooden crossbars, at which point the horse would come out and I would simply let myself drop onto its back. My heart beating wildly, I fell on the rump of the horse, but with one bound it dashed into the courtyard, and there I was with my butt on the ground. After turning its head briefly toward us, as if to say "So long, kids!" our guest trotted away, down the same path Anh Lo had taken the other evening. My father was relieved to learn that the horse had returned to its home.

My pastoral childhood ended when I started at the village school around 1920. I can still picture the horizon reddening at dawn as my mother and I left home on that journey into the unknown. After leaving the hamlet, we went through some woods, the songs of invisible birds troubling my timid heart.

My schoolmaster's name was Thay Giao Dong (Worthy Teacher). He looked very tall to me, and even his smile seemed stern. He lived a hundred paces down the same stony road as the school, in a gray straw hut hidden behind a thorny hedge.

To the right of the house a grassy track faded into the fields: this was the path we took to school. On the left was a cluster of several other straw huts, dark and dusty. They adjoined the village Communal House, an old one-story structure of wood with a tiled roof, whose façade opened onto a verandah with columns of whitewashed brick.

What distinguished our school—the Little Market School—

from the other straw huts was its roughly whitewashed plank walls and a verandah that sheltered us from the sun and rain during recess. The caretaker's hut was on the left. The narrow courtyard surrounding the buildings was entirely enclosed by a dense hedge of prickly bamboo. Along the back hedge stood a line of small, oval-shaped earthenware jars. The schoolchildren urinated in them during recess, and the old caretaker collected the liquid to fertilize his meager market garden. Under the scorching sun, the stench from those piss-pots behind the school became unbearable. For our other needs, we had to cross the hedge and hide behind the underbrush.

Our schoolmaster taught two classes, small children and older ones, totaling about thirty peasant children from our village and the surrounding hamlets. During recess we were allowed to quench our thirst by dipping a coconut shell fitted with a handle into a large earthenware jar in front of the caretaker's hut. If the jar was empty, we had to beg water from the local fishmongers.

The schoolmaster's wife sold fowl and vegetables. Every morning she set off, carrying a pole on her shoulders with a woven bamboo basket hanging at either end, to buy chickens, ducks, guinea fowl, cucumbers or bamboo shoots from peasants on their way to the market. She then sold her goods to merchants who resold them in Saigon and Cholon.

My mother awoke every morning at cockcrow, at the end of the fifth watch heralding the Hour of the Dragon. What is a "watch"? Nighttime was divided into five watches, each lasting about two-and-a-half hours. The middle of the third watch, the Hour of the Rat, was at midnight. At the Communal House a watchman, appointed by turns from among village youths in good health by the Council of Notables, marked the beginning of each watch by striking three times on the *cai mo,* a large resonant wooden cylinder set on trestles. The sound could be heard from afar. With a continuous drum roll, the watchman warned the village in cases of disaster—a fire or a fight or piracy—signaled by the victims' cries of *"Lang xom oi!"* (Village and hamlet, help!)

Around five o'clock each morning we gulped down our first rice. As soon as we saw the first crimson rays of dawn break over the horizon, we set off for school. During the rainy season, the sky was often overcast, but usually my mother still managed to see us off on time. If it did happen that on the way we heard the ominous drumming of the distant tomtom, we knew we were late and would set off running so fast we lost our breath.

The big red tomtom, which hung from a beam at the back of the schoolroom, signaled the beginning and end of the recess period and of the school day. Sounding the drum was not assigned to any particular pupil. The master simply waved his finger, and one of the older children would leap to the tomtom. That red tomtom exerted an irresistible attraction on me. One day, aided by one of my older brothers who hoisted me onto a desk, I succeeded in grasping the round-tipped stick and, taking careful aim at the center of the circle, made the red monster thunder.

From time to time, an unpleasant surprise awaited us on reaching school in the morning—a cleanliness inspection. Any boys who had dirt behind their ears were made to squat naked around the well like skinny toads. Then one of the sturdier boys in the class, perched on the edge, lowered a woven bamboo bucket into the well, drew up water, and doused his unfortunate schoolmates. The cold water made them flinch, then jump around frantically. With their frail hands they scrubbed behind their ears. At the end of the session some were still shivering, and rubbed themselves down feverishly before getting dressed. The girls, who stayed shut up in the classroom, were spared this vexing experience.

During the rainy season, our schoolmaster sometimes let us shower ourselves under the torrents gushing from the roof—rare moments of joy when we could frolic about freely.

One of my classmates was assigned to fill the teacher's water jars, which meant trotting back and forth several times to fetch water. The teacher once sent my brothers and me to gather deadwood for his cooking stove. A hundred meters from the school, we entered the same woods we crossed every day. I kept the lookout while my brothers climbed up the trees to break off dead branches. I could hear the sharp sound of the wood cracking. Suddenly the silhouette of an old man appeared at the edge of the woods. It was our father! I was rooted to the spot.

"What are you doing here?" he asked.

"I'm waiting for my brothers—they're gathering firewood for the teacher."

My father caught sight of them climbing around in the branches and began beating a path toward them through the undergrowth. They came down hurriedly and tried to dodge his slaps.

"If your teacher wants firewood, all he has to do is let me know and I'll bring him cartloads. You're not to climb trees. You could break your arms and legs!" From then on, we were excused from the chore of collecting wood.

Sometimes the teacher got bored. He would take several swallows of rice liquor from a flask he hid behind the map on one of the wallboards. In a state of euphoria, he would then set off for the old caretaker's hut to play chess, leaving the class under the supervision of one of the pupils. One evening upon the teacher's return, the pupil assigned to this rank of informer denounced several of his classmates for rowdiness. His face pale with rage, the master seized stiff stalks ripped from the guava tree near the fence and thrashed the wrongly accused boys with all his might. The scene terrified me.

An unusual event occasionally interrupted our daily routine— the School Inspector's visit. One day toward the middle of a sunny morning while we were at recess, an elegant cart drew up in front of the school. The barefoot Annamite driver jumped to the ground and held the horse's reins and a man dressed in an impeccably white French suit buttoned up to the neck descended ceremoniously. It was Inspector Tuan. Like a flock of sparrows, we darted back into the classroom, sat at our desks, and folded our arms over our closed exercise books. An unusual silence reigned. When the Inspector entered the classroom, at a signal from our teacher we all stood up in unison. With a gesture of his right hand, the Inspector motioned us to sit down. Although he was Annamite, he spoke with our teacher in French. None of us could understand what they were saying. He stood by my desk and, without saying a word, leafed through my exercise book, then took a small tube out of his pocket from which a pen sprang as if by magic. On the last page he scribbled a cabalistic sign *"vu"** in the margin to indicate that he had seen my work. Then he returned his pen to the tube.

During midday break, pupils who lived nearby went home to eat. Those who like me lived farther away brought their lunch over the long dawn hike—a lump of cold rice topped with a piece of dried fish or sugar cane, the whole wrapped in a dried areca palm leaf. After gulping it down, we would wander off into the countryside. I sometimes crossed the empty lot behind the school to the Phuoc Tuong pagoda a few hundred meters away. In the torrid midday heat I was drawn to the calm of this religious site, shaded by old trees. In the cool, dark silence of the main pavilion a giant golden Buddha was enthroned on the altar, legs folded on a seat of lotus petals. Eyes half-closed in meditation, Buddha dominated a group of smaller Buddhist deities, gilded or brightly painted. It was there that I first understood who the otherworldly being was that my mother invoked every time some misfortune befell us.

Gradually I became more familiar with these sacred precincts. The few monks living there ignored my presence, but the Venerable Superior noticed the young schoolboy's frequent visits. Once when my father came to the pagoda, the Superior proposed to accept me as a novice. For small peasants, such a proposal was attractive and much sought after. Thus it was that I almost ended up leading a life of asceticism, head shaven clean, wearing the robes of an apprentice monk, and being taught Chinese characters so that I could piously pore over sacred texts and copy Buddhist sutras. Had this been my austere fate, I would have followed in the footsteps of Shakyamuni (Buddha) down the path to ataraxia, renunciation of worldly life, of the ephemeral world, *phu the,* where every living being inexorably experiences the four sufferings: birth, sickness, old age and death. As I traversed this ocean of misery, *bien kho,* I would have striven to extinguish in myself all passions and desires. To this day I still shudder when I think of it.

One evening Elder Brother Seven took us to this pagoda for the great celebration in the Buddha's honor, where those who were wealthy and pious made sumptuous offerings. This rare occasion gave rural laborers from the surrounding villages, young and old alike, an opportunity to gather together, meet, flirt, and generally enjoy themselves. Before the Buddha's altar, in flickering candle-light and swirls of sandalwood smoke, youngsters clustered wide-eyed to watch figures of four hieratic animals made of brightly colored fruits, flowers, and leaves—Dragon, Ky Lin (a sort of unicorn), Tortoise, Phoenix—as they moved, animated by an invisible mechanism. At the end of the ceremony, huge amounts of fruit and multi-colored sweets in charmingly arranged offerings were distributed to everyone amid general gaiety. On the way home that night Brother Seven explained the venerated preacher's sermon to me, but my mind was still on the festival.

The Communal House about a hundred meters from the school was another place that especially attracted me. I often sought shelter there from the fiery midday sun, until the day that it ceased being a refuge and turned into a place of horror.

The Communal House was the village's administrative center, where the Council of Notables gathered from time to time to debate and "dispense justice." Otherwise no one was there except the care-taker, who lived in an adjoining hut. A closed room at the back of the house served as a cell. On the floor lay a long iron bar fitted with shackles that the notables used to fetter anyone arrested—usually peasants who were late in paying their capitation tax.*

One day at noon I entered the courtyard of the Communal House and stumbled upon a scene of beating. A poor wretch in rags was lying face down, his arms and legs pinned to the ground by three others. His tormentor was holding a long flexible rod at arm's length

Two styles of Communal House (drawings by Ngo Van)

and raining blows on the man's lower back. At each of the twenty-some blows, the victim cried out and jerked convulsively. The solemnly dressed notables seated inside looked on impassively at the punishment of the man they had just condemned. It was the notables' self-appointed right to intervene in disagreements between villagers and to judge and punish the poor people at their mercy. This scene of cold-blooded cruelty marked me for life.

I remember the time my family was the victim of a denunciation. At dawn one morning, a group of French and Annamite customs officials burst in on us. After searching the house from top to bottom, they confiscated the large earthenware crock and rudimentary equipment that my father used to distill rice liquor for offerings—at night, of course, and concealed in the woods. The spirits that were sold in the market from the monopoly distilleries of Thu Duc were truly disgusting. No one could possibly offer them to the deceased on the anniversary of their passing. After the officials had made an inventory of every one of our meager possessions, including the number of roosters, hens and pigs, these "buffalo heads" and "horse faces" took away Brother Seven in place of my sick father. The fine for Brother Seven's release from civil imprisonment in Saigon was crushingly high. My mother had to borrow a gold necklace from Great Aunt and pawn it at the Chinese pawnshop. In the face of such adversity, did the invocations to Buddha comfort my mother? Perhaps.

Around that time my father began suffering from chronic spasmatic pains. He let lie fallow the patch of ricefield he had in the neighboring village, near the house of his eldest brother, Uncle Four. My mother was at her wits' end. The conical hats she made for peasants out of latania leaves did not bring in enough for our daily rice. My two brothers stopped going to school and started working as plowhands and rice threshers, with or without our own buffalos, for farmers in and around our village. I was the only one still attending school, though I had to "play hooky" once to look after the buffalos in my brothers' place because they were overburdened with work. The morning I returned to school, the teacher gave me two resounding slaps for being absent without permission.

We knew what deprivation was. To fill our stomachs, we had to add potatoes to our staple diet of rice. When the potatoes ran out, we hunted in our woods for *cu nang,* a farinaceous bulb-shaped root with spiny tendrils. To make the tubers edible, my mother peeled them and cut them in slices which she soaked for days, changing the water several times. One day I saw my father stagger like a drunkard, and then my brothers and I fell ill. The *cu nang* flour had not been soaked long enough. This incident reminds me of the kindness of a distant cousin, living in the next village at three hours' walking distance. He often "loaned" us unhulled rice, which we went over to pick up in a buffalo cart borrowed from our neighbor.

After two years at the communal primary school, I was initiated into *quoc ngu,* the vernacular form of writing. At the end of the second year, though, it was time to say farewell to the communal school. Just before summer vacation, my mother took a beautiful plump rooster and some traditional cakes to my schoolmaster's house. He advised her to have me continue my education at the district school in Thu Duc.

I was then about ten years old. The school was an hour away by foot. Just outside our hamlet, I had to cross a wood stretching along a large stagnant pool that teemed with skinny frogs and dragonflies during the rainy season. The path opened onto a gravel road right beside Lady Hieu's huge banyan tree—*Cay da Ba Hieu.** This sacred tree sheltered the gods of the domestic hearth, *Ong Tao,* spirits of Lime embodied in the discarded lime pots and fragments of smoke-blackened terracotta blocks that were scattered at its foot.

Five hundred paces further on, I would pass the Catholic graveyard with its strange grayish tombstones topped by crosses, interspersed among the hevea trees. I was told that their priests removed dead people's eyes to offer them to Dog, the father of Jesus. My steps quickened as I imagined those souls wandering around blindly. All contact was to be avoided with Catholics, the *co dao,* who preferred to venerate a white spirit hanging on a cross rather than worship the dead and their ancestors. Long-standing mistrust of the Catholics, descendants of those who had helped the French occupy our country, stoked our imagination and gave rise to a tenacious legend in our village: that since the mother of Jesus had no husband, she gave birth to Jesus by coupling with a dog. This hateful legend is reminiscent of the Chinese legend about an emperor of China with an incurable wound on his leg, who promised his daughter to anyone who could cure him. The finest doctors failed, but a court dog licked his wound and healed it. True to his promise, the emperor put his daughter and the dog on a raft, which he had float downriver to the South, where they begat the ancestors of the southern barbarian tribes.

Returning home from school in the evening was even more frightening when an invisible chorus of cicadas atop the giant *cay sao* trees along the path began their clamorous chant. I was also filled with an uneasy dread when I passed Lady Hieu's banyan tree or walked in descending darkness by the haunted pool at the edge of the woods.

I was accepted in the preparatory course at the school in Thu Duc. Thay Giao Nai (Master Stag) was a gentle man who (most exceptionally for a teacher) never raised his hand against his students. The following year, I entered the elementary course under the authority of Ong Thiet (True Director), who was known for his severity. Every morning when he entered the schoolyard, the pupils had to line up on either side, fold their hands and bow down as he went by.

In class, if his forehead glistened with anger, we waited for the lightning to strike. He would point his finger like a dart at a "guilty" party and shout, "Come here!" The boy would prostrate himself at the master's feet. Immediately, the victim's lower back was bared and he would receive a violent caning. Ong Thiet's daily fury used up many canes. A large bundle of those horrid pliable stalks was stored alongside exercise books and record books in a cupboard at the back of the classroom. For a single "yes" or "no," any of us could be subjected to torture. Like the other pupils, my back knew the cane's wrath.

Our teacher Ung, newly graduated from the Teachers College, was in charge of the intermediate class. He used the cane less, but was adept at getting the pupils to do his personal chores. He was lodged behind the school. Many a time as we played marbles in the shade of the trees during break-time, he made us fill his water jars. It took two of us, bearing the ends of a wooden pole on our shoulders. On the way back from the public fountain, I walked in front of my taller companion, and the brimming tin oil drum swinging from the pole grazed my heels roughly at each step. Thay Ung also instructed me in the art of cleaning and whitening his canvas shoes.

At noon, after our cold rice, we sometimes ran off to one of the nearby sugar-refining shacks to be given scraps of cane sugar.

One night a nocturnal bird swooped down into the courtyard, flapped its wings furiously and let out piercing screeches before flying off again. My mother saw this as a terrifying omen, and so it turned out to be: our father, who had been ill for so long, died.

To this day I am very moved by the thought of my father. Sensing that he was soon to be united with his ancestors, he said to my mother, *"Ma bay tre, rang xoay xo cho qua ngay thang, dau sao cung dung do con."* (Mother of our children, try to get through the days and months as best you can, but never hire out the children at any price!)

My father had no doubt been affected by the fate of the four boys of our impoverished neighbor, Trum Nhut. Unable to feed them, he had placed them as ox-drovers and domestic servants with rich landowners, who had mercilessly abused them.

On my father's death, my family invited a monk from the village pagoda to conduct the funeral ceremony according to Buddhist rites. The next day, family members and acquaintances made their offerings, accompanied by strident funeral music performed by an itinerant troupe of musicians on tambours, oboes, cellos, kettledrums and wooden clappers. I stayed by my mother's side and naïvely tried to console her whenever she began to weep. The burial took place on the third day. The funeral procession, led by the monk, brought my dead father to his final resting place, a hundred paces from our house.

My father reposes in our woods under the shade of the old *cay go* tree. On the third day after the burial, the monk came to perform the "opening of the tomb door," a ceremony to allow my father to return home, where a shrine was dedicated to him. Every seven days my mother offered him a meal. At the end of a hundred days and then again on the first anniversary of his death, the eighteenth day of the eleventh moon, the family gathered to organize a commemorative offering. But after the second anniversary we discontinued any visible signs of mourning, since by that point we were supposed to have ceased to mourn him in our hearts.

With my father gone, my mother, faced with the worrisome task of providing our daily bowl of rice, redoubled her efforts to produce conical palm-leaf hats for peasants. I learned to help her, and my brothers worked as hard as they could in the fields so that I could continue going to school.

I started learning French when I was about eleven. The indispensable dictionary, *Larousse Élémentaire,* could only be acquired in Saigon, a fifteen-kilometer hike from Thu Duc. That journey marked a memorable moment in my life. I had to leave the house before dawn, in total darkness. Fatigue had no effect on me—I was too enchanted by my solitary walk through the night and then by the immensity of the rural landscape under the rising sun. At the Binh Loi bridge I gazed at the Saigon River, sparkling with lights. Up till then I had only known it as a blue line meandering across the gray map of Gia Dinh province.

I had gone to the teeming city of Saigon once before, on a trip with my father to buy bicarbonate in the hope of relieving his stomach pains. The pharmacy was opposite the Continental Hotel on Rue Catinat and next door to the Portail Bookstore.

In the early afternoon, under a blazing sun, I turned my steps homeward, the dictionary tucked under my arm. At each pause in the shade of a tree I could not resist the fascination of turning its pages to marvel at the plates of drawings, the illustrations, and the columns of words full of innumerable mysteries to penetrate.

At the end of the elementary year the teacher chose two pupils to enter a competition for a scholarship—myself and an older boy.

Ngo Van at the tomb of his father (1997)

On the eve of the big day, Brother Seven took me to Sister Five's house in Thi Nghe, so I could get to the Gia Dinh county seat north of Saigon on time the next day. The examination was to be held at the Ba Chieu school.

The afternoon was humid and swelteringly hot. We walked along the road from Hang Sanh to Thi Nghe. All of a sudden a monsoon hit, blowing huge clouds that obscured the sky and the earth. A few seconds later, great daggers of raindrops shot obliquely down on us. I held my Chinese umbrella tight as a blast of wind turned the lacquered brown paper dome inside out and thrashed at the tattered shreds clinging desperately to the broken bamboo spokes. I wondered if that foul wind was not a bad omen and if my prospects for a scholarship were not shattered also. We reached Sister Five's house at nightfall, completely drenched and my heart full of foreboding.

Nevertheless, I made it through the ordeal of competition without even forgetting the "s" in *torchis* during the French dictation. Then came the wait. In the meantime, one of our buffalos began refusing to eat and staggered around, moaning out of pain and exhaustion. With tears in our eyes we had to resign ourselves to leading it away to die in a distant wild wood.

A month later, the notable in charge of the village police summoned my mother, a widow with three dependent children, to investigate her financial situation. Eventually she was allotted 27 piasters every three months—a fortune for a poor woman struggling night and day to produce hats for 10 or 20 centimes (a centime was one-hundredth of a piaster).

Our schoolmaster, Venerable Thiet, was determined to see as many of his pupils as possible earn the *Certificat d'études* diploma, which would enhance the school's reputation and especially his own reputation as its principal. One evening after school, he took me and another classmate to Saigon in a horse-drawn carriage known as a "matchbox." He intended to "arrange" our upcoming *Certificat* exam. It was dark by the time we reached the city.

The coachman stopped the vehicle on a street in the Da Kao district. The master told us to wait there and vanished into a door a hundred paces further on. A silver moon shone bright in the sky. The horse, unharnessed by the coachman, grazed peacefully on wisps of grass beside the road and deposited droppings at the foot of an electric pole while we chatted with the coachman. When the schoolmaster returned, he looked very much out of sorts. Without a word to us, he signaled to the coachman to hitch up the horse. On the road home, no one broke the silence for a good while as the carriage tossed us about. Then, no longer able to contain his icy anger, he burst out: "Balls! He wanted nothing to do with it."

In other words, the colleague in Saigon refused to go along with his little scheme.

I supposed that he would try to enter into contact with other teachers in charge of proctoring

Ngo Van's mother (1955)

the next examination. But ultimately no one "helped" me in either the written or the oral exam. Nevertheless, on Venerable Thiet's demand, my mother had to pay him some thirty piasters as her share of his colleagues' compensation for "helping" me succeed. For her that meant producing quite a large number of hats.

The following month, I took the scholarship examination at Chasseloup-Laubat High School. Fate struck once again. When my name was called, I realized I had left my student card where I was staying at my cousin's. She lived in Thu Thiem, a hamlet on the other bank of Saigon River. The whole time from the school to her house and back, including the river crossing in a sampan, I was in a state of acute anxiety.

Then once again we waited for the result. Things looked hopeful when the head of the district summoned my mother to investigate her financial situation, a sign that I was admissible. Yet at the start of the new school year in September 1926, it was another "admissible" boy, from a well-off family, who prepared to enter Chasseloup-Laubat. His parents had taken effective "measures" to sway certain secretaries in the Saigon Department of Education, and he was the candidate chosen. This was a bitter blow, the first time I came up against the invisible wall that my mother was powerless to cross. We felt miserable and helpless. With my local primary-school diploma I was qualified to be a village teacher; but I was only thirteen years old! My teacher felt sorry for me and made one last desperate move. At his own expense, he brought me to the Huynh Khuong Ninh boarding school in Saigon, crowded with children of native notables, in the hope that I would be accepted free as a day pupil or at least as a boarder for a reduced fee. I didn't see how, in either case, my mother could continue feeding me for another three or four years. At any rate, all that bargaining was in vain because the purveyors of education turned their backs on anyone without money.

* * *

The most important person for me, as a child, was Anh Bay, Elder Brother Seven. When I was ten years old, he had to abandon his plough for a wrench and work as a mechanic's assistant in the Di An railway depot, an hour's walk from our house. A week before Tet—New Year's Day—we went with Brother Seven to weed the grass around the family graves. On the twenty-third day of the twelfth moon, the day for celebrating the departure of the spirit of the hearth, he put up the *cay neu*—a long bamboo pole—at the far end of the courtyard. A small bamboo basket attached to the top of this pole contained offerings to the spirit on its way to the heavens. On the eve of Tet, via this same *cay neu,* the spirit would return to earth to its own altar. Depending on the spirit's report, the Celestial Emperor would prolong or curtail one's life.

Elder Brother Seven also prepared bamboo firecrackers for our celebration and for friends in the village. I helped him grind burnt manioc stalks in a mortar into a fine charcoal dust. He explained exactly how much of each ingredient—charcoal, sulfur and saltpeter—I should add to make the powder, which I then packed in a cardboard cube. I learned how to encase the charge in long, finely

cut slats of bamboo to give
the firecracker a perfect cube
shape. Positioning the fuse was
a delicate operation. The qual-
ity of the firecracker is assessed
by the duration of the echo that
it produces when it explodes.
One time the mixture of powder in the mortar ignited spontaneously and almost set fire to
my brother's straw hut.

Much later, when I was
working in Saigon and Brother
Seven was scraping by as a
mason, living with Sister Five
at Thi Nghe in the northern

Anh Bay (Brother Seven)

suburbs of the town where I often went to see him, he was stricken
with malaria. I was able to stop his fever with intramuscular quinine
injections; but then, in his convalescense, he suddenly felt himself
transformed into a tamer of spirits and demons. Without warning,
he left Thi Nghe and returned on foot to our village. Instead of returning to the family home, he went to the temple of the Guardian
Spirit of the next village, walked straight into the inviolate sanctum,
parted the curtains, stared into the face of the Spirit (in statue form)
and began talking to him as equal to equal.

The much-feared occult influence of Guardian Spirits extended
far into the countryside. Sometimes people with a disagreement settled their differences in front of the altar. To free himself from a
false accusation, the accused would wring the neck of a live rooster,
beseeching the Venerable Guardian Spirit to strangle him, too, if he
spoke in bad faith.

This strange encounter of Brother Seven with the Guardian Spirit,
an unprecedented event in the region, endowed him in the eyes of
the rural world with a mystical aura and magical powers over the
forces of evil that inhabited the invisible world.

Often he remained silent. At other times, in the presence of family or friends, his words would come streaming forth, following a

logic different from ordinary language. Stretched out on a hammock night and day, he ate only at midday—a little rice with handfuls of red peppers. His way of drinking tea was to pour the boiling water directly into his mouth, onto the tea leaves resting on his tongue. He continued to baffle my mother and other brothers, who were extremely concerned about his condition.

The entry and exit of our house was by the two side doors, the front having been closed to outside view by horizontal slots of wood that allowed in light and air. One day of crisis, his face stormy, dazed and wide-eyed, Brother Seven suddenly "took off." Leaping through the narrow space between the roof and the upper crossbeam and down onto the courtyard, he disappeared like a puff of wind into the tangled undergrowth of the pineapple wood. What to do? Brother Twelve tried in vain to find him. Our anguished household did not catch its breath until Brother Seven suddenly reappeared, unharmed, relaxed, his face serene. Not one tear in his white clothes, not one scratch on his naked feet after plunging into the lacerating brambles and barbed pineapple leaves.

The crisis eased with time, and Brother Seven eventually regained his habitual calm. But he was no longer our former Anh Bay. A peasant from the neighboring village called him to help with a possessed man suffering an attack. As soon as Brother Seven arrived on the scene, the man stopped thrashing about and threw himself, shaking and mumbling, to Brother Seven's feet. As if the Evil Spirit had met its master, the poor victim was delivered. From that day on, the villagers came to consider Brother Seven not just as a healer but also as a seer, like the neighboring village's learned Tonkinese man, and even a magician, like the man who had inaugurated Great-Lady's little temple in our own village. He came to be able to remove ills and bring comfort. As the years went by, like the traditional itinerant doctor-healers, he prepared his remedies with plant-based potions used in the South as well as northern medicines that had come from China. Little by little, people began seeking him out, even from distant provinces. He lived on very little. In return for his help, people offered him shelter and a frugal bowl of rice. From poor people he asked nothing in return.

Most often, he arrived on foot, recognizable from afar by his lean, tall silhouette shaded by his white umbrella. The therapy practiced by Brother Seven remained an enigma. Perhaps the doctor friend who treated my father during his long illness had transmitted some tricks of the trade. Perhaps he had come across the medical compendium *The Essence of the Spiritual Art of Healing* in the form of "Questions and Answers between the Fisherman and the Woodcutter" by Nguyen Dinh Chieu, author of *Luc Van Tien,* the famous popular poem which Brother Seven knew by heart.

As he grew older, Anh Bay no longer traveled about. He was given lodging by the owner of a Chinese medicine shop in Thu Duc, and it was there that people came to consult him.

Chapter 3

YEARS OF APPRENTICESHIP

C'est une grande destinée que celle de la poésie! Joyeuse ou lamentable, elle porte toujours en soi le divin caractère utopique. Elle contredit sans cesse les faits. Dans le cachot, elle se fait révolte; à la fenêtre de l'hôpital, elle est ardente espérance de guérison; non seulement elle constate, mais elle répare. Partout elle se fait négation de l'iniquité. (Baudelaire)

[Poetry has such a great destiny! Whether joyous or mournful, it always bears within itself a divine utopian character. It ceaselessly contradicts reality. In the dungeon, it turns into revolt; at the hospital window, it is the ardent hope for a cure; it not only records, it restores. Everywhere it negates iniquity.]*

One of my cousins, a real country beauty, had married an employee of the Saigon branch of Descours & Cabaud, a French metal products company. She was pleasant, a gambler (sometimes for rather high stakes), and she liked me. She took me in as a lodger for eight piasters a month in September 1926, when I left my hamlet for Saigon to prepare once again for the scholarship competition.

I was entering a city that had been shaken for several months by the winds of revolt.

All around me I heard the name Nguyen An Ninh whispered with respect. He had been thrown into prison three days after a memorable mass meeting right in the center of Saigon.

On Sunday, March 21, 1926, between two and three thousand people had responded to an appeal to protest the expulsion of a journalist to Annam. Despite an enormous police blockade, at dawn hundreds of coolies, factory workers, office workers and students streamed onto Rue Lanzarotte. In the Mango Garden, the assembly point, the crowd was so dense it was impossible to move; the branches of the mango trees sagged under the clusters of young participants. In this shoulder-to-shoulder fraternity, the common people of Saigon shouted their indignation, denounced deportations, and demanded freedom of the press, of education, of assembly and of travel, as well as the abolition of "physical detainment" for debt.

Three days later another assembly at the port, organized to greet the arrival of Bui Quang Chieu, the leader of the moderate-nationalist Constitutionalist Party,* on his return from France, turned into a huge demonstration of anger at the news that Nguyen An Ninh had been arrested after the previous rally. The entrance to the port and the surrounding streets were overrun by protesters as the offices, stores and workshops emptied. The authorities delayed the arrival of the ship carrying Bui Quang Chieu until nine o'clock in the evening, but the crowd refused to disperse and continued to grow. Some young people from the Jeune Annam [Young Annam] organization, together with some 800 Arsenal workers, surrounded Bui Quang Chieu as he disembarked to protect him from counterdemonstrators who had been mobilized by De La Chevrotière, editor of the newspaper L'Impartial, and who were shouting: "Kill him!" A crowd of demonstrators accompanied Bui Quang Chieu through the streets to his party offices, chanting: "Free Nguyen An Ninh!"

That same day, the venerable Phan Chau Trinh died after a life of relentless struggle against the "civilizers." Condemned to death in 1908 after the peasant revolt in Annam, his sentence had been commuted to deportation to Poulo Condore due to the intercession of the League for the Rights of Man. He was then exiled to France in 1911. He was eventually sent back to Cochinchina, where, racked by tuberculosis, he died after eighteen years of penal servitude and exile.*

The popular emotion aroused by Phan Chau Trinh's death, augmented by the arrest of Nguyen An Ninh, reached its peak. Thousands of men, women and young people, defying the omnipresent police, filed along Rue Pellerin throughout an entire week, lighting sticks of incense for the deceased. On April 4, 1926, Phan Chau Trinh's funeral was transformed into a massive demonstration against the masters. Crowded around the hearse were thousands of coolies and workers from the rice-processing plants of Cholon who had abandoned their work, along with students from the city and the provinces, workers and employees of the Arsenal, and peasants from Ba Diem and Hoc Mon.

At his first trial (April 24, 1926) Nguyen An Ninh was sentenced to eighteen months' imprisonment.

Phan Chau Trinh

When this sentence was announced, students in Saigon and from the primary school at Phu Lam in Cholon and from all over the surrounding regions (Ben Tre, My Tho, Vinh Long, Can Tho) deserted their classes en masse. More than a thousand of them were expelled.

I attended primary school from September 1926 to May 1927. But I was already fourteen, and I worried constantly about the eight-piaster monthly rent, which was too much of a burden for my mother. So I jumped at the chance of a job at Descours & Cabaud when a vacancy came up in the accounts department. I was hired for 35 piasters a month, which allowed me to live tolerably well. At that time coolies were earning only 15 piasters, or at most 18. Now it was my turn to help my mother—except on the all-too-frequent occasions when my cousin, usually in the middle of the night, begged me to hand over my pay, which she invariably proceeded to lose in the gambling parlors. Which is why I eventually moved to other lodgings.

That was the end of my formal education, but I continued to read everything I could get my hands on. I would buy used books from the Chinese bric-à-brac stalls across from the Saigon railway station, where French people sold their books before leaving the country. I read them all voraciously—books on science, history, philosophy. In this way one day I discovered with exaltation the writings of Rousseau. "The despot is the master only as long as he is the strongest. . . . Force is the only thing that keeps him in his position, and only force can remove him."*

My overseer at work, a half-French young man who didn't care for reading, gave me all the books he'd been awarded as school prizes. Among them was Baudelaire's *Les Fleurs du Mal* [Flowers of Evil], a handsome volume with gilt-edged pages. I knew nothing about the poet or his times, but when I read that he had been condemned for "offending public morality and good manners" and that he had suffered censorship, which was so familiar to us in the colonies, I was strongly drawn to him. It was also said that during the 1848 revolution he had been seen among the raiders of an armory, carrying a rifle and shouting, "We must shoot General Aupick!"

I have also not forgotten Jean Richepin's *La Chanson des Gueux* [The Song of the Tramps], with its magnificent engravings protected by tissue paper. I can still see the illustration of the venerable old Goat with the two little vagabonds sitting on his bony back, laughing and trotting very gently so that they would not fall off. Above all, I was moved by the vibrant couplet that replaced the censored passage from the "Idylle de pauvres" [Romance of the Poor]:

> *Ici deux gueux s'aimaient jusqu'à la pâmoison,*
> *Et cela m'a valu trente jours de prison.*

[Here two tramps loved each other to exhaustion, and that got me thirty days in prison.]*

A workmate who was better educated than I secretly gave me a copy of *Une histoire de conspirateurs annamites à Paris, ou La vérité sur l'Indochine* [A Story About Annamite Conspirators in Paris, or The Truth About Indochina] by Phan Van Truong. In this book the author described the plot hatched against him and Phan Chau Trinh by the French government in Paris in 1914. He clarified, in a way that made my blood boil with revolt and set my brain on fire, the "profession of being an Annamite," the unavoidably ambiguous and duplicitous attitude of the colonized:

It is said that the Annamite is withdrawn and that his soul is impenetrable. But has France, supposedly the country of freedom of opinion, ever allowed the Annamites to freely express their ideas and their feelings? The Annamite is a cheat and a liar, we are told. But if the Annamite tells the truth and it is disagreeable, he is gagged, persecuted, smashed into a thousand pieces. The Annamite, we are also told, is obsequious, groveling, vile. That may be so. But when he allows himself to be justifiably proud and dignified, he is called arrogant, insolent, rebellious, and again he is persecuted. The conclusion is inescapable: "being an Annamite" is a vile profession.*

I began to follow news of underground revolutionary movements more closely. The first event that caught my attention was the "Rue Barbier affair." On the morning of December 9, 1928, the Saigon Sûreté discovered the mutilated body of a man in a room at 5 Rue Barbier. That discovery set in motion a vast dragnet of the underground groups Thanh Nien Cach Mang Dong Chi Hoi (Revolutionary Youth League) and Viet Nam Quoc Dan Dang (National Party of Vietnam). I cycled past the scene of this drama.

In my new lodging I had an older roommate named Phung, who worked as an accountant at the Botanical Gardens. A former nurse in the rubber plantations, he taught me how to administer first aid. He was curious, but somewhat timorous. Nevertheless, despite not having a real spirit of revolt, he lent me a banned book that had appeared in 1929, Phan Van Hum's *In the Central Prison,* which recounted the struggles of Nguyen An Ninh and Phan Van Hum and their lives in prison. I learned that upon his return from France in 1923, Nguyen An Ninh had refused a position as magistrate offered to him by Governor Cognacq along with a concession of land. I was extremely moved by those who voluntarily refused to integrate themselves into

Phan Van Truong

colonial society, to become functionaries, and who chose instead to live side by side with the common people. I tried as hard as I could to follow events, amassing piles of press cuttings which I hid in a shoebox. There was omnipresent police surveillance and I was constantly running into people who were much too curious. My roommate Phung was scared to death.

From October to December 1928, denunciations and torture-induced confessions led to the arrest of hundreds of peasants on suspicion of belonging to an imaginary organization, the "Nguyen An Ninh Secret Society."*

I was struck with admiration for the daring of 35-year-old Phan Van Kim, who, disguised as a Chinaman, bluffed his way into court and shot Judge Nadaillat. When arrested, he declared that he had also wanted to kill the prosecutor and his deputy.

The second trial of Nguyen An Ninh began on May 8, 1929, along with that of Phan Van Hum and more than a hundred indicted peasants and day laborers. On the night of September 28, 1928, Phan Van Hum, while walking in Ben Luc with Nguyen An Ninh, had been stopped by the militia, who confiscated his papers. When he protested, a *cai* (militia chief) hit him with a cosh. Nguyen An Ninh reacted with his fists. Phan Van Hum was immediately arrested. A few days later Nguyen An Ninh turned himself in.

On the day of Nguyen An Ninh's trial, dense ranks of guards surrounded the Hall of Justice. Nguyen An Ninh arrived barefoot, dressed in black like an Annamite peasant. More than a hundred people pushed their way into the court. They were expelled as soon as the hearing began, and the trial took place behind closed doors. Even though none of the other defendants "identified" him, Nguyen An Ninh was jailed for more than a thousand days and fined 1000 francs for having formed a secret society. Phan Van Hum got eight months in prison and a 500-franc fine; the others, from two months to four years behind bars.

In February 1929 in Hanoi, Bazin, the director of the Bureau of Labor Recruitment for the rubber plantations (he received a bonus of 10 piasters for every recruit) was killed by a revolver shot.* A high-school student, Le Van Sanh, already marked for having distributed leaflets denouncing this recruitment, was arrested.

My roommate Phung told me what he had seen in the unhealthy, mosquito-infested rubber plantations where he had treated the coolies stricken by "forest fever," which was sometimes fatal. He described the beatings, the confinement in cells inside the plantations, the hunger, the impossibility of breaking the contracts, the attempted escapes that had been punished with torture. The living conditions and the work were so atrocious that the yearly death rate was sometimes as high as 40 percent.* In 1927 at the Michelin rubber plantation in Phu Rieng a hundred coolie conspirators, bound by a fraternal oath, had killed a notoriously brutal French overseer. A ruthless manhunt was unleashed. Seventy of the coolies were captured. The others perished in the forest while fighting their executioners or were devoured by wild animals, if they did not die of hunger or fever.

* * *

1930 was the year of the memorable insurrection of the Yen Bai garrison, where around twenty French officers commanded a thousand Tonkinese infantrymen. During the night of February 9, right in the middle of the Year of the Horse Tet celebrations, the insurgents attacked and took over the garrison. At daybreak, the surviving French officers regained control. Twenty-six of the rebellious soldiers and twenty-five civilian partisans fell into their hands.

I followed the drama day by day. Five planes, after dropping around fifty bombs on the village of Co Am, raked it and the surrounding countryside with machine-gun fire. The indigenous security police then razed the whole of Kien Thuy, Tien Long and An Lao. Straw huts, pagodas, temples of guardian spirits, fruit trees, bamboos—everything was reduced to ashes.

Between February and April 1930, two thousand people were arrested. At Yen Bai three of the rebels were beheaded in May, and thirteen more in June. At Phu Tho five were beheaded in November. There were undoubtedly many other legal assassinations that were never publicized.*

In 1931 I was gripped by Louis Roubaud's *Vietnam: la tragédie indochinoise,* a book that was eagerly grabbed up immediately on its arrival in Saigon. Roubaud's account made me appreciate more fully the massive extent of the revolt, which, though ignited at Yen Bai, had that same night inflamed other centers of the Red River delta: Lam Thao, Hung Hoa, Hanoi and, in the next few days, Phu Duc and Vinh Bao.

On the morning of May 1, as I was cycling to work, I found myself caught up in the disgusting dragnet for people without tax cards. It was the deadline for payment of the capitation tax, and in the streets of Saigon and Cholon, as all the coolies, workers and office employees were on their way to work, the cops stopped us to demand our tax cards, which also served as identity cards. Anyone who had no valid card was immediately shoved into one of the police vans that suddenly appeared on every street corner.

In the countryside the notables and the militia did the tracking down. Agricultural day laborers, seasonal workers and poor peasants all lived in fear. As a village schoolboy I had already seen those poor devils with their legs in irons in the Communal House for "tax delinquency."

The capitation tax (also referred to as the "personal tax") hit every coolie or peasant between the ages of 18 and 60. It amounted to a month's wages. The poor, already stripped of everything after the economic crisis of 1929, simply could not pay. And in Cochinchina, according to the Code de l'Indigénat, a mere delay in payment was punishable by imprisonment and a fine.

My workmate at Descours & Cabaud secretly handed me a zincographed copy of Co Do (Red Flag). I gleaned from it all the news I could about the processions of distressed peasants which, despite shootings and arrests, continued to form in practically all of Cochinchina, such as the May peasant marches in Cao Lanh, O Mon and Cho Moi. With women and children at the forefront, they demanded a reduction in the capitation tax, postponement of the deadline, payment for days of forced labor, and seizure of rice stocks from the landowners so they could be distributed among the poor peasants. A ferment not seen since the rural revolts of 1916! In the area of Saigon known as "the red neighborhood" blood ran in the streets: a dozen peasants were killed and many more were wounded.

Wholeheartedly at one with the starving people, I thrilled to news of their revenge. In July 1930, in Tan Tao village near Cholon, the *huong truong* (dignitary) Huot was gunned down. Toward the end of August, peasants attacked the Communal Houses where the notables assembled, including those of Xuan Thoi Tay, Tan Tru, Long Son, Chau Thoi and Chau Binh. In Tan Buu, they poured kerosene over the archives and set them on fire.

In Annam, on May 1, 1930, 1500 peasants from the Vinh area marched in silence, without placards, without flags and without arms, to the match factory in Ben Thuy to join the workers. The commander of the indigenous militia had stationed thirty men inside the factory and ordered them to open fire. Fifteen of the marchers were killed and countless others wounded. In the village of Hanh Lam (Thanh Chuong)* the peasants assembled to occupy the communal lands that had been annexed by a landowner, who was expanding his holdings at the expense of the village. Again, the same slaughter: 16 dead and 15 wounded. The villages of Yen Tha and Yen Phuc were burned to the ground.

The movement intensified across Annam, and from September on developed into an open insurrection. Demonstrators attacked the subprefectures of Nam Dan, Do Luong, Thanh Chuong, Nghi Loc (Nghe An), Can Loc, Ky Anh and Huong Son (Ha Tinh), cut telegraph lines, ransacked the native police stations, freed prisoners, set fire to railway stations and churches, and executed detested mandarins and notables. Two areas, Thanh Chuong and Nam Dan, were in total revolt. The militia no longer dared enter the villages. In October the insurrection reached Central Annam, where the subprefectures of Duc Pho (Quang Tri) and Son Tinh (Quang Ngai) were sacked.

In September 1930, in the villages of Nghe An, which had been abandoned by the notables and the local militia, the peasants began organizing themselves into soviets [democratic councils]. They took over the administration and, without touching the landed property, proceeded to share out the communal land that had been annexed by the landlords. They confiscated the rice reserves and distributed them to the starving, allocated agricultural work collectively, abolished taxes, imposed lower farm rents on the landowners, and launched a literacy campaign. These soviets extended throughout

Beheaded rebels (1908)

the provinces of Ha Tinh, Can Loc, Thach Ha and Huong Son.

Repression matched the scale of the insurrection: aerial bombardment and machine-gun fire were used to disperse gatherings of peasants. The Foreign Legion, the Colonial Infantry and the Native Guard set villages on fire, hunted to death the fleeing villagers, and executed prisoners. On September 12, 1930, at Hung Nguyen, three kilometers from Vinh, carnage was inflicted from the skies; six bombs dropped from a plane killed more than 200 demonstrators.

Nevertheless, on the thirteenth anniversary of the Russian Revolution, November 7, 1930, 1500 combatants launched an assault on the fortress of Phu Dien (Nghe An) and 600 attacked the military post at Can Loc (Ha Tinh).

In early 1931, insurgents killed the *tri huyen* (Subprefect) of Nghi Loc and threw his escort of militiamen into the river. In reprisal, 30 peasants were massacred and 200 arrested. In Quang Ngai province demonstrations multiplied, as well as marches on the local administrative centers, notably in Son Tinh and Mo Duc and in the center of the province.

In Cochinchina in March 1931 villagers sacked police stations, strung trip-wires across the roads, felled trees across the causeways, and dug little hollows in the road where they put planks full of nails to puncture the tires of any vehicles bringing reinforcements.

Parallel movements were taking place in the cities. Several days before May Day 1930 leaflets were already being circulated in the central markets and municipal workshops of Saigon, calling on workers to strike for the eight-hour day. Red banners appeared overnight in front of the offices of the Franco-Asiatic Oil Company and Standard Oil, bearing the slogans: WORKERS AND OPPRESSED PEOPLES OF ALL COUNTRIES, UNITE! DEMAND THE EIGHT-HOUR DAY! DOWN WITH FRENCH IMPERIALISM! WORKERS, PEASANTS, SOLDIERS, UNITE! INDOCHINESE COMMUNIST PARTY.*

The same day, the 250 coolies and workers at the Cho Quan central electrical works stopped work—an almost heroic act in the context of economic crisis and repression.

On January 13, 1931, a strike of 80 coolies broke out at Standard Oil in Nha Be in response to the firing of a fellow worker. Banners appeared in the districts of Da Kao, Tan Dinh and Khanh Hoi. In Saigon on Sunday, February 8, during the exodus from a soccer match a man spontaneously urged the crowd to commemorate the Yen Bai infantry uprising, which had taken place in February of the previous year. A Sûreté inspector, Legrand, tried to grab him and was killed by a revolver shot. That night, the zincographed pages of *Co Vo San* (Proletarian Flag) flooded the streets.

During March and April 1931, in Annam and Tonkin, committees and cells were broken up by the enemy. On May 1 alone, almost 500 demonstrators were massacred in Annam. Little by little, the movement disintegrated and dispersed into the population, which had been pushed to the limit by slow starvation as well as by the repression.

Between May 1930 and June 1931 I counted newspaper reports of no less than 120 peasant marches and more than twenty strikes in Cochinchina.

While the countryside was in turmoil, the trial in the case of the "Rue Barbier crime" opened in Saigon (July 15, 1930). Thirty-one members and sympathizers of the Thanh Nien (Revolutionary Youth League) had been indicted. Seventeen militants from other underground nationalist organizations were also appearing before the same court.

For me, the trial unveiled the mystery about the mutilated corpse found by the Sûreté in December 1928 and also revealed the implantation in Cochinchina of underground nationalist parties from Annam (the Tan Viet) and Tonkin (the Viet Nam Quoc Dan Dang—VNQDD). I was stunned at the verdict: death sentences for three of the Thanh Nien youth—Ngo Thiem, 22 years old; Nguyen Van Thinh, 24, and Tran Truong, 27; twenty years of forced labor for the prime instigator of the assassination, Ton Duc Thang, and eight years for Nguyen Trung Nguyet, 22, one of the two women implicated in the affair, whom I would later see in the Central Prison.

During the night of May 20–21, 1931, the guillotine was set up in front of the Saigon Central Prison for the three death sentences, while police cordons blocked off all the surrounding streets. Inside the prison during the hours and days that followed, the political prisoners—women and men—shouted unceasingly: "Down with the white terror! Down with French imperialism!" until fire hoses, bludgeons and leg irons finally enforced silence. On November 20, 1931, it was the turn of the teenager Huy (Ly Tu Trong), allegedly guilty of Inspector Legrand's murder, to be beheaded. The prisoners set up an enormous din that reached beyond the prison walls and shook the whole area. The repression was merciless. The Central Prison was so overcrowded with the mass of detainees that new detention camps of straw huts were set up in the nearby town of Thi Nghe.

Every Sunday I biked back to my village with clandestine newspapers and leaflets hidden in the handlebars and read them to my peasant friends. Afterwards, I kept them in a bottle hidden in the bamboo hedge.

I continued my reading of Marx at the Saigon Public Library after work, registering under a false name. I struggled to understand *Capital,* but was fascinated by Marx's notes giving concrete examples of capitalist barbarism.

I submitted an elegiac poem, *Bien Ca Chieu Hom* (Facing the Sea at Twilight), to an Annamite newspaper, and they published it as well as some short rustic vignettes about the hard life of the peasants. Some of my workmates reacted with friendly surprise. One of them, Phan Khanh Van, told me about what he had read at the My Tho high school—Balzac, Victor Hugo, Madame de Staël. He had written a novel and, wanting to submit it to a bourgeois journal, *Nam Nu Gioi Chung,* had met with one of its editors, Ho Huu Tuong. During their meeting Phan mentioned my attempts to translate the *Communist Manifesto.* Intrigued by this "pastime," Ho Huu Tuong wanted to meet me. From the beginning his manner was trusting and friendly. He sensed my eagerness to act, and arranged a first meeting in an isolated corner of the Botanical Garden, behind the enclosure where deer grazed.

Initiating me into clandestinity, Ho Huu Tuong introduced me to Anh Gia ("Eldest Brother"), with whom I would "work." Stunted in stature, Anh Gia looked older than his age to me. We soon became friends, and carried on numerous discussions sitting on the grass in isolated areas.

One day he gave me some pocket-format notebooks of handwritten texts duplicated on a jellygraph in violet ink. This was *Thang Muoi* (October), the theoretical organ of the Ta Doi Lap (Left Opposition). In it the Opposition criticized the Communist Party, a party that was oriented more toward the peasantry than to the workers, and the majority of whose leaders consisted of "Moscow trainees"* who were peasants rather than workers. Rejecting the model of the professional revolutionary formed by the Stalinist school, *Thang Muoi* argued that it was necessary to "bond" with the rank-and-file urban workers and build a "mass-based" party.

Unfortunately, at work I found hardly anyone with whom I could discuss current events. The coolies, truck drivers, and office employees seemed unconcerned with what was going on. Even the workmate who sometimes surreptitiously passed me communist leaflets showed little interest. Yet the brute force of the colonial regime was ever present and increasingly provocative. Among other acts of bullying, my stomach churned at the spectacle of the French foreman violently kicking one of my coolie workmates.

The repression was so great that people were afraid to use words like *cong hoi* (labor union) and *tranh dau* (struggle). So I tried, not without difficulties, to discreetly bring together most of the coolies and the two truck drivers in a kind of "mutual-aid association" for

AVIS DE RECHERCHES

Sont recherchés et à conduire à la disposition de l'autorité compétente ou à celle du Chef local des Services de Police en Cochinchine, à Saigon :

★ 13153. — ĐÀO-HƯNG-LONG dit HAI LONG dit TƯ LONG dit THIÊN dit Thầy BA dit Anh BA dit ĐƠN dit TÔ-LIÊN dit Ông ĐỐ, ancien commissaire des chaloupes «Đong-Sanh», «Đồng-Phát» et «Vinh-Thuận», âgé de 23 ans, né à Phước-Long (Rachgia), inculpé de participation : 1°/ à l'attentat, commis en Novembre 1931 à Tân-Thạnh (Baclièu), sur la famille du linh Trần-văn-Chuổi ;

2°/ à la tentative d'extorsion de fonds, commise le 25 Août 1930 à Saigon, au préjudice du Docteur Trần-ngọc-An.

Signalement : taille moyenne, corpulence faible, cheveux coupés à la manille. Marque particulière: une incisive aurifiée ou argentée à la mâchoire supérieure, entre 2 dents manquantes.

Renseignements : connaît très bien les caractères chinois, — exerce actuellement le métier de peintre.

★ 13154. — PHAN-VĂN-HAI dit SƠN dit TRÍ dit HẬU dit NHUNG dit HAI dit NHƯỢNG, né en 1911 à Xóm-Chiếu (Saigon), de feu Phan-văn-Nhiều et de Trương-thị-To, déjà arrêté à diver-

ses reprises pour menées communistes et libéré faute de preuves.

Signalement : taille 1ᵐ64. Marque particulière: nœvus à 5ᶜᵐ en arrière de l'angle externe de l'œil gauche.

Prière de prescrire des recherches actives en vue de découvrir ces deux individus qui sont membres de premier plan du parti trotskyste.

EXÉCUTION DE MANDATS DE JUSTICE

13155. — THỊ-DẬU dite THỊ-SÁU, — figure au Bulletin N° 134, signal. 11653, — inculpée de recel de produits provenant d'un vol qualifié commis au préjudice de Lê-văn-Thỏng.

Mandat d'arrêt N° 6950 R. P. de M. NOEL, Juge d'Instruction à Saigon, en date du 18 Août 1932.

Wanted poster for Dao Hung Long ("Anh Gia") and Phan Van Hai

the purpose of helping each other in cases of death, illness or other misfortune, as well as to foster a minimal sense of wage-slave fraternity. From time to time thirty or more of us would cautiously get together at one or another of our homes, on the pretext of celebrating a birthday or a marriage, or simply having a dinner party. (A meeting of more than 19 people without prior authorization was illegal.) I hid the record of the money collected in the lining of my cap.

One morning on arriving at work, I was pleasantly surprised to find that the coolies had refused to enter the workplace when the gates opened, and remained standing on the street. This was the first strike of the lowest-paid workers at Descours & Cabaud during the crisis-ridden years of endemic unemployment in the 1930s.

The next day they gathered again, sitting on the pavement on the other side of Boulevard de la Somme, 100 meters from the gates of the coolies' entrance, presumably awaiting some response from the bosses. I put the money of our fraternal association at their disposal. In the afternoon they decided to go in and tell the *Tay* (the French) what they wanted. I acted as interpreter for the exchange between them and the company manager, Guyon, a snarling bald man with a huge paunch. Suddenly Péret appeared, my immediate boss, a thick, stocky guy who was sometimes rather paternalistic when he was in the mood. He grabbed me by the arm and dragged me to the corner where I worked in the other building. Jabbing his index finger in my belly, he shouted, "Keep out of it, asshole, or you'll be out on your ass! Understand?"

The strikers demanded better pay and denounced the beatings and filthy insults. The slave-drivers gave no ground for the moment, but at the next payday the lowest wages were slightly raised.

At the beginning of 1932, Huynh Van Dam, who was alleged to have killed a Sûreté informer, was sentenced to death and guillotined. It was the third year of the economic crisis. Public works day laborers in Saigon were forced to accept a cut in their wages in exchange for no firings. Rickshaw pullers, who had been paying one piaster for a four-year license, were now obliged to obtain a new license lasting only one year for the same money. Reduced to beasts of burden, these men went on strike in Gia Dinh.

From August to November 1932 there were searches and arrests in Saigon-Cholon and police roundups in the provinces. Some sixty conspirators of the underground "Communist Left Opposition" group and a similar number from the Communist Party (which was in the process of reconstituting itself) were caught in the dragnet. Horrible statistics appeared in the *Dépêche d'Indochine* of February 2, 1933: between 1930 and the end of 1932, more than 12,000 political prisoners had been taken, of whom 88 were guillotined and almost 7000 were sentenced to years of prison or hard labor in the penal colonies. Three thousand detainees were still waiting in prison to learn their fate.

I was living beside the Cho Quan church in a partitioned apartment next to Anh Gia. One night in October 1932, I heard an alarming disturbance on the other side of the dividing wall: the Sûreté cops had broken in and were taking Anh Gia away, along with his eighteen-year-old partner Chi Muoi (real name Tran Thi Muoi), who had been one of the first Oppositionists within the Communist Party in 1931. The police turned the lodging house into a trap. I quietly slipped away, but when I pictured Anh Gia and Chi Muoi in the hands of the Sûreté torturers I felt like a part of myself had been captured. During the routine of my job, I rehearsed to myself the instructions in case of arrest. And as the days and weeks passed, I thought of the courage of those two, of all they must have suffered without breaking, since the police had not come to arrest me. I learned later in what condition the torturers had left Anh Gia. For a long time he was unable to stand up. I did not know then that my initiator, Ho Huu Tuong, had also been seized in the same raid. I learned what happened to my friends at their trial.

Anh Gia was one of the 21 militants from the Communist Left Opposition group (*Ta Doi Lap*) who were tried on May 1, 1933. Most of them were very young. He was sentenced to a year in prison, then sent to break rocks in the Chau Doc quarries. The main organizers, Ho Huu Tuong and Phan Van Chanh (but not Ta Thu Thau, who was tried later), who had both returned after some years in France, were given suspended sentences of three and four years. The others received prison terms of between four and eighteen months. But Nguyen Van Thuong and Pham Van Dong (who plunged a file into his throat when he was arrested) were hit with five and four years, plus restricted residence* of twenty and ten years, for the possession of revolvers. Pham Van Dong was kept until his death at Poulo Condore. Chi Muoi was acquitted. Despite the torture she had endured at the Sûreté, she did not hesitate to return to the struggle: it was she who, in 1935, distributed the clandestine pamphlets and leaflets of our Left Oppositionist group in the Stalinist-dominated rural regions.

On May 3, 1933, the enormous trial of 121 Communist Party members took place. The detainees were taken out of the Central Prison, handcuffed and chained to each other, and led across Rue Lagrandière to the Hall of Justice in the midst of chants, shouts and weeping from parents, wives and children, who were held back by the police. The courthouse was surrounded by a mass of civil guards and soldiers with bayonets fixed on their rifles.

This was the final act of the 1930–1931 peasant tragedy in Cochinchina. The majority of the participants came from the lower ranks of agricultural laborers, but also included coolies, typographers, electricians, lesser notables, teachers, office workers and soldiers, led by a handful of professional revolutionaries who had been trained in Moscow or Canton.

The tribunal accused them en bloc of "constituting a secret society, plotting against state security, and criminal conspiracy"; disseminating propaganda leaflets and newspapers; clandestine formation of labor unions and peasant unions; organizing marches of the poor to demand reduction of taxes in 1930; stealing arms from the Camp des Mares in 1929; executing three police officials and killing a militiaman during a skirmish at Nha Be in 1930; and attacking a transport ship at My Tho. Rushed through in five days, the trial ended before dawn on May 7 with a verdict of death for eight of the accused. Ninety-eight were sentenced to the penal colonies—for life in the case of nineteen of them, including an 89-year-old man.

With the peasant movement decapitated, several insurgents, most of whom had passed some time in France—Nguyen Van Tao (a Stalinist communist), Ta Thu Thau, Phan Van Chanh and Huynh Van Phuong (Trotskyist Opposition communists), Tran Van Thach and Le Van Thu (Trotskyist sympathizers), and Trinh Hung Ngau (an anarchist)—regrouped around their elder, Nguyen An Ninh, and took the initiative of legally opposing the colonial regime during the Saigon City Council elections of April–May 1933.* They launched a weekly French-language newspaper, La Lutte [Struggle], thereby evading the requirement that every publication in the indigenous languages had to obtain prior authorization. Thus it was that the two communist tendencies, Stalinist and Trotskyist, formed a common front in 1933 within *La Lutte*. This unique alliance, at the very moment that in the USSR and everywhere else in the world Stalin and the Communist Parties loyal to him were hunting down anyone even remotely suspected of "Trotskyism," lasted nearly three years. Stalinists and Trotskyists, in a joint struggle against their immediate enemies, the colonial regime and the bourgeois Constitutionalist Party, worked together to publish a newspaper for the defense of the workers, coolies and peasants. Nguyen An Ninh was the real linchpin. Every week, thanks to a network of well-placed sources, *La Lutte* assembled all the news and eye-witness reports it could find about workers (strikes, unions, wages, workplace accidents . . .) and peasants (plundering by landowners, extortion by notables, brutality of the colonists), and about trials, torture, police violence, and other abuses of the administration. For my part, I was also able to contribute news of movements in the plantations.

The Workers' Slate (*So lao dong*) for the election was headed by the Stalinist Nguyen Van Tao and Tran Van Thach, who was close to the Trotskyists. I attended the meetings in April 1933 at the Thanh Xuong Theater, which was filled to overflowing by the common people of Saigon and infiltrated by Sûreté cops. The enthusiastic audience raised their hands to vote that Nguyen An Ninh should chair the meeting. Thus it was that I finally saw the face of the man whose struggles had gripped and inspired me since 1928–1929. He was flanked by Ta Thu Thau and Tran Van An.

For the first time workers and coolies heard through the voice of Tran Van Thach someone talking openly about the right to belong to a union and to strike, about the eight-hour day and universal suffrage. The candidates' speeches were studded with taboo words— *cong hoi* (labor union), *tu ban* (capitalist), *vo san* (proletarian), *bai cong* (strike), *giai cap tranh dau* (class struggle)—which until then had only been secretly deciphered in clandestine leaflets.

In order to raise the large deposit needed for each candidate in the elections, Nguyen Van Tao had opened a small beer bar in the Old Market district. I took my workmates there in the evenings. On May 7, Nguyen Van Tao and Tran Van Thach were elected in the municipal elections. I, and I think many others, felt somewhat strengthened by this challenge to the arrogant colonial society—two candidates from a "Workers' Slate" becoming part of the Saigon City Council. Nguyen Van Tao and Tran Van Thach became, as far as was possible, the voice of the dispossessed within this municipal body—until three months later when their election was annulled by the colonial regime.

At the beginning of September a third trial of communists began. Among the sixty-odd prisoners charged with reconstituting a party was Lu Sanh Hanh, a dissident who had been in touch with the Trotskyist Left Opposition in 1932. Meanwhile, I attended talks at the Center for Mutual Education given by Ta Thu Thau and Phan Van Hum on dialectics—a subject that, despite its difficulty, engendered enthusiasm in many young people, office employees, workers and teachers in those tumultuous times. But under pressure from the Sûreté, the Center soon closed its doors to these discussions.

I learned from the *Dépêche d'Indochine* that the spirit of rebellion had reached the forests. Unsubdued by "civilization," the Moi tribesmen of the mountain area of Ba Ra had killed the Regional Administrator in October 1933. Militiamen and police responded by setting fire to all the straw huts in the Moi village and to the fields where the harvest was still waiting to be cut. Other recalcitrants of the forests, the Phnongs, retaliating for the "pacification" in the Haut-Chlong area, attacked military posts and inflicted severe losses on the colonial troops.

In 1934, I discovered Ta Thu Thau's *Trois mois à la Sûreté rue Catinat* [Three Months at the Sûreté on Rue Catinat]. Ta Thu Thau described what happened in that gruesome building, situated on the liveliest and most beautiful street in Saigon. One evening, a cop pulled him out of his cell to take him up to the torture room at the top floor, shouting: "Ah! This strapping fellow will be able to tolerate lots of blows!" Ta Thu Thau started to yell. Lacombe, the chief, appeared, and assured him he would not be mistreated. Which turned out to be true. Lacombe preferred to work on him through his comrades, who were being tortured with no respite.

From his cell, Ta Thu Thau looked for a way to communicate with the other detainees. First he would hoist himself up to the spyhole at the top of the door to watch for the guards; then he would

la lutte

Malgré le coup de force du Gouvernement,
Tao et Thach
sont candidats quand même, et légalement

Opinion unanime de cinq avocats de Saigon

APPEL

Votez en bloc

Dans la 2ᵉ circonscription
Pour :
Duong-bach-Mai.
Nguyen-van-Tao.
Trân-van-Thach.

Dans la 1ʳᵉ circonscription
Pour :
Phan-van-Hum.
Hô-huu-Tuong.
Nguyen-van-Nguyên.

candidats de l'opposition ouvrière

NOS CONSULTATIONS JURIDIQUES

Tao & Thach
maintiennent leur candidature

"La Lutte" (February 23, 1935). The articles concern the "Workers' Slate" candidates in the Saigon City Council election.

flatten himself on the cement floor, pressing his mouth and his ear in turn against the opening at the foot of the door. In this way he made the acquaintance of the young Nguyen Van Hoang, whose voice was so soft and so fragile. One evening Hoang, who had been horribly tortured, called out to him: "Brother! I can't bear it any more . . . They'll start again tomorrow. I want to end it all tonight." With all his strength, Ta Thu Thau begged him not to let himself be broken. A little later, he heard a dull, heavy thud, then silence. The next morning, the cops found Hoang still alive; they left him there in his cell, naked, with his legs in irons, for two months. Every night, Ta Thu Thau would hear him rattling his chains weakly.

One night, there were dreadful moans again. The cops were bringing a woman on a stretcher back into her cell. Ta Thu Thau tried to speak to comrade Nguyen Thi My, but she was consumed by suffering. The next day she was transferred to the Central Prison, then to the hospital at Cho Quan. She died shortly after her release from prison.

On some nights Ta Thu Thau would hear other comrades, Nguyen Van Be, Nguyen Van Thuong and Dong, being dragged off for torture every two hours.

* * *

"The wide world belongs to the vagabond" (Nguyen An Ninh).

Saigon-Shanghai-Osaka, an account by a journalist engaged as a cabin boy on a Messageries Maritimes ship, was for me an irresistible *invitation au voyage,** and I dreamed that some day I would take the same path toward the West (*di Tay*). Often, in the evenings after I left work (Descours & Cabaud was right on the port), I would sit on a bench at the edge of the Chinese Arroyo near the signal post and watch the comings and goings in the harbor, fearing that my dreams would all evaporate in the course of time like the plumes of gray smoke rising from the ships' funnels.

But one day, among the straw huts next to the docks, I managed to make contact with the wife of a sailor named Ty, who was in charge of the laundrymen on the *Aramis.* If I coughed up 50 piasters— a whole month's wages—he would introduce me to his boss. This boss took me to the enrollment office to obtain the necessary maritime passport, an impressive document which featured all my fingerprints and described me in full anthropometric detail. And there I was, signed on to the laundry team aboard the *Aramis,* the first diesel-powered vessel of the Messageries Maritimes. I embarked without informing my family, my friends, my employer, or anyone else except my comrade in underground activity, Ho Huu Tuong, who gave me the address of a Trotskyist friend in Paris.

The ship weighed anchor in Saigon on March 3, 1934. The laundry team consisted of a dozen guys, natives of Annam and Tonkin except for Ty and me, who were both from Cochinchina. I was assigned to iron sheets. We worked in the poop and slept in the hold, lying on planks in rows like sardines. The Canton Chinese, employed in hostelry, and those from Shanghai who worked in the engine room, had separate sleeping quarters. The Italians were cabin boys and we saw them only rarely. Above the entrance to the Cantonese sleeping quarters was hung the inscription *Bang huu nhu van*

Ngo Van's maritime passport (1934)

(Friends are like the clouds), calligraphed on a strip of white muslin. The dark room, full of sleeping bodies, was fitfully illuminated here and there by the sputtering oil lamps of the opium smokers.

In the Indian Ocean, a heavy swell rocked the boat. The pitching and rolling made me so nauseous that I couldn't stand up without vomiting. I dropped my work and ran to the hold to lie down. Annoyed at my desertion, my workmates came and pulled me from my plank berth. Finally I was transferred to sorting the linen.

On some days, the sea was so calm that a plate could float on it— *bien tha dia khong chim,* as my Tonkinese companions said. Flying fish, porpoises or dolphins preceded us, leaping out of the sea. . . .

After an interminable week in the Indian Ocean, the *Aramis* dropped anchor at Djibouti, an arid city of squat houses surrounded by wretched shantytowns. Not a single tree. The colonists took shelter, it was said, in the shade of palm trees made of zinc imported from France. . . .

The Red Sea; chains of black mountains, bare and torrid; then Suez. The ship slowly made its way through the canal bordered by deserts, passing silhouettes of camels advancing across the sand dunes. Then Port Said, where Arab peddlers clung to the topmost masts of their swaying craft, then leaped on board our ship to sell things to the crew—what, I don't know. . . .

It was dark when the ship passed through the Strait of Messina, with its formidable currents, and it was there I saw for the first time a volcano: Stromboli, smoking in the dark sky. When we finally reached Marseilles, the journey had lasted three weeks.

The "Aramis" on the Saigon River

Bassin de la Joliette. I was captivated by the animation of the port, the fast, decisive way men moved, and the women on high heels: clack-clack-clack . . . I had entered another time, another world, where life seemed accelerated.

But then I discovered that I had landed there in vain. In my haste to leave Saigon, I had not understood that you were only paid upon your return to the port where you signed on. My dream of going to Paris was crushed. It was a bitter blow. There was nothing I could do but resign myself to wandering around Marseilles for three weeks before embarking for the return. The *Aramis* was laid up and placed in dry dock; the guys in our laundry team showed up only to receive our rations of rice and *nuoc mam* [fermented fish sauce]. At night we returned to our sleeping quarters.

My first encounter was with Tu Cao (Fourth Razor), a somewhat elderly barber. He came to the port with his little work case every time a ship docked. He was originally from Saigon, and asked me what was happening in our country. He cut my hair for nothing and that evening invited me to a local pub. Standing at the bar, side by side with men sweating from their day's labor, I drank for the first time a white wine cut with lemonade while listening to Tu Cao's advice to be prudent. He then entrusted me to his friend Hon, who had time to show me around Marseilles a bit.

A former sailor who had been fired for drug smuggling, Hon was a stocky man whose adventures and misadventures (including some prison time) appeared etched on his craggy face. He hung around the docks, waiting for suppliers coming in from Constantinople or the ports of black Africa. He was also sought out by certain French opium addicts—I sometimes noticed them sneaking into the hold of the *Aramis,* where the Cantonese sleeping quarter was transformed into a temporary smoking den.

What Hon lived on in between the arrivals of suppliers was not clear. Odd jobs, minor trafficking in blue denims from Shanghai or unmarked cigarette lighters from Singapore . . . He knew all the tricks for slipping things past the customs officers.

One night, when he was taking me through the slum areas clustered around the Old Harbor where the drawbridge still operated, he suddenly darted into one of the dives full of smoke and deafening jazz. I stopped in the doorway. A very beautiful young woman came out. With a seductive smile on her lips, she said, "Hey, honey, do you want to come with me?" She beckoned me to follow her up to her garret. Panic-stricken, I ran off as fast as my legs could carry me.

The *Aramis* weighed anchor late one afternoon. France slipped into the distance like the promised land. I arrived back in Saigon on May 13, 1934.

* * *

I was able to return to my job at Descours & Cabaud. My bosses swallowed the stories I made up to account for my disappearance. Back in the daily grind, I revived our "fraternal association." Among my workmates, only the coolie Vo Van Don was awakened to social struggles, and we often found ourselves together during subsequent adventures.

I met again with Ho Huu Tuong, who introduced me one day to Lu Sanh Hanh, a former Communist Party dissident who had just been released from prison. On May 2, 1935, a thunderbolt hit the opponents of the imperialist order: Stalin and Laval signed the "Franco-Soviet Mutual Assistance Pact," which officially approved of France's development of military power. The French Communist Party would henceforth strive to stifle any antimilitarist spirit and to defend the integrity of the French Empire. The Indochinese Communist Party (ICP) gradually aligned itself with this position, despite inevitable internal resistance. *La Lutte,* the journal in which Stalinists and Trotskyists collaborated, kept silent. There was an urgent need to criticize the new line imposed on the ICP, but the legal Trotskyistes were bound by their agreement to a common front with the Stalinists in *La Lutte.* Faced with this submission to Stalinist nationalism, Lu Sanh Hanh and I and another comrade named Trinh Van Lau decided to create the League of Internationalist Communists for the Construction of the Fourth International.

We feared that the victory of Vietnamese nationalism over French imperialism would simply mean the rise of an indigenous bourgeoisie, and that the desperate condition of the exploited workers and peasants would remain the same as ever.

While providing for my daily rice kept me chained to Descours & Cabaud during the day, my nights were occupied in working with a young typographer to set up a clandestine printing press, which we put together with salvaged components. I learned to set type, and we were able to bring out one issue of a printed theoretical journal, *Cach Mang Thuong Truc* (Permanent Revolution), which circulated clandestinely. Toward the end of 1935, our group also started a mimeo newsletter, *Tien Dao* (Vanguard). Faced with *La Lutte*'s silence on the Laval-Stalin Pact, in our clandestine newsletter we denounced the alliance between the USSR and French imperialism.

The first practical action of our group was to support the striking wagon drivers. The drivers of the "matchboxes" (light two-wheeled carriages) were up in arms against harassment aimed at eliminating them in favor of the French Streetcar Company [*Compagnie Française des Tramways*]. By December 25, 1935, almost 100% of the workers had joined the strike. The next day, delegates representing some 3000 drivers from Saigon-Cholon and from the suburbs of Ba Diem, Phu Nhuan, Khanh Hoi, Cho Dui and Cho Quan demonstrated in Saigon's Central Marketplace, demanding that the newly elected Stalinist and Trotskyist city councilmen intervene.

The repression was fierce. The Sûreté took over the *La Lutte* office and arrested Nguyen Van Tao, Tran Van Thach, Duong Bach Mai, and the recently elected councilman Ta Thu Thau, charging them with interfering with the freedom to work.

We were in increasing danger, and moved our printing press several times.

The attempt to rebuild the Communist Party in Cochinchina by a group of "Moscow trainees" led by Tran Van Giau was completely destroyed. At the trial of forty Communist militants, Twenty-four were sentenced, most of them being deported to Poulo Condore.

For our part, we continued our underground agitation in the workplaces and continued to discreetly distribute—including in Stalinist circles—our newsletter *Tien Dao* and our journal *Cach Mang Thuong Truc*.

Then, in June 1936, explosive news arrived from France. With the coming to power of the Popular Front government, led by Léon Blum and supported by the Communist Party, French workers had gone on strike and occupied factories throughout the country. Had the days of hope also finally arrived for us colonial slaves? Our Internationalist League decided to call on our brothers and sisters to storm the gates of hell.

It was at that moment, Wednesday, June 10, just as we were going into action, that our group fell into the hands of the Sûreté.

Chapter 4

IN THE CENTRAL PRISON

As though we had a silent rendezvous, every morning I was one of the prisoners who pressed their faces against the bars overlooking the small yard of the women's quarters as the female prisoners emerged, two by two, carrying out the waste pails. Among them were Chi Nguyet, a tall slim silhouette, her face a pale full moon, and her companion, the delicate-featured Chi Day. Both of them would throw us quick, radiant glances, and every morning they smiled at us. *Innocent paradis plein de plaisirs furtifs . . .* [Innocent paradise full of furtive pleasures].*

Nguyen Trung Nguyet, whom we called "Chi" (sister and comrade), was 29 years old. She was the longest held of the female prisoners, having already been in confinement for seven years. She was born into a family of literate peasants. Breaking with tradition, when she was still a teenager she disguised herself as a boy and stowed away on a ship to Canton to join the Revolutionary Youth League (*Thanh Nien Cach Mang Dong Chi Hoi*). Under the name of Bao Lan, she wrote in the "Women's Tribune" section of the League's newspaper. Her radiant charm and the freedom of her relations with men were worrisome to the Thanh Nien leadership, who issued numerous warnings against the disturbing influence of "frivolous love affairs." This did not prevent several comrades from falling madly in love with her. Back in Cochinchina, she was arrested on June 7, 1929, at the age of 22, for involvement in the much-publicized "Rue Barbier crime."

During the night of December 8–9, 1928, the leadership of the Cochinchina section of Thanh Nien had passed the death sentence on a comrade named Le Van Phat. His crime was his love affair with the female comrade Thi Nhut and his consequent inability to "put aside personal considerations in order to devote himself totally to the revolution." The "revolutionary tribunal," presided over by Ton Duc Thang, the "hero of the Black Sea" (so named for his part in the mutiny of April 1919 on board a French warship, where he had raised the red flag), designated three of the youngest Thanh Nien members to be the executioners. The hidden motives behind this premeditated crime—wounded pride and/or amorous rivalry—naturally remained obscure. This Rue Barbier tragedy made me sick at heart, showing as it did how readily a party of professional revolutionaries can end up imposing authoritarian control over every aspect of life.

Once the body was discovered, the French justice system entered the drama. On July 15, 1930, the Saigon court condemned the three young murderers to death. Ton Duc Thang, who had presided over the Thanh Nien tribunal, was sentenced to twenty years' penal servitude. This dark episode in the life of the "historic hero" Ton Duc Thang, who in 1969 became the successor to Ho Chi Minh as the leader of the country, has completely disappeared from the official history of the "Socialist" Republic of Vietnam. Pham Van Dong, Ho Chi Minh's future prime minister, was condemned to ten years' imprisonment during the same trial.

The particular role of Nguyen Trung Nguyet in this affair is not known, but she was a Thanh Nien member and a relative of Ton Duc Thang's wife. She was sentenced to eight years' incarceration.

Chi Day (Nguyen Thi Dai), her companion, was 23 in 1935 when she was sentenced to five years in prison and ten years of restricted residence for having produced political leaflets. And their fellow women political prisoners Le Thi Dinh, Nguyen Thi Ba, Nguyen Ngoc Tot, who were sentenced at the same time—what became of them?

I remembered the big May 1933 trial of those other women combatants at the heart of the anticolonial revolts, who were also tortured in the chambers of the Sûreté and condemned to harsh sentences. Were they still there, invisible, somewhere behind those walls? Nguyen Thi Sau, 21 years old, who printed underground leaflets and newspapers; Nguyen Thi Nho, 25, and Pham Thi Loi, who had taken part in the "revolutionary tribunal" that condemned to

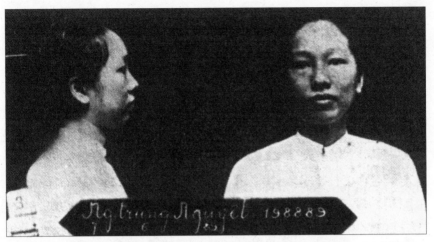

Nguyen Trung Nguyet

death the police notables of Huu Thanh; Nguyen Thi Nam, 22, who was active in the peasant demonstrations in the Cao Lanh region; Tran Thi Hanh, originally a teacher in Vinh Long, and Tran Thi Day, both of whom got jobs at the Franco-Asian Oil Company in order to carry out revolutionary action among the women coolies.

The monotony of confinement was broken twice a month by visits on the first Tuesday of every fortnight. Our close relatives, who mostly came a long distance in from the countryside, arrived in Saigon the night before and improvised a lodging as best they could so as to be at the prison early the next morning. The comrades from *La Lutte* helped them fill out their visit requests on stamped paper to present to the office at the earliest hour and gave them food to bring to us.

The guards made those who had visitors squat down along the inside of the courtyard wall, facing the Head Guard's office and the wire barrier. The visitors would squat on the other side, each one across from their prisoner, and put their packages on the ground in front of them. The guards rummaged through the food packages from top to bottom, fingering our cigarettes and eavesdropping on our conversations. Head Guard Agostini himself took part in the surveillance and made our visitors move off as soon as the search was complete, with no regard to the amount of time officially allotted for visits.

Despite the guards, we managed to pass prison news to *La Lutte*. Conversely, the pieces of local newspapers that the food came wrapped in provided us with bits of news of the outside world.

One evening, two weeks after we had been incarcerated, about forty men appeared one by one in the yard, their faces marked more deeply than ours by longer or more severe imprisonment. They were political prisoners brought back from Poulo Condore. Many of them had been sentenced the year before, militants of the ICP or simply members of the clandestine peasant unions. Our first contact with them was silent and guarded—they knew we were Left Opposition-ists.

I knew them by name from the newspaper articles I had read during their trial in June 1935. Here was Tran Van Giau, 25 years old, trained in Moscow, a "professional revolutionary" as he had proudly described himself before the tribunal on June 24. His vivid, piercing eyes shined with the fierce energy of rigid adherence to his cause. Nguyen Van Dut, a tall, gaunt figure, taciturn and prickly. ("It's the convict labor that made me this way," he would say in his defense.) Tran Van Vi, with his prominent red cheeks, former scribe to the Council of Notables in Vinh Kim village, had a certain arrogance, perhaps because he was an alternate member of the Central Com-mittee. I still remember some of their faces: Chau Van Giac, who showed his prominent canine teeth when he laughed; Nguyen Huu The, who looked like a provincial schoolteacher; Pham Van Kinh, whose dark complexion gave rise to his nickname "An Do" (the Indian).

Among the Poulo Condore returnees was a group of peasants from Mo Cay (Ben Tre) who, the previous year, had refused to stand up in the Court of Appeals to hear the verdict and had raised their clenched fists and shouted: "Down with French imperialism!" The judge immediately added five years to their sentence, to which they responded by shouting once more: "Down with French imperial-ism!" Despite the fury of the club-wielding police, the shouting con-tinued until the prisoners were returned to the prison. As they were led back, they were surrounded by a crowd of passersby who had rushed there to show their solidarity.

Still waiting to be judged, the peasants of Duc Hoa were held with us in Cell 6, while the Poulo Condore returnees were confined in Cell 5. But during the hours when the doors were opened, everyone met in the little yard and it was there that contacts, cautious but often sincere, were established between us. They, adherents of Stalin, and we, inspired by Trotsky, tacitly agreed that we should not provoke tension between us in the territory of our mutual enemy.

Ton Thanh Nien (Ton the Young), as his friends called him, cheerful and full of laughter, humorously recounted to me his "stay" at the Sûreté prison in Ben Tre. The detainees had been put on a diet of rice cooked in salt, and deprived of water. After a session when they were beaten on the soles of their feet with rattan canes, they were forced to run over the sharp stones in the Commissariat yard under the burning midday sun. Tortured with thirst, Ton stopped and despite the blows that rained on his body, drank the repugnant pond water polluted by ducks.

I liked to talk with one blind old man, whose eyes were completely veiled by opaque clouds. I admired both his youthful enthusiasm and the serenity and firmness of his face. Accused of having raised a red flag one night on a coconut palm tree in his hamlet, he was sentenced to three years in prison plus six years' restricted residence, then sent to Poulo Condore. People called him Van Tien, the name of the hero of the popular epic poem *Luc Van Tien,* about a young educated man who loses his sight through weeping over the death of his mother.

Tran Van Giau told me about the hunger strikes and the strikes against forced labor on Poulo Condore to protest the rotten food and the brutal treatment. Those strikes had suddenly appeared on March 1, 1935. The prison guards, armed with clubs, had burst into the cells like a pack of dogs, yelling, "We'll make you bastards see reason!" beating them mercilessly with all their strength. The cries of "Down with imperialism!" shouted in chorus grew weaker and weaker under the violence of the blows. The guards cleaned the blood off their clubs in the basins in the yard, then resumed their savage attack on the split skulls, the lashed backs, and the broken arms and legs until the clamors of the victims died down into silence. Nguyen Van Nu, his head shaved like a young Buddhist monk, would later give me his *Memories of Poulo Condore,* written in a sort of notebook put together with pieces of coarse brown toilet paper.

On August 6, 1936, our twelve peasant companions from Duc Hoa were taken to trial. Upon their return to the prison, in response to our anxious questions, all they could tell us was that they had declared in court that they had been tortured and that they had confessed whatever their torturers wanted. As witnesses, the court had simply called upon the inquisitors themselves: the Administrative Delegate from Duc Hoa who had had them arrested and Political Police Chief Gélot, who had tortured them. Moreover, the accused had no way of understanding the witnesses' statements, the prosecution's indictment or the speech for the defense, since they were all conducted in French. Nobody translated for them, as if it was none of their business. Nguyen Van Sang, a great strapping man, was sentenced to a year in prison plus five years' restricted residence, and the eleven others to between three and six months.

From the newspapers that wrapped the food our visitors brought, we soon learned that the "subversive plots" in Nguyen Van Sang's case were limited to his "intention" to hoist a red flag in a school on May Day, while his companion Lo allegedly distributed leaflets in the ricefields. They were also accused of holding meetings to discuss the redistribution of land and of having belonged to an association whose subscription was one centime per person per month.

News reached us that a Commission of Inquiry was to be held under Colonial Minister Marius Moutet, and we wanted to make our voices heard. The Poulo Condore returnees proposed that we conduct a hunger strike to demand the status of political prisoners.

During the night, by short sharp taps of a small stone on the cement floor, the strike project was communicated in Morse code to the women imprisoned in the cell underneath us.

Nguyen Van Sang, the most combative of the Duc Hoa peasants, proclaimed firmly, "Whatever happens, I will go the whole way!" As for me, I couldn't help thinking of the popular saying: *Nam that nu cuu* (A man dies after seven days of starvation, a woman after nine).

On Tuesday, August 11, 1936, about eight o'clock in the morning, Head Guard Agostini arrived as usual, accompanied by a French guard with a revolver in his belt and the jail-boy. At the end of his inspection of the cells—nothing abnormal about the ceiling, nothing unusual on the walls—just as he was about to leave us in peace, we came out with our declaration of war. Nguyen Van Dut, our delegate (diplomatically appointed in my stead because of the Head Guard's hostility toward me), went up to him and announced: "We all demand that the government give us political prisoner status, and to back up this demand we are refusing all food from today on." Without saying a word, Agostini gave us a pencil and paper and agreed to convey our list of demands. Those demands were: application of the same political prisoner status as in France; return of all the political prisoners deported to Poulo Condore, Lao Bao, Son La, Guiana and Inini; improvement in food (the daily ration for European prisoners was 80 sous' worth of food, while that of the Annamite prisoners was only 6 sous' worth). We also asked to be allowed to receive newspapers and books and to be allotted paper, pens and ink; and that sick prisoners not be shaved and shackled when in the hospital.

As usual, at mealtimes the tubs of rice were set out in the yard by the nonpolitical prisoners. We remained inside, lying down. Three-quarters of an hour later, the untouched food was taken away. No one went out into the yard during the period when the doors to the court were open.

The first days of the fast, I felt profoundly empty, and sweated profusely at mealtimes. The following days, I felt very weak, but the hunger pangs diminished—except for the day they brought us tubs of rice accompanied by eels fried in citronella, with its appetizing aroma. But nobody flinched. On the fifth day, Nguyen Van Sang, without saying a word, led some of his companions to the row of rice tubs, to the silent indifference of those who remained inside.

The days seemed longer to me than the nights. At the seven-day mark, I could see that none of us, even the elderly Van Tien, were on the point of rejoining our ancestors. To the oldest and to those who looked about to faint, we gave a little sugar that we had hidden in the walls.

Every morning around eight o'clock Agostini came and took an impassive glance at the bodies stretched out flat on the floor like sardines.

Day eleven, still no reaction and the strikers were reaching the limits of their strength. We decided to announce the end of our strike to Agostini the following day. In the morning, the guards brought us tins of condensed milk and boiled water. Our exhausted bodies immediately sprang back to life and a certain fraternal euphoria took hold of us all, even though it seemed that our strike had failed.

Around midday, we doused ourselves abundantly with water in the tank used for washing, and water gushed out of the pipe in the outside wall on Rue Filippini. That was the signal to the *La Lutte* comrades that we had ended our action. (They had their meeting place next to the prison, and had kept watch at this time every day since August 11, when we had begun the hunger strike.)

On Monday, August 30, 1936, we went to trial. Together, we had tried to prepare a minimal response to the judges, while at the same time trying to avoid making statements that could be used against us by the Stalinists. Handcuffed and escorted by armed militia, we crossed Rue Lagrandière to reach the Hall of Justice, which was just across the street. Large numbers of plainclothes and uniformed policemen were posted all around.

We were seated in the front rows of the benches in the courtroom. The room was packed with cops and journalists. In front of the black row of magistrates—Presiding Judge Lavau, with his emaciated, masklike face and Charlie Chaplin moustache, and Public Prosecutor Bouin, brawny with bloated pink face—the white-clad Annamite interpreter sat behind his little table, puffed up with self-importance.

This ritualistic stage setting left me feeling strangely detached. I even allowed myself a certain measure of carelessness. The Presiding Judge looked over his glasses at me and grunted, "What's wrong with that one? Is he ill?" A lawyer came up to me and discreetly urged me to uncross my legs and sit up straight; then, going up to the platform, he said something to the judge as though imploring his indulgence.

Lu Sanh Hanh was interrogated first. He was accused of having formed, in 1935, a group called the League of Internationalist Communists for the Construction of the Fourth International, whose aim was to overthrow the government and set up a communist regime; and of having published the journal *Cach Mang Thuong Truc* (Permanent Revolution) and distributed *Tien Dao* (Vanguard), a paper printed with a French mimeo machine. And we were all charged with "membership in a secret society" and with "subversive activities" for having taken an active part in the wagon drivers' strike of December 1935. Lu Sanh Hanh declared that we simply wanted to help workers and peasants gain the freedom to form unions. The Prosecutor returned to the charge, quoting French translations of excerpts from our newsletter indicating that the League aimed to destroy the colonial regime by insurrection and to establish an internationalist communist regime.

Then it was my turn. As a member of the League, I was accused of having organized the printshop. Asked about my activities at Descours & Cabaud, I replied that I had tried in vain to organize a labor union among the coolies and drivers. The judge pointed out that I had abandoned my job the previous year to go on a merchant ship. Then he asked, "Is it your intention to overthrow the government and set up a communist regime in this country?"

"We haven't thought about that yet. We are struggling to obtain democratic rights . . ."

From the rest of the interrogations I sometimes learned more about the occupations of my co-accused: Trinh Van Lau, whom I had never seen except during our secret three-person meetings in the little Chinese eateries on Rue Paul-Blanchy, was pursuing his secondary studies while giving lessons in a private school; Ngo Chinh Phen was a commerce clerk; Van Van Ky, the "baby" of our group, was a typesetter at the Nguyen Van Cua Printshop (from which he "liberated" metal letters and ink for our clandestine printshop); Vo Van Don, a coolie at Descours & Cabaud, was wise enough to keep silent about our "fraternal association" and confessed only to having sold newspapers and having put up a red banner one night on the road to Giong Ong To on the opposite bank of the Saigon River, a route that many workers and coolies took to their work in town early every morning. The banner had called for a general strike.

When it was his turn in the witness box, our torturer-in-chief, Superintendant Perroche, talked about our group as though it was a vast subversive organization with considerable influence. He concluded that to destroy our group, at least 500 people would have to be arrested.

"Well, there are only eight of them here," interrupted a lawyer. "What have you done with the other 492?"

"We couldn't arrest any more of them because we lacked material evidence," the cop replied.

Then Prosecutor Bouin took over. He recalled how at the previous trial only poor peasants of Duc Hoa had been involved, whereas now the Tribunal was dealing with people who were more educated, and therefore more dangerous. He quoted articles from our agitational paper *Tien Dao,* translated into French, emphasizing the passages in which we had denounced all nationalism and advocated the transformation of anti-imperialist war into civil war. On those grounds, he demanded heavy sentences.

Trinh Dinh Thao and Le Van Kim, the lawyers for the defense, expressed their surprise at the Prosecutor's use of the term "Communist virus," considering that Communists were part of the current Popular Front government in France. They argued that our demands for labor union rights should not be punishable because at that very moment throughout the country action committees were drafting lists of demands to the government without being prosecuted (alluding to the "Indochinese Congress" movement that was then under way).

The French defense lawyer Loye continued the same argument: "You see before you eight poor wretches with no money, no resources and no weapons. What have they done to disturb public order except to meet at the Saigon library, or at Descours & Cabaud, or in a cheap eatery?"

The arguments for the defense ended at nightfall. I was worried about Lu Sanh Hanh because he was a repeat offender. The verdict came fifteen minutes later: Lu Sanh Hanh, 18 months; Ngo Van Xuyet, one year; Trinh Van Lau and Ngo Chinh Phen, eight months; Van Van Ky, six months; Pham Van Muoi and Vo Van Don, six months suspended sentence; Van Van Ba, acquitted. Not as bad as we had expected.

It was dark when we left the court. A group was waiting for us on the pavement outside, opposite the prison. With a surge of emotion, I recognized the slender silhouette of my mother. She looked lost in the dim street light, so far from her village. I could only murmur some words of reassurance to her as I passed.

A silver-white moon shined above the prison walls. The heavy iron door clanged shut behind us.

As a delayed response to our hunger strike, in September 1936 we were given a blackboard in each room (instead of the paper, pen and ink we had asked for, with which we could have put together leaflets) and allowed to receive occasional newspapers from France. This was how we eventually heard the astonishing news of the first Moscow Trial of the 1917 revolutionaries.* We were utterly stunned and bewildered by those abject confessions, nineteen years after the revolution:

> ZINOVIEV: We burned with hate against the Central Committee of the Party and against Stalin. We were convinced that the leaders should at all costs be replaced by us, in collaboration with Trotsky.
>
> KAMENEV: The terrorist plot was organized and led by me, Zinoviev and Trotsky. . . . What led us to this point was our hatred for the leadership of the Party and the country.
>
> PROSECUTOR VISHINSKY: Liars and fools, pathetic pygmies, wretched little dogs yapping at an elephant! . . . I demand the death penalty for these mad dogs! For every last one of them!
>
> (Moscow, August 19, 1936)

The sixteen accused were shot.

We refrained from referring to this event in our conversations with the Stalinists. But we were profoundly disturbed, troubled by a thousand unanswered questions.

On September 27, 1936, I learned that Nguyen An Ninh and Ta Thu Thau had "arrived." They were incarcerated in Cell 7, which was cleared of all the other prisoners. But during the hours when the cell doors were open, we could meet them in the yard. On October 3, Nguyen Van Tao joined them.

The program of the French Popular Front included sending a Parliamentary Commission to look into the aspirations of the colonial peoples. Ta Thu Thau and *La Lutte* had therefore called for the formation of action committees and for the designation of delegates to an "Indochinese Congress,"* which was seen as the first step in forming a local Popular Front. A campaign for this Congress was launched and thousands upon thousands of leaflets were distributed. The action committees spread like wildfire. In the Saigon-Cholon region they were set up at the French Streetcar Company, at the cigarette factory, at the Indochina Distilleries in Binh Tay, at the Nha Be oil depots, on the railways, in the printworks, among the coach drivers of Tan Son Nhut . . . A popular ferment was building up like a sweeping tide. The colonial administration took fright and alerted Paris. On September 8, Colonial Minister Moutet prohibited "the holding of a congress in Saigon of many thousands of persons, because of possible disturbances." A new wave of arrests followed. This was why Nguyen An Ninh, Ta Thu Thau and Nguyen Van Tao had joined us in the Central Prison. With its leaders behind bars, the Indochinese Congress movement was beheaded. Cochinchina Governor Rivoal ordered the dissolution of the action committees.

During the same period the seventeen peasants from the Ben Luc action committee also joined us in prison.

* * *

Neither the Stalinists nor the Trotskyists sought out Nguyen An Ninh. To both sides he was only one nationalist among many, a man of the past who represented an outdated tendency. But for me his arrival was a great event: perhaps I would have the opportunity to get to know the man whose battles had gripped and enlightened me for ten years. In my eyes he was the person who had chosen to give his combative newspaper the title of a poem by Baudelaire, *La Cloche Fêlée;* the person who had sown the seeds of disrespect for the colonial regime; the person who had "shaken a corner of the southern sky, striking terror into the hearts of corrupt, servile sycophants as though an axe had been hurled down at them from the heavens" (a description I had been thrilled to read in Phan Van Hum's *In the Central Prison*).

One day I saw Nguyen An Ninh alone and silent, leaning against the bars. He seemed to be contemplating the tops of the tamarind trees that rose above the prison walls, and the clouds farther off in the distance. Burning with naïve curiosity, I went up to him and blurted out: "Brother Ninh, could you tell me about your agrarian program?"

He turned his head in surprise, looked at me for a few seconds without saying a word, then, apparently ignoring me, he raised his eyes again toward the tamarind trees and began to sing:

> *Dans les jardins de mon père les lilas sont fleuris,*
> *Tous les oiseaux du monde viennent y faire leur nid.*
> *Auprès de ma blonde, qu'il fait bon, fait bon, fait bon,*
> *Auprès de ma blonde, qu'il fait bon dormir.*

[In my father's gardens the lilacs are in flower, all the birds of the world come there to nest. Lying beside my darling is sweet, so sweet, lying beside my darling, that's the sweetest sleep.]*

I no longer remember how I extricated myself from that wretched first encounter.

But a few days later, a small, simple human thing brought us together and overcame the silence. Nguyen An Ninh had perhaps noticed that I was reading Malraux's *Le Temps du mépris,** which had showed up in the prison soon after its publication. Reading in French was not too common.

"Here, read this!" he said to me, handing me Céline's *Voyage au bout de la nuit* [Journey to the End of the Night] in two faded, square-shaped paperback volumes, their covers decorated with attractive woodcuts.

My heart leaped with joy—he had not, after all, taken offense at my awkward questioning the other day. I took the book as a special message from

Nguyen An Ninh

the moment I read the epigraph on the first page:

Notre vie est un voyage
Dans l'Hiver et dans la Nuit,
Nous cherchons notre passage
Dans le Ciel où rien ne luit.

[Our life is a journey through winter and night, we seek our passage in a sky without light.]

For me it was a revelation, this speaking in everyday French to express the essentials, the poetry of the world and all the deadly hypocrisies of the prevailing society. I drank in these words that so splendidly debunked patriotism and religion:

La religion drapeautique remplaça promptement la céleste, vieux nuage déjà dégonflé par la Réforme et condensé depuis longtemps en tirelires épiscopales.

[The religion of the flag soon replaced the cult of heaven, an old cloud that had already been deflated by the Reformation and reduced to a network of episcopal money boxes.]

It exploded like lightning, flashing through the monotony of prison life, a formidable howl of rage:

Je vous le dis, petits bonshommes, couillons de la vie, battus, ran-çonnés, transpirants de toujours, je vous previens, quand les grands de ce monde se mettent à vous aimer, c'est qu'ils vont vous tourner en saucissons de bataille.

[I tell you, little men, life's fall guys, beaten, fleeced to the bone, sweated from time immemorial, I warn you, that when the princes of this world start loving you, it means they're going to grind you up into battle sausage.]

In Céline's clear and brutal evocation of the life of workers, I recognized all the meaning of my own revolt:

"Ça ne vous servira à rien ici vos études, mon garçon! Vous n'êtes pas venu ici pour penser, mais pour faire les gestes qu'on vous

commandera d'exécuter . . . Nous n'avons pas besoin d'imaginatifs
dans notre usine. C'est des chimpanzés dont nous avons besoin . . .
Un conseil encore. Ne nous parlez plus jamais de votre intelligence!
On pensera pour vous mon ami! Tenez-vous-le pour dit." . . . On en
devenait machine aussi soi-même à force et de toute sa viande en-
core tremblotante dans ce bruit de rage énorme.

["Your studies won't do you a bit of good around here, son. You're
not here to think, you're here to make the movements you're told
to. We don't need imaginative types in our factory. What we need
is chimpanzees. . . . Let me give you a piece of advice. Never mention your intelligence again! We'll think for you, my boy!" . . . We
ourselves became machines, our flesh trembled in the furious din.]

And in the peculiar peace of the prison, I continued the *Voyage* to
the land of dreams:

> *Ferme tes jolis yeux, car les heures sont brèves . . .*
> *Au pays merveilleux, au doux pays du rê-ê-ê-ve.*

[Close your lovely eyes, for the hours are short . . . in the wonderful
land, the beautiful land of dr-e-a-ms.]*

That was my last and only meeting with Nguyen An Ninh. He returned to prison in 1937 for two years, then was placed under house
arrest at My Tho in 1939. In 1940 he was deported to Poulo Condore, where he died on August 15, 1943, at the age of 43.

I had first seen Ta Thu Thau at meetings during the 1933 Saigon
municipal elections. I had also listened with enthusiasm to his talks
on dialectics at the Center for Mutual Education, along with a crowd
of office and factory workers and high-school students.

I was pleased to meet him, though I knew that he had taken issue
with the action of the underground League we had formed at the
time of the Laval-Stalin Pact in 1935 (he had referred to our League
as "infantile"). He was an open-faced man, full of cheerful energy,
who refused to let imprisonment get him down. "Once I get settled,"
he said, "I can stay here as long as it lasts." From the beginning we
got along very well. He helped me compose a French-language letter
to the judge that was both dignified and firm, requesting—for form's

sake—the return of my books that
had been seized by the Sûreté, on
the grounds that they "constituted
my entire fortune." He also helped
us understand certain economic issues more clearly.

One morning, a discussion about
the Popular Front drew together all
the prisoners at the far end of the
yard. In a veritable aping of Vishinsky, the prosecutor at the Moscow
Trials, the Stalinist Tran Van Giau
called the Trotskyist Lu Sanh Hanh
a "mad dog." Ta Thu Thau tried to
calm things down. The Stalinists
agreed that we should be allowed
to speak, and my comrades asked

Ta Thu Thau

me to speak for our group. Not an easy task. I tried to explain how
the French Communist Party, in making an alliance with the Radical Party and the Socialist Party on the pretext of preventing the rise
of fascism, had broken the revolutionary momentum of the working
class after the huge wave of strikes and factory occupations. As we
saw it, it was the Popular Front that was paving the way for fascism
by preventing a revolutionary mobilization, the only force capable
of bringing about a definitive victory. And in Indochina, as in all the
other colonies, wasn't the Popular Front government carrying out
the traditional policy of colonial repression? Wasn't our own situation a living proof of this?

Some in the Stalinist camp seemed to agree with me, but their
leader Tran Van Giau defended the Popular Front, talking about
"conjunctures" and "realism" . . .

At the end of October 1936, Ta Thu Thau, Nguyen Van Tao and
Nguyen An Ninh left us, being evacuated to the hospital at Cho
Quan after a hunger strike. I can still see all three of them, stretched
out side by side on a straw mat on the cement floor in the gloom
of the small Cell 7. I can hear Ta Thu Thau shouting at the French
doctor brought in by Agostini: "Get the hell out of here!"

Sometimes, inside our four walls with our imagination aroused by the agitation outside, we were like caged wolves. The price of a liter of rice had jumped from 40 to 70 centimes. We were delighted to learn that strikes were erupting throughout Indochina. In the rice-fields, the rice planters were on strike for higher wages. The coolies in the workshops for the unemployed in Bac Lieu refused to work in protest against their ill treatment. At the Michelin rubber plantations in Dau Tieng, Quang Loi and Binh Truoc the coolies had stopped working in protest against low wages, the brutality of the overseers, the use of private prisons on the plantation, and the beating to death of escapees. At the Société des Plantations in Ben Cui a spontaneous strike broke out, an explosion of anger provoked by the news that an escaped worker had been beaten to death. In November and December 1936 actions were begun in the woodworking shops, brickworks, sugar refineries and soap factories.

In November 1936, in the hellish coalmines of Hongai-Campha in the north, more than 20,000 miners started a strike against "physical cruelty, beatings with rattan-canes, blackjacks, fists and feet," and for improved wages. Similar events occurred at the Haiphong cement works. Our visitors told us excitedly that in Saigon itself more than 1200 workers and coolies from the Arsenal had gone on strike. They were being supported by villagers in the surrounding countryside, who brought them food. More than a thousand railway workers, mechanics, drivers, train guards and coolies from the depots in Saigon and Di An were joining in at the same time that the strike was spreading to the streetcar workers and bus drivers. To the north of Saigon, 400 coolies and workers in the sawmills in Bien Hoa had stopped work and *occupied their workshops!* This had *never* been seen before in Indochina—it demonstrated the depth of the agitation and made us delirious with joy.

In France, the Popular Front government of Blum and Moutet hypocritically changed one article of the Labor Code, so that the "compulsory public service work" that was unpaid in Indochina was renamed "community work." The Code did not provide for any labor union rights or recognition of workers' delegates. Just as before, any Indochinese labor unionist could be imprisoned for membership in a secret society.

On January 11, 1937, when the new Popular Front–appointed Governor-General Jules Brévié arrived, we began a hunger strike to obtain better food, the right to read newspapers, and the end to mistreatment in the prison infirmary and at the Cho Quan hospital. But above all, we intended it as a gesture of solidarity with the agitation outside the walls.

As was reported in *La Lutte* of January 17, 1937, on the day of Brévié's arrival the local governor of Cochinchina had put hundreds of workers into preventive detention in the Botanical Gardens and stopped the multitudes of peasants at the outskirts of Saigon who had come to demonstrate in the city from Gia Dinh, Hoc Mon, Thu Dau Mot, Ba Diem, Ba Queo, Ba Hom and Cholon. Police roadblocks were everywhere. Streetcars had to turn back to the station. Buses were searched. Despite all this, in mid-afternoon ten thousand demonstrators, under banners proclaiming "Full amnesty!", "Democratic and union rights!" and "Aid for the unemployed!" streamed onto the wharfs. When the *Aramis* appeared, bearing the Governor-General, the police and soldiers attacked the crowd, beating people with incredible brutality and forcing them back into the nearby streets. Everyone they arrested was taken to the Sûreté headquarters, where they would be tortured.

Thus began the rule of the new satrap of the Popular Front. Ten days later, as strikes were spreading throughout the country, he summoned four comrades from the *La Lutte* group and tried to win them over with vague promises of reforms.

The workers in thirty-five rice-mills of Cholon greeted him with a work stoppage, demanding pay raises and the implementation of social laws. The bosses gave in after ten days of total paralysis in the mills. In a sign of the times, the Chinese coolies came out in solidarity with the Annamites. Strikes also erupted at the Indochina Distilleries in Binh Tay. In the countryside, angry peasants destroyed rice threshing machines.

Less than a week later we ended our hunger strike in the Central Prison.

At the beginning of February, we prepared to celebrate the new year, the Year of the Buffalo, which began with the new-growth leaves on the tamarind trees surrounding the prison. We shared between us the food, Tet cakes and cigarettes that we received in abundance from our visitors.

As is done by peasants, who decorate their houses for Tet with strips of red paper bearing calligraphed good-luck sayings, Tran Van Vi, an old village scribe, designed and mounted two sentences in Chinese characters: "In community we can build without relying on the outside world." "With the right skills, we can produce everything." The first words of these two phrases, *Cong* and *San,* when joined together, read "communist."

For New Year's Day we constructed a huge game of chess with pieces moulded out of breadcrumbs and cardboard. The game was played in the yard between two teams—my friend Vo Van Don and I on one side, and two peasants from Ben Tre on the other. Our tactic was to confuse our opponents by discussing our game plan out loud, but in a convoluted manner. They, on the other hand, discussed their moves out of earshot. Then, following the saying in Sun Tzu's *Art of War,* we "attacked where the adversary was not protected, suddenly, when it was least expected."

* * *

The festivities were over. Terrible news for our group reached us, of a new trial of the "old Bolsheviks" in Moscow, held on January 23, 1937, a trial brought against the "Anti-Soviet Trotskyite Center," which was allegedly implicated in a "conspiracy of sabotage" by leaders of the transportation and coal industries. The same sort of "full confessions" appeared: Piatakov went into detail about relations between the conspirators and Trotsky and between Trotsky and the Nazis; Radek, toward the end of the trial, shouted: "If they do not learn from our example, the Trotskyists of France, Spain and other countries will pay dearly!" The tragedy culminated at dawn on February 1, 1937, with thirteen executions.

The Trotskyist-Stalinist united front in *La Lutte* now seemed to us more than ever a total paradox. In Moscow, Russian Trotskyists were being treated as poisonous vipers, imprisoned, deported, or massacred. How long could the Trotskyists in Indochina escape the condemnation of Stalin and his local followers?

While Ta Thu Thau and his comrades persisted in trying to maintain unity within *La Lutte,* we learned in March 1937 that our comrade Ho Huu Tuong, in opposition to their enforced silence, had relaunched *Le Militant,* "organ of proletarian defense and Marxist struggle," and in it published Lenin's *Testament,* with its warning against Stalin's brutality and deceitfulness.*

We were somewhat heartened by news of a strike at the Arsenal, brought to us one day in May 1937 by Ta Thu Thau. (I should mention here that he and Nguyen Van Tao were once again back with us in prison. Although both had been reelected the previous month to the Saigon City Council, Governor Pagès had had no hesitation in locking them up in response to the new wave of workers' struggles triggered by the Arsenal strike.)

The strikers held out for five weeks, from April 6 to May 12, 1937, supported by their comrades in other factories and once again fed by the surrounding villagers. They succeeded in obtaining the reinstatement of fired workmates and the promise of higher wages. In Nha Be, the coolies of the Franco-Asian Oil Company went on strike against the firing of one of their comrades. A thousand coolies rebelled at the Michelin rubber plantation in Dau Tieng. In the countryside, the peasants of Can Duoc and Ba Diem demonstrated against new regulations governing tobacco production.

One Sunday morning I was very moved to see that one of the new prisoners was my old friend Anh Gia, whom I had not seen since 1932. He had received a one-year sentence in 1933 and been sent to forced labor in the quarries at Chau Doc, where he had led the nonpolitical prisoners in their refusal to do forced labor, and then in their subsequent hunger strike.

He told me that his arrest had happened during a large secret meeting organized by the Trotskyists on the evening of May 29, 1937. For the first time, delegates from some forty factories and workshops in Saigon-Cholon (including the Arsenal, the Artillery workshops, the railways, the streetcars, the ship repair yards [*Forges, Ateliers et Chantiers d'Indochine*], the Post Office, the East Asiatic Company, the Rubber Manufacturing Company, the Water and Electricity Company, the Portail, Ardin and Union printing companies, the city's three big garages, the Indochina Distilleries, and porters in the ricefields of Hiep Xuong, Duc Hiep, Hang Thai, and Extrême-Orient at Cholon, etc.) had gathered together to set up a Syndicalist Workers Federation (*Lien Doan Tho Thuyen*). In the midst of the meeting Anh Gia, along with the sixty-odd worker delegates present, was seized in a brutal police raid by the Sûreté.

Among those imprisoned with Anh Gia were Ta Khac Triem and Nguyen Van Kim, who had been active in the strikes at the Arsenal, and Vo Buu Binh and Nguyen Kim Luong, whose house in the north of Saigon had been the venue for the secret meeting. Vo Thi Van (Lu Sanh Hanh's partner) was also incarcerated.

The Trotskyists were making their presence felt in the workers' movement as never before, and the Sûreté was alarmed: "The influence of revolutionary agitators sympathetic to the Fourth International has increased in Cochinchina, particularly among workers in the Saigon-Cholon region. . . . The workers are supporting the Trotskyist party more than the Indochinese Communist Party." The Stalinists did not want to go against the Popular Front policy by setting up labor unions, and argued instead for the creation of "fraternal societies."

* * *

When I was finally released from the Central Prison, it was with a sense of joy mixed with sadness for the friends I left behind. It was a sunny June morning. A prison guard escorted me to the Sûreté headquarters, where an inspector asked me what I was going to do now, and warned: "Watch your step! We'll have our eyes on you!"

I returned to our village to see my mother. A burden having been lifted from her heart by our reunion, my mother made an offering of thanks to the Guardian Spirit of the village. In her distress, the human world had seemed to her entirely without recourse, and she had often turned to invisible spirits. Then I went to visit Sister Five, who lived on the outskirts of Saigon. Her husband, who suffered from asthma, worked as a stonemason. They had trouble making ends meet but, as always, they welcomed me with generosity.

In a poor quarter of Cholon, I met Ho Huu Tuong again at his home in company with another comrade, a modest, reserved man.

Ho Huu Tuong introduced me to him, saying simply, "He's some-one in the background," without revealing the identity of this "third man." We shared a meager roast pigeon with our bowls of rice. This was how I first met Phan Van Hum, the man whose narrative *In the Central Prison* had so moved me. It was also to be the last time I ever saw him.

Chapter 5

FROM ONE PRISON TO ANOTHER

On May 19, 1937, Marcel Gitton, of the Colonial Section of the French Communist Party, wrote to the Stalinist members of the *La Lutte* group: "According to the directives we have received concerning you, we consider it impossible to continue the collaboration between the Party and the Trotskyists. We have received a letter from a comrade about the situation in Indochina and the collaboration with the Trotskyists. We are going to transmit this letter to Moscow, along with our personal judgment."

This secret message was delivered to *La Lutte* by a French sailor. But amusingly enough, he mispronounced the name of the person it was addressed to—the Stalinist Tao—and it fell into the hands of Thau, a Trotskyist.

At the end of May, the Stalinists left the *La Lutte* group and hurriedly launched the newspaper *L'Avant-garde* [The Vanguard]. In it, submissively echoing the line from Moscow and the French Communist Party, they wrote:

> The Popular Front is not a form of class-collaboration between the proletariat and the bourgeoisie, as has been deceitfully claimed by the Trotskyists, those twin brothers of the fascists. . . . Our comrade Stalin, in his speech to the plenary session of the Central Committee of the Communist Party of the Soviet Union on March 3, 1937, noted that Trotskyism has ceased to be a political current in the working class, as it was seven or eight years ago. . . . Trotskyism is the ally and agent of fascism.

This abrupt split between the Trotskyists and Stalinists in the *La Lutte* group profoundly disoriented their supporters, who knew little or nothing about the differences between the Third and the Fourth Internationals.

In June 1937 (just as I was released from prison) our newspaper *Le Militant* featured an evaluation of twelve months of Blum's Popular Front government. It noted the budget of 30 billion francs for war, the failure to intervene in Spain, the seizing of revolutionary newspapers, the disbanding of the *Étoile Nord-Africaine* organization, and the repression of the strikes in Indochina. The article also noted that in March the police under Minister of the Interior Dormoy (a Socialist) had fired on workers demonstrating in Clichy [a Paris suburb], killing five and wounding more than 150, and that in Metlaoui in North Africa riot police had killed 21 strikers and wounded several hundred others.

In Saigon, we pounced on copies of André Gide's *Retour de l'URSS* [Return from the USSR].* The poet Bich Khe even made a quick translation of it in *quoc ngu.* This book, which introduced me to Gide, also confirmed what the Moscow Trials had revealed and made me even more aware of the inevitably explosive nature of our relations with the Stalinists, despite the fraternal bonds formed with some of them in prison. "In the USSR today," wrote Gide, "Trotskyism is referred to as the spirit of counterrevolution. Submission and conformity are the qualities demanded now. Anyone who expresses dissatisfaction is denounced as a 'Trotskyist'."

I was looking for work and found a proofreading job at *Le Flambeau d'Annam* [The Torch of Annam], a French-language newspaper that had just been launched by the indefatigable Constitutionalist Nguyen Van Sam following the suppression of his previous paper, *Duoc Nha Nam,* its equivalent in the Annamite language. Anh Gia, who earned his living as a sign painter, offered me a bed at his place on Rue Lacotte in Saigon.

At the Rubber Manufacturing Company [*Compagnie du Caoutchouc Manufacturé*] the police had just arrested four worker militants in the underground labor union, in an attempt to prevent a strike in solidarity with the railway workers. I wrote a short article about this for *Le Flambeau d'Annam*. The boss calmly gave it back to me with the remark, "By using this tone, are you trying to get them to close down our newspaper?"

In the *Flambeau*'s review of the press, I discreetly inserted excerpts from French newspapers denouncing the judicial farce of the Moscow Trials. The Stalinists made sure that the *Flambeau* received bundles of the complete official reports of the trials, which I of course filed in the waste basket.

With a sense of urgency I wrote a pamphlet in Annamite, *Vu an Moscou* (The Moscow Trials), which violently denounced the murders perpetrated by the Stalinist legal system almost twenty years after the October Revolution. Anh Gia designed the cover, and we published it under the name *Chong Trao Luu* (Countercurrent Publications). The pamphlet, which was banned as soon as it appeared, narrowly escaped seizure and was distributed via the underground network. Later, the Sûreté would come upon copies during searches in Annam and Tonkin. In the same series Anh Gia and I issued other pamphlets (all in Vietnamese) on the topics of syndicalism and action committees.

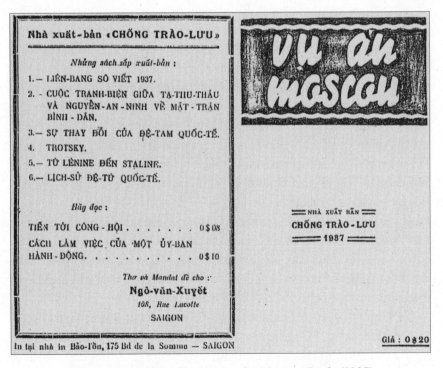

Ngo Van's pamphlet denouncing the Moscow Trials (1937)

Then, in Saigon in July 1937, a hundred dock workers appeared on Rue Catinat, fists raised, marching on the Board of Factory Inspection to protest against firings. And 150 workers at the Saigon Navigation Company downed their tools in reaction to the dismissal of three comrades. And sixty workers from the Stacindo factory demonstrated in front of the 3rd Arrondissement police station to demand the release of workmates who had been arrested. Strikes started breaking out everywhere.

I offered as much support as I could to the women strikers at the Guyonnet Delicatessen, whose delegates asked me to help them formulate their demands in French.

The Sûreté—to which Cochinchina Governor Pagès had given carte blanche "to carry out all the searches and arrests it considers necessary"—swooped down on the militants of the *La Lutte* group, which was now entirely composed of Trotskyists since the departure of the Stalinists. Cops also searched the office of the labor union committee led by Tran Van Thach at 133 Rue Lagrandière, where 45 factory delegates were holding a secret meeting (June 22, 1937). The Sûreté also descended on the *L'Avant-garde* group. All of them, Trotskyists and Stalinists, had to appear in court and were hit with prison terms for taking part in illegal gatherings.

But the repression had not stopped the railway workers from launching a general strike over the whole rail network, from the north to the south of the country. For the first time ever, from July 10 to August 9, 1937, the Trans-Indochina line linking Saigon and Hanoi was at a complete standstill. The strikers won a 15-percent increase in wages and an end to punishment for "damage to tools," but they had to concede to the employers' refusal to reinstate several hundred of their fellow workers. Governor Brévié refused to recognize workers' delegates and refused to grant any labor union rights. Chinese workers at the Saigon rail depot who had come out in solidarity with the strikers were deported. This struggle marked the culminating point of the 1936–1937 strike wave.

In August 1937, as Governor Brévié was on his way to Can Giuoc, a thousand peasants presented him with petitions for the abolition of the capitation tax and a demand for democratic liberties. Brévié threw their representatives in jail, as he had done when he arrived at Rach Gia. During the evening of August 23, an enormous uproar emanating from the Central Prison shook the streets of the city. The prisoners had revolted against the chaining up of a young man, yelling: "Down with repression! Free the peasants of Can Giuoc!" A hail of truncheon blows followed by jets of water from the fire hoses reduced them to silence.

Also in August, the 500 workers in the municipal workshops and depots went on strike against dismissals, and won their demands. In October and November 300 coolies working for Texaco and Socony in Nha Be stopped work. The dockers deserted the port. Outside the city, the carriage drivers of Trang Bang (Tay Ninh) struck against bullying by managers.

* * *

The dawn light was still faint when violent blows smashed through our door and loud shouts jolted me from sleep. Cops burst into the room. A French cop grabbed me by the arm and dragged me out of bed. My head was still in a fog. My body trembled and he asked:

"Have you got a fever?"

"No."

Meanwhile, his henchmen clapped handcuffs on Anh Gia and his partner, both still half-asleep, and on two other young comrades. They turned our place upside down, confiscated our forbidden pamphlets, and took us in a covered truck to the Sûreté on Rue Catinat.

Herded into the yard, we found a dozen other comrades together with their families, who had all been rounded up the same night. Among them I recognized Vo Buu Binh, Ta Khac Triem, Doan Van Truong and the young Nguyen Van Soi. In the partition wall of the latter's straw hut, the cops had discovered duplicating materials and copies of the *Appeal* of the Saigon-Cholon Workers Federation, along with a list of money collected (about 1000 piasters) in different workplaces and at the Arsenal. A record of the time from the Sûreté, which continued to be worried about Trotskyist influence among the workers, mentions these "judicial operations carried out in Saigon on September 2, 1937, against members of the Fourth International in Cochinchina."

We were taken to the Central Prison. I passed the night with a dozen strangers in the cell of those condemned to death. A tiny spy-hole at the top of the steel door was the only opening. A weak electric light faintly illuminated the huge dungeon.

The next day I was placed in solitary confinement. When I was pulled out to be presented to the judge at court, the French screw announced in an aggressive tone: "Prison clothes." With a sense of déjà vu, I donned the rough canvas prison overalls, which as always were too small. And I couldn't help chuckling to myself at the sight of my pal Anh Gia in the same ridiculous get-up, as the prison guard dragged him across Rue Lagrandière to the court.

After a night in solitary confinement, I found myself once more in the cell of political prisoners. I was very moved to see again the friends I had left in June. I also met four workers from the Rubber Manufacturing Company—Duong Van Tu, Nguyen Van Tien, Nguyen Van Man and Nguyen Van Nho.

We were together for about a month. Then one morning a guard came for Anh Gia and me. We barely had time to say goodbye to our comrades.

My new prison friends received heavy sentences at the trial of November 18, 1937: Le Van Oanh got two years in jail and ten years' restricted residence; Duong Van Tu, Nguyen Van Tien, Nguyen Van Man, Doan Van Truong and Ta Khac Triem each got one year plus five years' restricted residence; Nguyen Van Nho, Nguyen Van Trong, Duong Van Tuong and Nguyen Van Soi were sentenced to six months in prison. All of them had been totally involved in the strikes and the illegal labor union movement of 1937. Le Van Oanh and Ta Khac Triem, who had been very active in the railroad workers' strike at the Trans-Indochina Railway Company, had formed groups of comrades in Quang Ngai, Annam and Tonkin.

When I was released from prison, Vo Buu Binh's partner Chi Sau, who sold beansprouts in the Central Marketplace, gave me a generous welcome. Her small house often served as a haven for quite a number of comrades in difficulty.

My sole immediate preoccupation was obtaining my daily bowl of rice. I walked the city looking for work. Eventually a hardware firm, Indochina Trading Posts [*Comptoirs Généraux de l'Indochine*], offered me a place in their Cambodian branch at Phnom Penh. I was upset at having to leave the friends I had only just rediscovered upon coming out of prison, but breathed more easily knowing I would no longer have to live at their expense. I was also relieved to be eluding police surveillance by leaving town. This was foolishly naïve: I had scarcely arrived in the Cambodian capital (at the end of 1937) when my landlord, a young Annamite who owned a bicycle company, warned me that the Sûreté had their eye on me. Soon afterwards my French boss told me, "You know that you're being watched. I'm going to help you to work here, but don't try any agitation; you would risk being deported from Cambodia." I was surprised at his sympathetic attitude, which was very rare among the colonists. I later learned that he was a radical socialist and that his wife was Laotian.

In 1938 I made the acquaintance of the typographer Tu Van Hon and some other readers of the newspaper *Tranh Dau/La Lutte* and the journal *Thang Muoi:* Diet, who worked at the customs; Huong and Binh, two young men who worked at the Phnom Penh branch of Descours & Cabaud; and finally a journalist. All of them were pro-Fourth International.

Despite our efforts, our circle was not able to make contact with native Cambodians. Language was the main barrier, but there was also an instinctive distrust inherited from the Annamites' conquest of the south during the seventeenth century, when they seized Khmer land in Cochinchina and established their rule over the whole kingdom. *Cap youn* (cut off the Annamites' heads), an expression of revenge still fresh in their memory, evoked the massacres of Annamites by the Cambodians during the 1920s. The colonial regime intentionally encouraged this hostility by giving better jobs to Annamites than to indigenous Cambodians, who were generally less educated. We were among the estimated 27,000 Annamites living in Phnom Penh, serving as functionaries, commercial employees, workers, craftsmen and merchants. There was a Catholic neighborhood that was exclusively Annamite, where the old French priest lent money to his flock. If any of them was unable to pay it back, he had the ownership of the debtor's fishing boat transferred to himself, so that the expropriated unfortunate was completely at his mercy.

I met the lawyer Lascaux, who was looked upon with ill favor because of his criticism of those in power. Alluding in conversation to the absurd "confessions" of the old Bolsheviks at the latest Moscow Trial, he remarked, "It's as absurd as if they had confessed to having stolen the bells from Notre-Dame!" Since I knew nothing about Notre-Dame, this only deepened the mystery for me. When we parted company, he made me the gift of an old typewriter.

A comrade who worked on the ferries plying the Mekong River between Saigon and Phnom Penh brought us banned newspapers and pamphlets from time to time. And Lu Sanh Hanh often came to see me, keeping us informed about what was going on in Cochinchina.

In February 1938, 4000 striking porters totally paralyzed the rice-mills of Cholon, refusing to unload the sacks of rice from 300 junks, which were immobilized in the harbor. After three days, the bosses capitulated. Sporadic strikes continued to break out during 1938 in the workshops manufacturing bricks, pottery, glassware and soap products, and on the river ferries.

That year—the Year of the Tiger—rice plants were attacked by mildew and the harvest was catastrophic. The specter of famine haunted the poor peasants in western Cochinchina. In September 1938, 1500 peasants, including women and children, demonstrated at Phuoc Long, demanding work and food. The Annamite Administrative Representative alerted the Administrator of Rach Gia, threw together some "relief workshops for the poverty-stricken," distributed some emergency rations, then blocked his door and posted a sign: "Closed due to illness." In the province of Bac Lieu, in one week hundreds of starving people emptied dozens of granaries belonging to local landowners. On October 4, 1938, 500 peasants demonstrated at Ca Mau. The militia responded with violence, wounding many of them. Those ricefield slaves were then sentenced to months and years in prison for challenging the sacred right of property and the established order.

I shared a lodging with my friend Diet very near the market. Amazingly enough, he had a gramophone! We could never get enough of listening to the tunes of Louis Armstrong and the songs of Tino Rossi:

Guitare d'amour,
Apporte-lui l'écho des beaux jours,
Va lui chanter pour moi
La chanson de mon rê-ê-ê-ve . . .

[Guitar of love, bring him the echo of the good times, go and sing to
him for me the song of my dr-e-a-m-s . . .]

One Saturday night, Diet took two other friends and me to a night-
club with the sign RO (*Régie d'Opium,* indicating a state-licensed
opium house). He got us in free because the Chinese owner had
"business" with him at the Customs House. As soon as I stepped
inside, I breathed in the sweet, soothing, incomparable aroma of
the drug. There was no other illumination but the glow of the oil
lamps, which cast a wan light on the faces of the smokers. The
owner considerately led us to a quiet corner apart from the regulars.
We stretched out on the wooden benches, our heads resting on per-
forated porcelain headrests, murmuring rather than talking. Along
with the smoking apparatus, we were brought a teapot and four small
cups. The opium pipe was made from a tube of varnished wood
about 50 centimeters long, closed at one end. Two-thirds of the way
down its length was the terracotta bowl of the pipe with a tiny hole
in the middle. Diet, already initiated into the ritual, dexterously held
the viscous brown ball at the end of a long needle, so that it sizzled
over a flame protected by a thick cone of glass. He kneaded it on the
polished convex edge of the bowl, reheated it, then mixed it again,
until it took on the color of a cricket's head. Then, with a deft twist
of his hand, he pushed the ball into the bowl of the pipe and pulled
out the needle. He held the bowl over the flame again and handed
me the pipe. I took several puffs, coughing out smoke. My more experienced friends breathed in a whole pipeful at once, then chugged
down a small cupful of strong tea before exhaling the smoke. I was
overcome with euphoria.

In February 1939 I became a correspondent for *Tia Sang* (The
Spark), a Vietnamese-language paper published in Saigon. In April,
under the pseudonym Tan Lo, I wrote an article there entitled "Ta
Thu Thau and Bolshevik-Leninist Politics," which dealt with the
ruinous contradictions within the old *La Lutte* group and harshly

criticized Ta Thu Thau and the legal Trotskyists for having formed a bloc with the Stalinists.

One day, I asked my boss for permission to go to Saigon for a few days to see my family. He agreed, commenting wryly, "Yes, and the elections also just happen to be taking place . . ."

He knew as well as I did that there was no prospect of my voting in the election for the Colonial Council, since only taxpayers could vote; but I was anxious to join my comrades for the pre-election agitation that was creating turmoil in Saigon in April 1939. The Stalinists, with their newspaper *Dan Chung* (The People) and their "Democratic Front" slate of candidates, were leading a campaign for democratic reforms in exchange for their support of the colonial regime's policy of "defending Indochina." The Trotskyist *Tranh Dau/La Lutte* group opposed this and denounced all compromise with the colonial regime. They based their propaganda on the need for a "united front of workers and peasants" against war, against the setting up of a national defense fund, against the raising of taxes and the creation of armaments taxes, and against the forced conscription of more infantry troops. They put forward their revolutionary project: set up factory committees and peasant committees to control the activity of the banks, industries, businesses, and agricultural companies; put the management of transportation and postal services in the hands of the workers; divide up among the poor peasants the lands belonging to the banks, the Church and the big landowners; entrust peasant committees with the task of abolishing feudal exploitation; and oppose war by working toward the eventual formation of a soviet federation of Asia.

On April 30, 1939, I was in the Place de l'Hôtel-de-Ville, which was jam-packed with people waiting to hear the results of the election. Suddenly a shout went up: "The whole Fourth International slate has been elected!" There was an explosion of joy. Spontaneously, a procession moved toward the *La Lutte* offices, shouting "Long live the united front of workers and peasants! Down with the Democratic Front!"

One might have thought that the subversive program of the supporters of the Fourth International would have estranged lots of voters; but many people seemed to have been primarily motivated to protest against the new taxes for National Defense. Hence the paradox of Ta Thu Thau, Phan Van Hum and Tran Van Thach from the *La Lutte* group being elected to the ruling Colonial Council by a suffrage based on income tax. On the other hand, the Stalinist candidates Nguyen Van Tao and Duong Bach Mai ended up losing, despite (or, rather, because of) their second-round collaboration with the bourgeois Constitutionalists. Some of the disgruntled voters went so far as to characterize their slate as "pro-government."

It should be remembered that a year earlier (May 1938), when the Daladier government had launched a bond measure of 33 million piasters for the defense of Indochina and decreed the conscription of 20,000 additional indigenous infantry troops, some in the ICP went so far as to propose offering bonds of 5 and 10 piasters (rather than 100) so that poor people could afford them! An ICP circular dated July 1, 1938, explained to members: "The covetous glance Japan is casting toward the island of Hainan directly threatens the security of Indochina. In the face of these fascists' territorial designs, the Indochinese Communist Party approves of the measures taken [by the government]." In other words, the colonial regime had become a possible ally for the Stalinists. The ICP's Central Committee, sensing the unpopularity of the bond measure, ended up by abandoning their ardent propaganda for it, but continued to support the government: "If we don't do that, our position will be confused with that of the Trotskyists, who protest against the strengthening of our country's defenses."

In the *Dan Chung* of April 1, 1939, the Stalinists proclaimed: "The Trotskyists have sold out to Japan and fascism." Phan Van Hum replied, in the *Tranh Dau* of May 19, 1939: "As long as the people suffer poverty and misery, there is nothing to defend. They point to 'our' ricefields, land, houses . . . but on looking more closely we can see that the splendor and beauty and wealth all belong to the big bourgeoisie. The ten categories of new taxes include taxes on sugar and matches, two daily necessities. . . . Why should the burden of 'National Defense' be loaded onto the backs of the poor?"

There were disturbances in the recruitment centers, where 20,000 infantrymen were being press-ganged into the army by a system of drawing lots, including instances of self-inflicted mutilations and arrests for inciting others not to sign up.

On May 20, 1939, Governor-General Brévié sent a telegram to the Colonial Minister expressing his appreciation of Nguyen Van Tao's position: "While Nguyen Van Tao and the Stalinist Communists have understood that the interests of the Annamite masses require them to ally with France, the Trotskyists under the leadership of Ta Thu Thau have not hesitated to incite the natives to revolt so as to take advantage of a possible war in order to gain total liberation."

* * *

The Sûreté at Phnom Penh had not lost sight of us. On the eve of July 14, 1939, Tu Van Hon and I were summoned. I was first taken into Arnoux's office. As the door closed behind me, I found myself standing in front of the chief cop, who was deeply settled into his leather armchair behind a vast empty desk. To his left stood Inspector Brocheton, whom I recognized from having seen him occasionally when he called on my boss. To his right, his hands resting on the edge of the desk, was Inspector Ouvrard, a Tonkinese half-caste who used to speak to me in Annamite when he came to the Trading Post to buy cartridges for his hunting rifle. The trio stared at me in silence, undoubtedly trying to intimidate me.

"We have left you in peace," Arnoux said at last, in a deliberate and monotonous voice. "We're asking you to leave us in peace too."

"But I don't see . . ." He cut me off and continued: "You know that Cambodia is a peaceful country, and we will not tolerate any disorder or any agitation."

"I'm here to work and earn my living. Besides, I can't speak Cambodian and I have no contact with people in this country . . ."

"But," interrupted the Tonkinese, "you have held meetings among yourselves?"

"No."

"Not even on your bicycles?"

I realized then that they must have followed us everywhere—even on our Sunday bicycle trips in the outskirts of Phnom Penh to Bak Touk, the Chinese area, and perhaps also when we took a sampan on the streams of the Mekong to the Chroui Changwar peninsula, the fief of the Malayan Muslims.

World events moved swiftly in the following two months: Stalin signed the "German-Soviet Nonaggression Pact"; German troops invaded Poland; France and Britain declared war on Germany; and mobilization was decreed in France and in Indochina.

In Phnom Penh, early in the morning two days after the posting of placards in the city announcing the general mobilization, the cops came to search my house and carried away my letters and books. The next day I had to present myself at the Sûreté to witness the unpacking of the seized material. I felt trapped like a game animal and wished I could disappear somewhere. But where?

Summoned once again to the Sûreté on October 4, 1939, our journalist friend Tu Van Hon and I found there another twenty or so people, most of them Annamites living in Phnom Penh, including a school principal, and also several elderly Chinese people, probably suspected of belonging to a secret society. An inspector, a customer at the Trading Post where I worked, barked at me:

"Are you involved in these affairs?"

"They tried to implicate me . . ."

A heavy door swung shut behind us—we were in their power. In the evening, we received food and blankets from the outside. We slept on the concrete floor, pressed tightly against each other. Family members brought us food toward the end of the following afternoon; messages and news from outside reached us in scraps of paper hidden in the duckweed packing.

The days passed, and after one and then two weeks we were all asking ourselves why we were being held in indefinite detention.

Kha, the school principal, recited classics of French literature to us all day long. The image of *"un ver de terre amoureux d'une étoile"* [an earthworm in love with a star]* has stayed in my memory.

One day a Frenchman was introduced into our ranks. He had been arrested for opium dealing, and was happy to talk to us in French.

During my third week in prison, I was called one morning to the Public Prosecutor's office. Despite the handcuffs, I was pleased to see the streets and people once more in the town where I had lived for two years.

The prosecutor was Indian. "We have a warrant to press charges against you, from the Prosecutor's Office in My Tho. Do you agree to appear before the tribunal of My Tho?"

"And if I do not agree?"

"We'll take you there by force."

My Tho was in the western part of Cochinchina. Why was I being sent there? I didn't understand. I was taken to the prison in Phnom Penh to await the next transport to Cochinchina.

It was afternoon. The sun was beating down. The Head Guard, a hideous wreck of an old colonist with bristling hair, was stretched out and rocking on a hammock in the midst of a nap. He suddenly jerked up, furious that his siesta had been disturbed. My escort went up to him, stammering something.

"No, no, no!" he shouted. "Get the hell out of here! No 'politicals' here!" So I was taken back to the Sûreté.

At dawn the next day, I was loaded onto a truck already full of prisoners. Squeezed into the same space were baskets of rabbits and huge semi-spherical latticework cages in which ducks, roosters and hens fluttered about, which the Commissioner in Phnom Penh was sending his colleague in Saigon (because they were less expensive here than in Cochinchina).

We stood, handcuffed in pairs, crammed against each other like sardines and holding on as best we could with our one free hand to the iron frame that supported the tarp. The guards wouldn't let us sit down on the cages. We crouched down as much as possible to avoid being hit in the face by branches, and the truck set off. I realized with regret that I was leaving Cambodia without ever having seen Angkor.

In Saigon, I was taken to the Sûreté headquarters on Rue Catinat, with its familiar odor of urine and fear. I met again the opium smuggler, my French fellow-prisoner from Phnom Penh. He shared his midday meal with me, ordered from outside (a privilege accorded to French prisoners). The next day, a military escort took me in handcuffs to the train to My Tho.

Chapter 6

IN THE MEKONG DELTA

On the little train from Saigon to My Tho, my fellow passengers (barefoot peasants for the most part), whether out of tact or indifference, appeared not to notice the handcuffed prisoner with his police escort. After almost a month of confinement in the Sûreté at Phnom Penh and with an unknown jail sentence ahead of me, it was a sheer joy to watch the repetitive landscape roll by, the sparkling expanse of ricefields, the herds of peaceful buffalos, the straw huts sheltered by clumps of bamboo. But why was I being transferred to My Tho?

As soon as we arrived, I was taken to the office of the examining magistrate, a native of India with a bloated, peevish face.

"Ah, a Trotskyite! You gang of saboteurs!"

It was strange that he was using this Moscow Trials–style terminology to attack me. He took a letter from a file and asked me to confirm that I was its author. I recognized it: it was a letter I had written to Canh, a friend who worked at the tax office in My Tho. He had asked my advice about which of Trotsky's books he should read. The letter was written in Vietnamese, but the titles *The Permanent Revolution* and *The Communist International After Lenin* were in French. Canh had forgotten the letter in between the pages of a tax ledger. His French boss had found it and taken it straight to the Sûreté. I learned in this way that Canh had been arrested.

"You are charged with subversive activities," the judge informed me.

The guard took me to the prison in the center of My Tho, where I was put in the holding cell with others under investigation or awaiting sentence. We were packed together like trussed poultry. Amid the suffocating stink of urine and the stench of the latrines, the prisoners were all sitting or lying on boards that oozed filth. My bare feet recoiled from walking on the slimy floor. One of the prisoners was relieving himself on an elevated platform at the back of the room; squatting over the hole, he tried to hide his nakedness with the plank of wood that served as a lid for the latrine.

Seven or eight peasants came up to me as I entered, welcoming me as though they had been expecting my arrival. Perhaps, like me, they had been seized after the declaration of war.

We were penned up in the cell all the time. Twice a day—in the morning around 11:00 and in the afternoon around 4:00—the single iron door would open and the herd would surge into the narrow courtyard and fall on the food, crouching and eating it off the ground where it had been left. Then we would be quickly herded back inside under the watchful eye of the screws. Apart from that, we had no access to the yard nor a single breath of fresh air.

During these feeding times we could see the female prisoners, crouched on the threshold of their cell. Among them I saw my partner's elder sister, Chi Nam Thin, who had been sentenced to three years. The only woman "political" in this jail, she had joined the ICP in the heroic days of 1930.

They soon separated us from the nonpolitical prisoners. The Thanh Loi peasants and I found ourselves confined in a cell no bigger than a corridor with my unfortunate correspondent, Canh, and with four religious cultists who were charged with political crimes just like we were.

Apart from the two brief periods when we were let out for food, we had no space for walking, so we remained sitting or lying on the planks in the cell. Outside, just underneath the barred window facing the yard, was a water jar. To get water out of it, acrobatics were needed. We had to perch on the windowsill, two meters off the ground, lower an empty can on a string through the bars, and fill it from the jar, so that we could drink and occasionally have a perfunctory wash.

Canh and I went to trial in November. Since we had no lawyer, we conducted our own defense. The dossier probably contained no more than the letter to Canh and my past Sûreté records. I stated that since leaving prison in 1937 and going to work in Phnom Penh, I had abstained from any political activity, and that my only "subversive action" had been to communicate to a friend the titles of two works by Trotsky.

"But in Saigon you were seen greeting Ta Thu Thau in the street," retorted the Presiding Judge.

"I knew Ta Thu Thau in prison, so naturally I greet him when I see him."

The verdict: six months' prison for Canh and eight for me. We decided not to appeal.

The Criminal Court convened the same day in the same place. At dusk, I heard heart-rending cries: as men were led off in chains back to the prison, their wives followed them, shrieking and sobbing, children in their arms. These men, condemned to forced labor, would be held in the gloomy cells next to our room, waiting to be transported to Poulo Condore. That same evening, as night fell, the vile magistrate arrived in the prison. This descendant of a slave, until recently colonized in the same way as his current victims, but now elevated to the dignity of a French citizen (because he was born in the Antilles), seemed proud of his lackey's role as he inspected the men he was sending off to the slow death of the penal colony.

In an isolated cell there was an escapee from Poulo Condore who was kept in irons day and night. His head was half shaved, from the middle of his forehead to the back of his neck, and the screws maliciously nicknamed him "the rooster."

I fraternized with the youngest of the religious cultists, and gradually also established a certain rapport with the three older ones, who were more distant and taciturn. The eldest, Nguyen Ngoc Dien, a stocky man in his thirties, had a pale face and an elegiac gaze, in contrast with his companions, whose faces were burned by the sun and battered by the mud of the ricefields. "He thinks he's descended from the Emperor Minh Mang," one of the old peasants from Thanh Loi informed me, "and he demands that the French restore the Annamite Empire."

It came back to me that in August 1937, during the year of turmoil in Saigon, I had been surprised one day to read in the newspaper that "General" Nguyen Ngoc Dien, head of a Cao Dai sect, had been incarcerated in the Central Prison for urging his followers not to pay the capitation tax.

Bit by bit, the young cultist told me about their prison Calvary. How they had been taken from the Central Prison to the psychiatric ward of the Cho Quan hospital. He described in detail the daily sight of the agonizing deaths of their fellow prisoners. When both of their feet stiffened, he said, it meant that their life—and their suffering—was finally at an end.

This is what the head doctor of the Cho Quan hospital wrote in his professional report: "Nguyen Ngoc Dien seems to pose no threat to himself, at least at present. . . . Staying with his family should be formally discouraged, however, since it would not prevent the transmission of his delirious ideas to the outside world and would therefore be a danger to society." Nguyen Ngoc Dien had already been confined three times to the mental asylum at Bien Hoa. This time they put him in a provincial jail along with us "politicals." The regime was still haunted by the memory of the peasant insurrections of 1916, which had been initially sparked by religious cultists.

Our cultists belonged to the sect called Tuyet Coc, or Abstention From Cereals. They subscribed to the Cao Dai (Very High) faith, a new religion born during the flowering of nationalist movements in 1925–1926. A section of the indigenous bourgeoisie—including former top administrators dissatisfied with their subordinate role in the colonial bureaucracy—tried to invent for themselves a transcendent space in the margins of colonial society where they could regain social preeminence. This new religion combined the three traditional religio-philosophical currents (Buddhism, Taoism and Confucianism) with Christianity and a cult of guardian spirits. Its pantheon included Buddha, Lao Tzu, Confucius, Christ, Mohammed, Brahma, Vishnu, the poets Ly Thai Bach, Nguyen Binh Khiem and Victor Hugo, and political figures such as Gandhi and Sun Yat-sen. Its central religious temple was at Tay Ninh, 90 kilometers north of Saigon.

Aided by the economic crisis and the crushing of the "communist" peasant movement of 1930–1931, Cao Dai achieved a rapid recruitment among the peasantry, who were oppressed by the large landowners and the rural notables. In 1932 this new religion counted around 350,000 adherents. In their quest for power, certain bourgeois Constitutionalists also converted to Caodaism.

Two years before we met, the rebel mystic Nguyen Ngoc Dien and his followers had made their way to western Cochinchina, in the Cao Dai diocese of Bac Lieu. Calling together all the priests and the faithful, he urged them to burn their capitation tax cards and henceforward to obey only orders from Heaven. That was how he came to be arrested. Because Nguyen An Ninh's name appeared on a list of donors he had on him when arrested, he was interrogated about him. Naïvely, Nguyen Ngoc Dien replied, "I know Nguyen An Ninh. I met him last June at Gia Dinh. I made him part of my mission to retake the land of Annam. He gave me a piaster and told me that he was sought by the Sûreté, but that I could always find him if I needed him."

One day there was an unbelievable windfall. Paper, envelopes and a pencil stub reached me, concealed in some clothes. This gave me the idea of writing an article for the *Dien Tin* newspaper defending the cultists (with their permission, of course). Aunt Two, my partner's mother, who often came to the prison to visit her other daughter, managed to get acquainted with the chief Annamite screw, Sergeant Khanh. She knew that he was an addict, and would thus turn a blind eye to anything if she slipped him a little packet of opium every now and then. That was how my article was able to leave the prison and get published.

My Communist peasant companions did not seem to take the cultists seriously. But they were friendly enough to Canh and me, even though we were Trotskyists. One memorable night in November 1939, Dau, a peasant of around 25, got up on a bench and improvised a passionate speech to celebrate the twenty-second anniversary of the October Revolution. One of the older prisoners sang in Annamite an anti-French song of the 1920s, which had been passed down by word of mouth: "In the midst of a storm, we share the same boat." I had learned by heart this epic lament, composed in honor of Duy Tan, the emperor of Annam who had been deported in 1916. It also denounced Khai Dinh, father of the current emperor Bao Dai.

> Annam, our country, lived in peace
> Until the Tay [the French] seized it. . . .

> Poor Emperor Duy Tan,
> Wise king with a heart for the people. . . .
> King Khai Dinh succeeded him,
> The king who went to France to sell out the nation
> Begging favors from the powerful. . . .

"You should join us at Thanh Loi," said my peasant friends. "We will help you. We'll rent you a bit of land and build you a straw hut (there are plenty of areca tree trunks and palm tree leaves in the area). We'll teach you how to plant sugar cane, and give you cuttings to start out with. When we get too hot at midday, we can jump into the river and swim in the clear, sparkling water—it's great!"

They saw the struggle as inseparable from their daily rural life, envisioning global social change in terms of how it would affect their own village community. Their sense of brotherhood moved me greatly. But it was only a daydream. At each release from prison our projects for the immediate future invariably dissipated as the current of life carried us to unexpected shores.

What became of my rural friends in the maelstrom of the Cochinchinese peasant insurrection in November 1940? Their village Thanh Loi, which was on the fringes of the Plain of Reeds, was apparently wiped out by machine-gun fire and bombs.

One morning in June 1940 I said goodbye to my companions in misfortune. I crossed the prison threshold and, with a light heart, strolled along the streets of My Tho, making my way to the sun-drenched market. I wanted to thank Phung (we referred to him as "Brother Six"), the town auto mechanic whose acquaintance with the prison guards had made it possible for me to communicate secretly with the outside world.

A girl on a bicycle suddenly stopped alongside me: "My uncle invites you to come see him." Perplexed, I hesitated, but then followed her and soon found myself facing Inspector Tran Chanh of the Sûreté Political Police. "Saigon has asked us to hold on to you," he said. He had me taken to the My Tho Sûreté office, where there was an old French Police Commissioner whose demeanor did not bode well.

My partner, with a toddler in her arms, brought me a mess tin of food, which I ate sitting on the stoop of the police office. The Commissioner stood behind me, then suddenly, for no apparent reason, started to yell: "It's not me that stirred up trouble!" I continued to eat without flinching. He disappeared. The Annamite interpreter endeavored to reassure me: "He was gassed during the war. Sometimes he flares up at me for no reason!"

Then, with horror, I caught sight of Chin Ngoc, my torturer from the Saigon Sûreté. With his full weight, he was stamping on the chest of a poor wretch lying outstretched on the tiled floor. "Confess, and you'll get off with a few years of hard labor and then be released. If you don't, you're dead!"

The next day I was taken back to the Sûreté in Saigon. For the written questions the Sureté posed I concocted answers as evasive as possible. I realized that the next stop for me could be a "special work camp" in the Bien Hoa forests or forced house arrest somewhere in the provinces.

It turned out to be the latter, in Tra Vinh, a town on an island in the Mekong Delta. I was handcuffed and escorted there by a militiaman, traveling in a rattling public transport bus a whole day to cover 150 kilometers. For me, the name "Tra Vinh" had a heroic resonance because of a popular poem that had been surreptitiously passed to my mother in the village market and which I enthusiastically learned by heart when I was ten years old:

> In Tra Vinh
> There lived a remarkable person,
> Chanh, a man of great boldness.
> At night, he brooded on his hatred of the Prosecutor,
> Nurturing his plot.
> He would not be at peace till he had gunned him down. . . .

I found out later that the hero of this poem was a real person, who had daringly assassinated the Public Prosecutor in 1893. I was also intrigued by the rebellious tradition of the region. As early as 1889, an indigenous rebel had stabbed the French Administrator while he was having dinner with his wife.

We arrived at Tra Vinh in the evening. I spent the night on the filthy wooden planks of the hut next to the guardroom. The next day

Thong Chanh,
assassin of Public Prosecutor Jaboin (1893)

I was taken to Administrator Montaigut in the Provincial Governor's office. His panther eyes locked into mine as he leaned toward my face and yelled: "Communist!" He ordered me to be taken to the police station, where I would have to report every two weeks. The militiaman who took me there told me about a hut for rent very close by.

I strolled through the streets, my first walk in the city. All of a sudden someone came up to me and took my hand: it was Tran Huu Do, an elderly cultured man who was also in exile here. He took me to a small eating place named *Lien Lac* ("Liaisons"—which for the initiated indicated a clandestine meeting place). The owner, Anh Sau, refused to let us pay for our meal and warmly invited me to come back: "We'll work it out later." He also gave me a small oil lamp. I was to find out later that Montaigut was constantly harassing Anh Sau and trying to break up this haven for exiles where I had discovered such a warm welcome.

My friends in Phnom Penh sent me a little money. A poor neighbor, who hated the cops and pointed out the most violent ones to me, showed me how to make rice cakes to sell in the market. Then I had a little stall selling dried fish. Then I sold coffee and root-colored aperitifs on the sidewalk. I also made medicines, using the traditional recipes I had learned in prison.

My forced exile within the limits of the small settlement of Tra Vinh kept me isolated from what was happening in the rest of the country, or even in the nearby area. So I was completely taken by surprise one dark November night by the arrival of a convoy of trucks on which dozens upon dozens of dead and wounded peasants were piled, flanked by French police and Annamite militiamen. Without knowing it, I found myself in the heart of the peasant uprising that engulfed the whole of western Cochinchina in November 1940 and lasted until mid-December. The insurgents attacked the Annamite militia posts to obtain arms, set fire to town halls and other official buildings, killed cops who were known torturers, attacked patrols, and tried to block roads and canals and to destroy bridges.

Martial law was declared. French and Foreign Legion troops, backed up by French police, Annamite militias and Sûreté agents, searched the villages after first bombing them and raking them with machine-gun fire. Sharpshooters from Tonkin and Cambodia were also brought in. Over a hundred insurgents were killed in combat; untold thousands of noncombatant villagers were slaughtered by bombs or gunfire or taken away to be tortured. Of the 5800 people arrested, 221 were condemned to death—the executions were held in public to serve as examples—and 216 others were condemned to forced labor camps. The prisons were so overloaded that the excess prisoners were cooped up in barges where, under metal sheeting broiling in the sun, they died like flies. I later learned that my friend Trinh Van Lau, who had been a member of our League, met his death on one of those barges.

* * *

After nine months in Tra Vinh, I began to spit blood. I obtained permission to return to Saigon for medical care. Two days before I left, my mother suddenly appeared. I couldn't believe my eyes. She had made her way all alone, across ricefields and through cities, to see me. Together we took a boat back to Saigon, traveling for a whole day and night.

I spent a month in the Gia Dinh hospital. Then, given shelter by Sister Five, I started looking for work.

Saigon had changed a lot. Behind the cathedral, a huge banner had been erected bearing a giant portrait of Marshal Pétain in front of a French flag, with the inscription:

UN SEUL CHEF: PÉTAIN.
UN SEUL DEVOIR: OBÉIR.
UNE SEULE DEVISE: SERVIR.

[A single leader: Pétain. A single duty: Obey. A single motto: Serve.]

This iron-fisted display was the work of Decoux, the fascistic admiral appointed as Governor-General by the Vichy government.* Charged with defending the "interests of the white races" against 25 million Indochinese, he had ordered villages to be bombed and the rebelling peasants of Cochinchina to be massacred.

For my illness I went to see Dr. Pham Ngoc Thach, a well-known opponent of the colonial regime. My X-rays revealed opaque nodules at the top of my lungs. He prescribed injections of calcium and rest, and did not ask for any payment.

I absolutely had to find a job. But I didn't even bother to look for work at the French hardware firms, since shipments from France had ground to a halt due to the war. French firms survived by collaborating with the Japanese. My friend Lam Thanh Thi, who had set himself up as a commercial agent during those hard times, found me a job in a Japanese firm, Dainan Koosi. My job was to sort buffalo hides destined for export to Japan. Considering the state of my health, working among all the dried skins impregnated with arsenic in an atmosphere of unbreathable dust was almost intolerable. An elderly, opium-addicted male nurse whom my friend had gotten to know in the opium dens advised me to take crisalbine, a type of gold salt used at that time as a remedy for tuberculosis. I managed to get some on the black market for an exorbitant price. The old man gave me intravenous injections with it and refused to let me pay him.

I kept going in this way for several months until I was overcome by exhaustion. Finally, my Japanese boss moved me to the accounts department. From time to time, I had to travel to the provinces to check the accounts of the brickworks installed all along the Mekong River. It was a unique opportunity to get to know western Cochinchina a little better, particularly Vinh Long, Can Tho and Sadec. In the course of these journeys, with the driver's help, I was able to practice driving. I had had a license for about twelve years without ever having touched a steering wheel. I still had the idea of studying

Can Tho (1995)

in Paris one day and of paying for it by driving a taxi.

Then Dainan Koosi opened an office in Can Tho and I was transferred there. My lung disease seemed to be stable even though I got out of breath easily. In the small brickworks I was able to observe the superexploitation of the proletariat by a rapacious rural employer class, in total complicity with the local notables. The wretched peons—men, women and children alike—were paid by the piece. Covered in mud, they ground up clay from dawn to sunset. What they earned was often not enough to pay off the loans plus interest advanced to them by the boss. Sometimes whole families were condemned in this way to a lifetime of slavery. Those who tried to escape were caught by the village notables and beaten by their exploiter as long as he felt like it. I will never forget the solid whip with its stingray cords hanging on the wall behind the owner's desk at the Van Xuong Brickworks in Vinh Long.

One day as I was at work at Dainan Koosi, I had a strange visit from a stocky, scar-faced man with a handlebar moustache and a mane of iron-gray hair. It was Nam Lua (Fifth Fire), feared leader of a well-known guerrilla gang in the Can Tho region. He had become a fervent convert to the "Mad Monk" sect and felt threatened by the French, so he was seeking the protection of the Japanese. That was how I found out about the existence of the Hoa Hao religious sect, named after the native village of its founder, Huynh Phu So. This young visionary, commonly referred to as "the Mad Monk" [*le Bonze Fou*], had begun in 1939 to preach a new kind of Buddhism marked by simplicity and ancestor worship that was well suited to appeal to the poor peasantry. The global slaughter currently under way seemed to confirm his prophecies announcing the end of the old world. His *Litanies for the People* alluded to the approaching end of the French occupation, and his prediction of the coming of the Buddha King promised the troubled rural poor a future of universal happiness. In their distress, many poor people found solace in this religion, or nourished their spirit of revolt with its mysticism. When the cult began rapidly spreading up and down the Mekong River, the colonial regime became apprehensive. The French Sûreté interned the Mad Monk as a mental case in the Cho Quan hospital . . . until he converted his doctor! He was then forced to live in the far west, at Bac Lieu. Then the Japanese police took him under their protection.

I learned that Chi Nam Thin, my partner's elder sister whom I had run into a few times at the My Tho prison, had been put under house arrest in Ben Tre after three years in detention. I knew she was on her own with two children. How was she managing? I decided to go to Ben Tre.

On the way there, on the ferry across the Mekong, I ran into Duc. We had met in the Central Prison in 1936. I was happy to be able to share a few piasters with him. He belonged to the Communist cell in Ben Tre, and gave me news about his comrade Tong, with whom I had become friends in prison. Little did I know that not long afterwards, in October 1945, this same Tong, promoted to be an agent in the Vietminh secret police, would try to capture me in the Thu Duc area. How is it possible to imagine

Huynh Phu So, the "Mad Monk"

that someone who faced the enemy together with you, who lived side by side with you in prison, could one day want to take your life?

During one of my trips to the brickworks along the Mekong River I came across yet another former fellow prisoner, Pham Van Kinh, a Stalinist party worker and veteran of Poulo Condore. He was wandering around at loose ends, living clandestinely. I got him hired at Vinh Long, and he set himself up in a straw hut on the bank of the Mekong. One evening, who should I see in the hut but Tran Van Giau. He told me he had escaped from the Ta Lai camp in Bien Hoa. He seemed to be relaxed and carefree, as though he was enjoying the state of being an escapee. We bathed together in the Mekong, then he disappeared.

It was balm to my heart to learn of the arrival of my friend Tran Van Thach, who had been exiled to Can Tho after his return from Poulo Condore at the end of 1944. He was the one who had gotten me the proofreading job at *Le Flambeau d'Annam* when I got out of prison in 1937. He was living in a room on the bank of the Mekong. I brought him my deep affection—and some soap. In the evening we would often go for a stroll together by the river. He once confided his dream to me, in English: "I would like to go abroad after the war." It never happened. In October 1945, while in the resistance movement in Ben Suc, he was shot by thugs hired by the Stalinists Tran Van Giau and Duong Bach Mai.

During this period I also ran into my old friend Ho Huu Tuong, who was also in exile in Can Tho after being released from Poulo Condore. This was a troubling reunion. He told me that he had broken with his past after years of "meditation" during his imprisonment. He now believed that the emancipation of humanity by the proletariat had been the biggest myth of the nineteenth century, and the revolutionary potential of the European and North American proletariat the biggest myth of the twentieth. I could find no words to refute this haughty, detached position of the very man who had initiated me into the struggle so long ago. I felt as though I had already been erased from his past. Our friendship slipped away before my eyes, like the flow of the Mekong.

* * *

On March 10, 1945, Can Tho woke up to martial law. As astonished crowds gathered in front of huge posters put up during the night, I saw the proclamation by the Commander in Chief of the Japanese Army, which ran roughly as follows:

> In view of the developing military situation against the Anglo-American attacks, the Greater Japan government feels obliged to assume sole responsibility for defending Indochina, while declaring that it has no intention of territorial conquest. The Greater Japan government will do everything possible to help the peoples of Indochina, hitherto toiling under the colonial yoke, to fulfill their ardent desire for independence. The Japanese army will annihilate only the present colonial government and its army, and does not consider native soldiers as enemies. . . .

During the night the Kempeitai (Japanese police) had imprisoned the French Administrator and all the French Sûreté agents and police. They had also rounded up all the French people and put them in large centers inside guarded perimeters.* The French colonial regime, after eighty years of crushing with terror, violence and corruption all the attempts of its slaves to break their chains, had collapsed in a single night, March 9–10, 1945. The Japanese replaced the French at the head of the system of oppression, presenting themselves as liberators. The Commander of the Japanese army, Tsuchihashi, replaced Decoux as Governor-General of Indochina. Under the aegis of the Japanese, Bao Dai, the Emperor of Annam,* proclaimed the "independence" of Vietnam on March 11, 1945, and called on Tran Trong Kim, a retired school inspector, to form an imperial government in Hue.

One evening, Lu Sanh Hanh turned up at my doorway. I hadn't seen him since Phnom Penh. He recounted his adventures during his five years underground. Having escaped the enormous roundup at the beginning of the war in September 1939, he went into hiding in the extreme west of Cochinchina, where he took a position as tutor to the only daughter of the brave farmer who hid him. I was moved by the story of his romance with this girl from the ricefields, and his heartbreak when he had to leave her.

Lu put me in contact with Nguyen Van Linh, an older comrade

who had played a significant role in the Indochinese Left Opposition group in France. He had returned to Cochinchina at the beginning of the war, and was now teaching in a private school in Can Tho. It was a warm and stimulating encounter. We gathered at his house to discuss the political situation, without yet formulating any plan of action. Finally back in the company of people who shared my ideas, I came to life again. Lu Sanh Hanh wanted to bring together the surviving comrades and reconstitute the League of Internationalist Communists.

In Saigon, the nationalist groups, which had been outlawed under Decoux, began to stir. The National Party for the Independence of Vietnam, led by intellectuals, joined with the Cao Dai and Hoa Hao mystico-religious sects in calling for a demonstration "to express the nation's gratitude to the Japanese army for freeing us from our French enemies." But the Japanese banned the demonstration. The Cao Dai sect, which commanded a paramilitary force of several thousand peasant followers trained by the Japanese, had participated in the coup alongside the Japanese troops. The Hoa Hao, until then relatively unknown, came on the scene at the bidding of their leader, the Mad Monk, who had emerged from his hiding place in the Japanese zone. In 1945, in their fief of Chau Doc, the Hoa Hao followers forged spears, knives and sabers and underwent military training. The sect set up its own security force and wielded a certain amount of de facto power. In July 1945 many of its members enlisted as auxiliaries in the Japanese army.

In April 1945, with the blessing of Minoda, the new Japanese Governor of Cochinchina, Dr. Pham Ngoc Thach and a handful of intellectuals launched the JAG (*Jeunesse d'Avant-Garde/Thanh Nien Tienphong*) [Vanguard Youth]. Imbued with a jingoist ideology of the Stalinist Komsomol and Hitler Youth type, this movement contributed to the maintenance of order by the Japanese and to civil defense. In the remotest countryside as well as in the urban areas, it mobilized everyone over the age of thirteen into brigades that demanded an oath of unquestioning obedience to superiors. Uniformed and armed with sharpened bamboo sticks, these boy scouts marched under a yellow flag with a red star, singing "On the March," an anthem praising the ancient heroes who had defeated the Chinese at

Chi Lang and at the Bach Dang River. Those who failed to join this organization were accused of not loving their country. A parallel organization of "Vanguard Women" was set up to carry out a similar role with female youth. In the cities, the movement soon became the de facto power in every factory, every office, every workshop and every school. Branch sections were in every area of the public services. It was the same in the countryside, from the main county towns to the smallest hamlet. At the beginning of August 1945 the JAG held a mass swearing-in ceremony in Can Tho.

During this period there was a huge Anglo-American air offensive. In the west, I had been far away from the war. But one day when I had come to Saigon I got caught in a bombardment and ducked into a ditch. After the piercing whistle, followed by the explosions, I felt the ground tremble. The large trees bordering Boulevard Norodom were literally cut to pieces. The neighborhoods of straw huts were in flames. The dead and wounded lay everywhere under the onslaught of shrapnel and fire. JAG teams gathered up the corpses and cleared away the rubble. These massive air attacks were a daily occurrence. The B-29s flew at very high altitudes so as to evade the Japanese antiaircraft guns. Sky-high flames blazed from burning fuel depots.

When I went to see my mother and brothers in the village, my peasant friends showed me the cartridge cases they had picked up after low-flying planes had strafed the villagers, in the belief, perhaps, that they were Japanese troops in camouflage.

"Your boys are in danger," my prophetic Brother Seven had told my cousin, who thought that Brother Seven had foreseen the misfortune because the Japanese had concealed antiaircraft guns under the trees surrounding the house. But nothing disastrous happened until later, after the Japanese retreat, when soldiers of the French Expeditionary Corps, in a "mopping-up" operation, rounded up all my cousin's sons and shot them at the place called Cau Sat (Iron Bridge) and threw their bodies into the river.

Chapter 7

CAUGHT IN A CROSSFIRE

The Japanese army surrendered on August 15, 1945. The victorious Allies put the defeated forces in charge of maintaining order in Indochina until the Allied occupation army arrived. Nevertheless the troops of the Vietminh entered Hanoi on August 18.

Saigon was reported to be in turmoil. Unable to stay away, I quit my job in Can Tho and set out for Saigon with Nguyen Van Linh. We reached a checkpoint outside the city at Tan An and there, standing right in front of me, was Nguyen Van Tao, the Stalinist leader I had known in prison. He, too, was naturally on his way to Saigon. He clapped me on the shoulder: "Listen, don't do anything stupid! Think before you act!" His protective attitude was like that of an older brother toward a wayward boy. He knew very well that I belonged to the underground Trotskyist group.

I went to Tan Lo, the hamlet 15 kilometers north of Saigon where my mother was living. Her house soon became the main contact point for the League. Many of its members showed up there—Lu Sanh Hanh, Nguyen Van Nam, Nguyen Van Linh—as well as new comrades such as Liu Khanh Thinh, who worked for the Chinese at Cholon, and Le Ngoc, who was on the action committee set up by four hundred workers in the streetcar workshop at Go Vap. Under the Japanese occupation this combative committee had managed to win a pay raise and recognition of their elected delegates. Our League had a very active nucleus there.

* * *

Ho Chi Minh and Vo Nguyen Giap with their
American OSS advisors (September 1945)

One day the poet and printer Tran Dinh Minh arrived from Hanoi with news from the North that both excited and alarmed us. He told us that in 1944 and 1945 he had been putting out a "samizdat" newspaper, *Co Do* (Red Flag), and that the writer Nguyen Te My had published a "Manifesto" criticizing the Stalinist Vietminh for its contacts with the imperialist Allies, denouncing it for sowing the illusion that it was possible to obtain "national liberation" by making a deal with the imperialist French and the Allies. In the Dan Phuong area (Ha Dong), Luong Duc Thiep and his friends had circulated a news-sheet called *Chien Dau* (Combat), which urged workers and peasants to rise up against all imperialists without exception, Allied as well as Japanese. The students Nguyen Ton Hoan, Phan Thanh Hoa and Tuan had gone to talk to the miners about the problems of the struggle, striving to counter the jingoistic propaganda of the Vietminh and to criticize the strategy based solely on a demand for national independence. Because in the final analysis, what sort of "liberation" would it be if the workers and peasants were still slaving away in the mines or on the plantations for private profiteers?

A burst of wild hope filled us when we learned that the 30,000 miners of the Hongai-Campha Coal Mines had taken their fate into their own hands and elected workers councils to manage the coal production themselves. The miners were now in control of the public services in the area, the railways and the telegraph system. They were applying the principle of equal pay for all types of work,

whether manual or intellectual. They had even begun a literacy campaign, setting up courses in which those who were literate taught
their fellow workers how to read. In this working-class "Commune,"
life was organized with no bosses and no cops.

But we were already afraid this could not last. Everything that
Tran Dinh Minh reported showed us that not only was social revolution not on the agenda for the Stalinist Vietminh, who were now in
power in the North, but also that they were prepared to repress it at
any cost in order to retain total political power. They had not even
waited to be formally installed in the government before starting
to physically eliminate those they called "Trotskyist traitors to the
Fatherland." Tran Dinh Minh told us about a young and very active
Trotskyist, Nguyen Huu Dung, who had been pursued in a sampan
through the flooded ricefields and assassinated by a young Vietminh
member; and about the death under torture of his friend Tran Tien
Chinh, a teacher and an Oppositionist, in a Vietminh jail at Bac Kan.
What, then, would be the fate of the miners' Commune at Hongai-
Campha? Torn between hope and fear, for a long time we had no
way of finding out what was happening. But thanks to those miners,
we had a better understanding of what we were fighting for.

* * *

In the South the parties and political groups that had developed during the Japanese occupation had formed a working alliance to confront the imminent return of the French. The National Party for the
Independence of Vietnam and the other nationalist groupings (the
Cao Dai and Hoa Hao sects, the JAG, the State Employees Federation, the Intellectuals' Group, and the Buddhist Anchorites Group)
all came together in a National United Front and called for a demonstration on August 21, 1945, under the slogans: "Down with French
imperialism!" and "Independence for Vietnam!"

We took part in the demonstration under our own banners: "Arm
the people! Form people's committees! Land to the peasants! Workers' control of the factories!" What a joy it was to be once again
with my old comrades, marching shoulder to shoulder in passionate
and fraternal solidarity, immersed in the crowds of coolies, work-

ers and peasants who had joined us! But I felt a knot in my heart at the absence, suddenly cruelly evident, of those who had died in the torment of the past few years: Trinh Van Lau, Vo Van Don, Van Van Ky . . .

That same evening cars drove through the streets of Saigon blaring out from loudspeakers: "Everyone behind the Vietminh!" We read in their leaflet: "The Vietminh has collaborated closely with the Allies in the fight against the French and the Japanese. We will thus be in a good position to negotiate [for independence]." Bluster and boasts from the Stalinist Tran Van Giau, worming his way into power.

Sensing the way the wind was blowing, Dr. Pham Ngoc Thach, the leader of the JAG, left the National United Front to join the Stalinist party, putting at its service the formidable instrument of control and power that the JAG had become. The next day the JAG's banners were proclaiming: "All power to the Vietminh!"

The State Employees Federation formed a bloc with the JAG. The Cao Dai and Hoa Hao sects also aligned themselves with the Vietminh. Everything was set for the Stalinists to take power.

The evening after the march, I met Kinh An Do, my workmate at Vinh Long.

"We're ready to take power," he confided to me. "The proclamation's already printed."

So he was in on Tran Van Giau's coup plans. Walking through the big city park, I came across JAG groups carrying sharpened bamboo poles, drilling in military formation.

On the evening of August 24, 1945, a massive square column draped with a red muslin banner appeared in front of the City Hall. In huge letters, it proclaimed: "Nam Bo* Provisional Executive Committee: President and Minister of Military Affairs, Tran Van Giau; Foreign Minister, Pham Ngoc Thach; Minister of the Interior, Nguyen Van Tao; Minister of State Security, Duong Bach Mai." Thus was announced the self-appointed de facto government of our new masters. It would be a purely Stalinist regime, though for appearance's sake they had included a few token non-Party figures. They announced that the following day, August 25, there would be a demonstration that would function as a plebiscite. We decided to attend it and make our dissenting voice heard.

In the dawn hours of August 25, the whole native population of Saigon began to arrive for the demonstration. People from the straw huts outside the city, the lower classes from the inner suburbs of Gia Dinh, Go Vap, Thi Nghe and Khanh Hoi, all converged on the city center, which was already crowded with peasants from rebellious areas such as Ba Diem, Hoc Mon, Duc Hoa and Cho Dem. They poured onto Boulevard Norodom, where an impressive platform had been artfully erected behind the cathedral. No one had ever seen such an enormous crowd. There was a surge of hopes and an intoxicating feeling of unanimity. Everyone wanted to experience the end of the colonial regime, and to do so they were prepared to throw themselves into combat for a future that was still uncertain.

The League, with its radical slogans, "Land to the peasants! Factories to the workers!" aroused the enthusiasm of this exploited population, who had come with the hope to be done with all masters, whether white or yellow. To the Stalinists who shouted "All power to the Vietminh!" we replied: "All power to the people's committees!" And we sang the "Internationale" in response to the JAGs, who were singing "On the March," a song about "the eternal heroism of the Vietnamese." In fact, the Stalinists went so far as to declare: "The Communists, as the militant vanguard of our people, are prepared to put the interests of the Fatherland before class interests."

At the press conference held the next day by Tran Van Giau in the City Hall, Tran Van Thach, a member of the *La Lutte* group, posed the question: "Who elected this 'Nam Bo Provisional Executive Committee'?"

Tran Van Giau, beside himself with rage, replied, "We have provisionally taken over the government at this stage; later we will transfer it to you."

Then, fingering his revolver, "As for my political reply . . . I will give that to you elsewhere."

And so he did: two months later, in October 1945, Tran Van Thach was shot dead by Tran Van Giau's thugs.

The Allied Commission was due to arrive in Saigon at any moment in order to disarm the Japanese troops and send them home. Tran Van Giau asked the people to "cooperate with the government in welcoming the Allied Commission with solemnity. Every building, public or private, should display the national flag of Vietnam, surrounded by the flags of the British, the Americans, the Russians and the Chinese." On September 2, 1945, Tran Van Giau organized an armed demonstration and harangued the crowd from his podium. Not content with celebrating independence, he already denounced "a certain number of people who are traitors to the Fatherland. . . . We must punish the gangs who are stirring up trouble in the Democratic Republic of Vietnam, thereby giving our enemies the opportunity to invade us." These threats were obviously aimed at us, as well as being a warning to other potential rebels. We understood that the elimination of revolutionary opponents, already well advanced in the North, was now also threatened in the South.

Nevertheless, we were astonished to see that the armed procession included a group of men who were naked to the waist and covered in tattoos, carrying their own banner with the bizarre appellation: ASSASSINATION ASSAULT COMMITTEE. They were Binh Xuyen river pirates, hired by Tran Van Giau and Duong Bach Mai as policemen and bodyguards. They took their name from a poor, almost uninhabited area south of Cholon that was reputed to be a nest of outlaws. We soon learned that the main portion of their band, which was based near the Y-shaped bridge over the river between Saigon and Cholon, was in control of the Chinese Arroyo, the bypass canal, the southern part of Saigon and almost all of the developed portion of Cholon. In addition to these pirates, Tran Van Giau's "People's Army" was composed mostly of brigades of riot police, militiamen and gendarmes, the French repressive force which had been maintained by the Japanese and which now switched over to the service of the new potentates.

The JAGs paraded around with banners displaying the Tran Van Giau government's pet slogan in English, Russian and Chinese: WELCOME TO OUR ALLIES! The Cao Dai sect marched behind their own leaders, as did the powerful nationalist army known as the "Third Division"* and the Hoa Hao, armed adherents of the Mad Monk, who had a messianic belief in the imminent return of the Buddha King. Everywhere you could see banners in French or in Annamite: DOWN WITH FRENCH COLONIALISM! BETTER DEATH THAN SLAVERY! TOTAL

INDEPENDENCE FOR VIETNAM!

At about four o'clock, as the procession was passing the cathedral, shots rang out. "The French are firing at us!" the crowd shouted, and started running in all directions, panic-stricken.

Groups of armed men rushed toward the House of Missions. A kindly chaplain named Tricoire, whom I had known in prison, was stabbed and fell on the courtyard. There were more scattered shots coming from various directions, including Boulevard Bonard and the Central Marketplace. At nightfall a torrential rain brought calm. A rumor spread that five French people had been killed.

The next day, Tran Van Giau decreed that no weapons were to be carried in the streets, except of course by his own cops and supporters. Fortunately, no one paid any attention to this order.

We put out a leaflet in the name of the League of Internationalist Communists and distributed it in the Central Marketplace, calling on the population to arm themselves, to organize themselves in people's committees and to set up people's militias. It should be noted here that in a book published in Saigon in 1994 called *Histoire de la Résistance, Saigon-Cholon-Giadinh 1945–1975,* the servile authors slanderously attributed to the League the racist slogan: "Exterminate the whites!" Wretched hired penpushers!

Everyone was looking for ways to get weapons. In Saigon, large numbers of people's committees (reminiscent of the 1936 action committees) arose spontaneously as organizations of local administration. In August the workers in the Phu Nhuan district had already elected such a committee, which had proclaimed itself "the only legal power in the district." The Ban Co district followed suit the next day. Embryonic people's councils were springing up everywhere: the dynamism appeared irresistible. The League took part in the coordination of this movement. We opened premises at 9 Rue Duclos in the Tan Dinh district where the elected delegates could meet, protected by armed workers. These delegates issued a declaration in which they affirmed their independence from the political parties and resolutely condemned any attempt to restrict the autonomy of the decisions taken by workers and peasants.

I continued living clandestinely, spending my time going to and from the village in order to hide weapons there that we had managed to pick up, mostly on the black market.

One day, I ran into Kinh An Do in the city. He told me that in the provinces of My Tho, Tra Vinh, Sadec, Long Xuyen and Chau Doc the peasants had spontaneously taken possession of the land. "The land to those who work it" had been a Communist Party slogan in 1930; now some Stalinist militants very nearly got themselves lynched for trying to restrain those who were carrying it out. A communiqué appeared in the press from the Commissar of the Interior—who was none other than my old acquaintance Nguyen Van Tao. It declared: "Those who are encouraging the peasants to take over landed property will be punished without mercy. The communist revolution, which will resolve the agrarian problem, has not yet taken place. Our government is a democratic and bourgeois government, even though the Communists are in power." Now that my old prisonmate Nguyen Van Tao had become the master of the "crushing machine," he had the power of life and death over us all. When we had met at Tan An, his advice to take care had been tinged with genuine concern. Now it sounded like a serious warning.

* * *

The Allied Commission arrived on September 6, 1945, under the command of British General Gracey. Despite his ceremonious reception by the Vietminh, Gracey immediately ejected the latter's de facto government from the Cochinchina Governor's Palace and installed himself there. Tran Van Giau and his team had to move to the City Hall. Under an order from Gracey, the Japanese commander Terauchi ordered Tran Van Giau to dissolve all armed groups and to totally prohibit any possession of arms.

Tran Van Giau soon found his scapegoat. He lashed out against our League: "An irresponsible group has called on the population to demonstrate at the Saigon marketplace with the demand of 'arming the people,' thereby giving foreigners a pretext to attack our sovereignty. This is an abuse of the democratic liberties that we, the Executive Committee, have promulgated."

A hate campaign was unleashed against us. The Stalinists, in their paper *Dan Chung,* called the Trotskyists *Viet gian* (traitors to the Fatherland). On September 7, the *La Lutte* group put up posters announcing that Ta Thu Thau had been arrested in Quang Ngai in front of his group's meeting place. When he was challenged about this, Tran Van Giau issued a terse press statement that said, "The Nam Bo Executive Committee has the right to judge Ta Thu Thau."

In fact, Tran Van Giau continued to have various groups of armed men at his disposal, which constituted a sort of Stalinist secret police, and he also controlled the police stations and the prison, which were run by his crony Duong Bach Mai. On September 14, 1945, Duong Bach Mai sent his cops to surround the meeting hall of the Tan Dinh people's committees, in which the League had been very active, in order to arrest some thirty delegates, including our comrades Lu Sanh Hanh and Nguyen Van Chuyen, and to seize weapons. The prisoners were locked up in the Central Prison—a place that was all too familiar to nearly all of them from the days of the French.

These tumultuous events came to a head with the arrival of a battalion of Gurkhas* commanded by English officers, charged with disarming the Japanese soldiers and maintaining order in the southern half of Vietnam.

On September 17, the de facto Vietminh government called a general strike. On September 20, Gracey banned the entire Annamite press and ordered all Vietminh proclamations to be torn down from the city's walls. The Vietminh then urged the population to disperse into the countryside and to "remain calm, as the de facto government hopes to obtain negotiations." On September 21, Gracey declared martial law. The following day, the British took control of the Central Prison and delivered to the French Sûreté our League comrades who had been arrested by the Stalinists.

Gracey also freed and rearmed the French soldiers held by the Japanese as prisoners of war, who then unleashed a reign of terror in the city against the Annamites. At about 4:00 a.m. on Sunday, September 23, these French soldiers stormed the City Hall, which Tran Van Giau and his men had already abandoned, and shot the Annamite sentries. They tightly bound together about fifty other Annamites and retained them as prisoners.

Filled with terror and rage, the people of the city quickly built bar-

Prisoners of the Sûreté (September 23, 1945)

ricades with chopped-down trees, overturned vehicles and piled-up furniture in order to bar the passage of patrols and troops. It was a desperate resistance. You could hear the rattle of machine-gun fire until six the next morning. Eventually the city center fell to the French, supported by the Gurkhas. French soldiers and sailors went from door to door in the city center and on the waterfront, shooting out the houses' locks and taking the inhabitants away, incarcerating them in police stations and any other available public buildings. At the Central Post Office more than a hundred men, women and young people under guard were made to squat on the ground with their arms shackled tightly above their heads.

But the outskirts of the city and the suburbs, where most of the poor lived, belonged to the insurgents. Saigon was surrounded. In the south, the Binh Xuyen pirates controlled the Chinese Arroyo all the way to Cholon; in the northwest, the Cao Dai controlled the Tay Ninh road and the Tan Son Nhut airport. The Vietminh militias operated in the district immediately to the north of the city and on the banks of the Arroyo de l'Avalanche as far as the Gia Dinh road.

Simultaneously under fire from two sides—the Anglo-French and the Stalinists—Nguyen Van Linh and I hid out at Nguyen Van Nam's house in Cau Kho, on the edge of town. Early one morning we were awakened by the din of the JAGs assembling nearby. Since Nam knew all the insurgents from his street, we were able to leave without any problem. We learned that in the Da Kao neighborhood on September 23, the same day the French had attacked the city, the Stalinists had assassinated Le Van Vung, the secretary of the Saigon-Cholon district committee of *La Lutte,* while in Can Giuoc they had killed Nguyen Thi Loi, a labor unionist teacher from the same group. Since all our fighting units in the inner city had been smashed by Tran Van Giau's secret police, Linh and I decided to leave the city in order to regroup. Nam found us a man who ran a boat on the Chinese Arroyo. We dashed on board under a hail of bullets.

Late that afternoon, a group of Binh Xuyen insurgents came up the Chinese Arroyo toward Boulevard de la Somme to join with another group that was advancing into Saigon along Rue de Verdun and heading for the Central Marketplace. From there and from Boulevard Bonard they had the city center, Rue Catinat and the Continental Hotel within their range.

We flattened ourselves on the bottom of the small boat. The boatman moored as far from the banks as possible, right in the middle of the river. We had to wait for the rising tide in order to leave. Half-submerged corpses were floating on the water. I witnessed a horrible manhunt on the river bank. Showers of whistling bullets landed like storm-driven rain around the boat. Night fell. On the left bank flames leaped into the sky: the central power station at Cho Quan was ablaze, plunging the whole town into darkness. Insurgents also dynamited the waterworks.

The next day we reached the Kinh Te Canal, which connects with the Saigon River and which was still not under the control of the colonial enemy. We were stopped by some Binh Xuyen who were patrolling the canal, but Linh showed them an old safe-conduct pass and managed to convince them to let us go.

Just as we emerged from the canal onto the river, a convoy of barges passed us, going upstream toward Saigon. The Japanese soldiers guarding them saw our boat drifting toward them in apparent distress and threw us a rope. They towed us out into the middle of the river and that was how we managed to pass through the port Customs. We left the convoy as night fell, tying up at the Binh Loi bridge. Saigon burned red in the distance. Our boatman dropped us off near Thu Duc, generously offering us a pot of stewed beans at the expense of the Chinese client he was supposed to be delivering them to. Nguyen Van Linh and I reached my mother's house in the middle of the night.

In the hamlet we organized a self-defense group. Linh taught the young people how to use a revolver. Although they all belonged to the JAG, they were quite friendly to us. However, my presence upset their leader, a retired elementary school teacher: he was afraid it would give him a bad name with the Stalinists who were in power in Thu Duc.

Close to the hamlet, there stood a building at the entrance to a rubber plantation. It had been abandoned by its French owner and in it we found a massive library that had been trashed, with books scattered all over the floor. I was delighted to find a copy of Georges Coulet's *Sociétés secrètes en terre d'Annam* [Secret Societies in the Country of Annam], a collection of dictionaries of native languages, and some old sepia photographs showing dead insurgents who had been shot at the Chi Hoa fort after the failed attack on the Central Prison in February 1916. Our young comrades hung these photos on the walls of their meeting place, a hut they had erected on our land.

Our friend Nguyen Van Nam had also managed to get out of the encircled city. He described life there without water or electricity, plunged into a scene of slaughter and famine. The insurgents had attacked the police station of the port and set fire to the Rubber Manufacturing Company, the warehouses, the Central Marketplace and the French-owned rice warehouses.

One memorable evening Le Ngoc arrived with amazing news. Together with his comrades, the workers at the Go Vap streetcar workshops had decided to join the insurrection while remaining totally autonomous. In the internationalist spirit of the League, they had taken to heart the appeal to arm the people: They had broken with the Vietminh labor union organization, the General Confederation of Labor (renamed "Workers for National Salvation" by the Vietminh), and formed a "Workers' Militia," a name inspired by the Spanish Civil War. There were about sixty workers in this militia, organized into groups of eleven, each under the responsibility of a comrade chosen by the group. They had elected Tran Dinh Minh as military leader. As the French, backed by the Gurkhas, attempted unsuccessfully to break out of their encirclement in Saigon, the Workers' Militia took up position at Cau Moi (Ba Chieu–Gia Dinh), the center of the front line of the eastern front, which extended to the right along the Hang Sanh road as far as the Thi Nghe bridge and to the left as far as the Binh Loi bridge.

On October 3, 1945, an order reached the front from the Vietminh Executive Committee, which was discussing a ceasefire with General Gracey. It called on all insurgents to fight only the French and to allow the British and Japanese to pass freely through the lines. This was an appalling and deadly folly: Detachments of Gurkhas and Japanese, who were being used as auxiliary troops by Gracey, immediately passed through the zones controlled by the insurgents without having a shot fired at them, and took possession of the most strategic positions. This enabled the French to break through the resistance at Ba Chieu, Binh Hoa and the Binh Loi bridge and on the Hang Sanh road toward Thi Nghe. At the Thi Nghe bridge around two hundred Trotskyist fighters from *La Lutte* were massacred.

After several days of fierce encounters with French tanks, the Workers' Militia fighters retreated to Bau Tram. There, fighter planes dive-bombed the hamlet and strafed it with machine-gun fire. Twelve comrades were mowed down, including Chi Quy (the Militia's nurse), Thien, Dong, Tran Quoc Kieu, Le Van Huong and Ho Van Duc. The survivors retreated further to the west, where the "Third Division" had camped. In order to avoid being at the mercy of the Vietminh, the Militia joined up with this latter "army" of partisans. Tran Van Thanh met his death alongside them in guerrilla fighting near the Cambodian frontier during a French counteroffensive on Loc Giang.

Le Ngoc left us to rejoin the Militia, carrying with him a statement of our political aims.

As for Nguyen Van Linh and me, at the alarming news that the Vietminh had arrested our comrade Nguyen Van Vang in Bien Hoa, where he had set up a people's committee, we decided to set out on a search for him. When we reached Bien Hoa, Linh had a parley with the Vietminh while I waited for him, hidden on the river bank. Hours passed in increasing despair. He came back empty-handed. The jailers claimed to know nothing about our friend. We later learned that they had executed him.

Back at the hamlet, my cousin warned us that the Vietminh's local police spies had been snooping around inquiring about us. It was time to move on. The next morning at dawn we left our guns with my Brothers Ten and Twelve and my nephews Bo and Xung, for the use of the hamlet's self-defense group, and said a discreet goodbye to my mother. Nguyen Van Nam went back to Saigon, while Nguyen Van Linh and I chose to join the Workers' Militia. On the way, Linh, who was sporting a blue Vietminh cap that he'd found somewhere, received several undeserved greetings. We found the Workers' Militia in Loc Giang: what a joyous relief to join with our comrades in that atmosphere of combative solidarity!

Our life in the Militia became more organized. We got on well with the local peasants, explaining to them that we were fighting not only to "drive out the French" but also to get rid of the indigenous landlords, to end the forced labor in the ricefields, and to liberate the coolies.

One day, however, planes flew over Loc Giang, a sign that an attack was imminent. When the Third Division broke camp, the Militia decided to do likewise. We requisitioned local people with their ox-carts to help us move out.

During this exodus, we saw a guy with a rifle standing at the roadside next to a huge pile of bikes. Anyone who rode past on a bicycle had to leave it with him—an example of the power deriving from mere possession of a gun. Some Third Division men disarmed him and he fled.

After crossing vast, mournful stretches of marshland on foot or in ox-carts, we continued our odyssey by small boats on a canal that went through a desolate immensity of alum-permeated swamps. This was the Plain of Reeds, where the first insurgents had set up their base when the French arrived in the nineteenth century. Even today tanks still find it impenetrable. But there are airplanes. . . .

We made our way across the Plain of Reeds via waterways—hundreds of men with their families, women and children in a stream of sampans and little boats. Eventually we made a stopover with some fishermen and peasants. They naturally were not very welcoming—there were too many of us and their lives were already so difficult.

We had hardly finished digging ourselves into trenches when a French reconnaissance plane appeared in the sky. A few hours later, formations of French fighter planes dropped bombs and strafed the hamlet with machine-gun fire. The poor people who had suffered our presence wept at their burned-out thatched houses, damaged fish tanks and destroyed gardens. We had to quickly move on. We ended up further away in the vicinity of western Vai Co.

We needed a radio receiver for the Militia: I set out with a companion to try to unearth one. Some Vietminh guards hiding in a straw hut on the riverbank arrested us. They searched us, confiscated my revolver and my copy of *Les Sociétés secrètes en terre d'Annam*, and tied us together on a bench for the night. In the morning, they took us further inland to their leader. I claimed that we belonged to the Third Division, while of course omitting any mention of the Workers' Militia.

"Are you the ones who've been threatening to blow the brains out of the people on the river? Where did you get that book? What's your religion?"

"Buddhism," I lied.

We were shoved into a small boat and taken along the left bank of the river till we reached a Guardian Spirit temple that had been turned into a prison. There were already around thirty detainees, including two women—a fishwife and a girl whom the jailers called "crazy"—and four Japanese soldiers. None of the prisoners seemed to have any idea why they were there.

A numbing, torpid sense of powerlessness overcame me at the sight of the supposedly "crazy woman" bound by arms and legs to a post in the muddy yard in the pouring rain, and struggling furiously. "Trong wants to kill me!" she was yelling. "He wants to kill me! That damn teacher, seller of Chinese medicines . . . what did I do to turn him against me like this? What have I done?"

I soon discovered that Nguyen Van Trong, the leader of the gang, had been put in charge of this region by Tran Van Giau.

General Leclerc's tanks were making a dash for My Tho. Nguyen Van Trong realized that they would have to pass through Tan An, so he had moved further into the interior. In order to control everything that went up and down the river, he had hired former indigenous police agents from the French Sûreté. After the destruction of the French colonial regime by the Japanese, these cops had managed to escape having their throats cut during the Saigon uprising and had hidden out in the countryside. Some of them were now offering their services to the Vietminh chiefs.

The exodus from Tan An had left it completely deserted. Whole families had crammed themselves into junks and set off upstream. Any Catholics among these fugitives, or any who were thought to be Catholic, were arrested by Nguyen Van Trong's henchmen, their new master having decided that all Catholics must be on the side of the French. To seal his authority, Nguyen Van Trong needed prisoners—victims over whom he held the power of life and death.

We heard rifle shots and thought it was a French attack. It turned out to be the execution of three Catholics by the Vietminh. From now on, I thought, I must be ready for anything. By some miracle I still had a bit of paper and a pencil stub. I scribbled down some information about my past struggle against the colonial regime and how I had continued the fight in the Go Vap streetcar Workers' Militia. I kept this piece of paper carefully, as a trace, in case my life was to end there.

A night of horror. . . . Through the wooden partition we heard shouts: "Admit that you informed for the French! Say it!" The shouts were followed by the dull thud of a heel being driven into someone's back, then a knee going into someone's chest, then the sound of fists smashing a face. We heard a man howling in pain, mingled with the frightened cries of a child and the racking sobs of a woman. This went on all night. The only words they could wrench out of their victim were: "This is injustice! Oh, heaven and earth!"

The torturer was also our jailer. I mentally called him Buffalo-Head, and his mate Hawk-Beak, after the demons in the Buddhist hell. The next morning, Buffalo-Head interrogated two of the accusers—ex-cops from the French Sûreté who had been hired by Nguyen Van Trong for his police, and who in order to demonstrate their zeal to their new master had uncovered a "nest of spies" on the river! It turned out that their "evidence" was some bits of red, white and blue string—the colors of the French flag—that had been "discovered" under a heap of potatoes piled on the flimsy boat that carried this poor peasant family and their crops. Fresh prey for the torturer.

Two days later, we witnessed the execution of one of the cops who had instigated this farce. The Vietminh assembled all the prisoners and a crowd from the village. At dusk the condemned man, blindfolded and with his hands tied behind his back, was brought out into the open by the executioner, a hefty man stripped to the waist with a revolver in his hand. A hush fell on the spectators, and Hawk-Beak pronounced the death sentence. Some of the crowd applauded feebly. Turning to the peasants who had been tortured the previous night, Hawk-Beak made a great show of offering them a 100-piaster note as compensation. I looked away. The sound of a shot. The kneeling victim collapsed, twitching on the ground. His head was split open, and red blood was soaking into the trampled grass.

Three days later it was the turn of the other cop, at the same place and with the same audience. A cloth was tied round his eyes and the wretch was forced to his knees. Buffalo-Head knelt down too, facing him, about three meters away, and pointed his gun at the victim's chest. Click! The man flinched but the gun didn't go off. Someone took off his blue jacket: he was wearing a dirty white vest underneath. At the third shot he fell over. As he lay dying, Hawk-Beak leaned over him and shot him in the head. The body was still writhing weakly. Hawk-Beak fired again. The victim's family wrapped the body in a piece of matting and buried him alongside the other one who had been shot, next to the river.

Some time later, there was an effort to primp up the place of executions as an elegant public square. A giant altar to the Fatherland was erected on the spot, and served as a platform for the ceremonial visit of the provincial Vietminh boss, Nguyen Van Trong. He arrived in a solemn procession, surrounded by fawning acolytes, and crudely mimicked the former French Administrators when they used to do the rounds of the villages. We could hear him bawling out his fervent but stilted sermon about how the children of the Mother Country were weeping for her in her illness. After the ceremony, when he passed near us, my companion dared to demand our freedom. Nguyen Van Trong shouted into his face: "You should consider yourselves lucky you're still alive!"

Then one day the jailers came for my friend and me. We tried to remain calm, but we were extremely worried. We spent two days and a night in a small boat going back up the Vai Co River. Then we were imprisoned in a little thatched church on the bank of the Mango River.

I was amazed and very moved to find there my friend Thu, who was a surveyor at My Tho. He told me that the Vietminh had imprisoned him because he had helped the peasants to divide up the land and ricefields that they had expropriated from the landlords. In so doing, the peasants had contravened the Stalinist party's order against interfering with property rights. With Thu were other *La Lutte* supporters. Around forty people were held in this prison-church, including some former officials of the colonial regime.

One pleasant old fellow said to me, "You were a prisoner of the French, and now under the Vietminh you are still in prison. How can that be?" I recognized him. He had been the secretary of the French Administrator at Tra Vinh, the guy who had registered me when I was sentenced to restricted residence there four years before.

We had no contact at all with the only female prisoner, who was held in separate quarters. She was there, apparently, because of her connections with the French. Some nights the guard, who had himself done time at Poulo Condore, took the unfortunate woman to a hidden corner behind the church for "interrogation."

There were no clocks. We could tell the time only by the appearance of the morning star. Every morning at daylight the guard ran up the Vietminh flag in the middle of the yard. Some young people sang "On the March" (*Len Dang*), the jingoistic Vietminh anthem, while I and my *La Lutte* friends sang the "Internationale." Then we hung around in the yard until our food ration arrived at midday. After that, more time in the open air, until being confined again at nightfall. Packed in rows like sardines, we slept on mats laid out on the hard-earth floor. During the day, whenever we heard the rumble of approaching aircraft, everyone ran for shelter into the church.

Thu and some of his companions kept themselves fit with *nei kong,* a kind of martial art, with the idea that we might have a chance to overpower the guards and escape. My body, enfeebled by tuberculosis, did not allow me to participate in these exercises, but did not prevent me from keeping an eye out for opportunities.

From time to time our guards let us wash ourselves in the Mango River. One sparkling sunny day I jumped into the clear current and was dog-paddling to keep myself afloat. A string of boats packed with armed men appeared. Then suddenly the shout: "Anh Duc!" (my name in the Militia). "Good heavens!" Someone raised his arm, and a small boat broke away from the convoy and came alongside me. Joy! I was surrounded by my friends in the Workers' Militia, who were moving west with the Third Division. I quickly told them what had happened to me, and that other *La Lutte* friends were among the prisoners.

"We'll come back for you," they promised, as they pulled away.

The next day my companion and I were released, following the energetic pressure applied to Nguyen Van Trong by the Third Division commanders. It was simply a matter of the relative strength of forces.

My Militia friends informed me of the deaths of Le Ngoc, Le Ky and the young Nguyen Van Huong. They had split off to go and reconstitute a base in Saigon. On the way to the city they had been rounded up and imprisoned by a French patrol, and when the latter released them, the local Vietminh had executed all three as *Viet gian* (traitors to the Fatherland).

Then we found out that our jailers had transferred all our former fellow-prisoners from the church onto a large junk that they had turned into a floating jail. The Third Division boarded the boat and liberated the imprisoned human cargo. As a result, all the Vietminh's prisoners, including the *La Lutte* supporters, joined the Third Division.

We were still in the Plain of Reeds, on the front between My Tho and Sadec, where Leclerc's armored columns were breaking through.

Exhausted by tuberculosis, I felt that I was a dead weight on the Militia. Seeing my debilitated state, a comrade, Nghi, suggested that I return to Saigon with him. We traveled the same road back across the Plain of Reeds. Crossing the vast marshes on foot and in a sampan, we managed to avoid the Vietminh checkpoints and to conceal ourselves at the approach of French patrols. All along the route the frames of burned huts and the ravaged skeletons of fruit trees gave silent witness to the distress of these deserted villages. Here and there were fresh mounds of earth marking graves, some marked with the names of the slaughtered persons. In one hamlet we saw the remains of a flimsy barricade made of sandbags and bundles of latex leaves. We were received with touching sympathy by the few surviving villagers, who told us about the French patrol that had fired on them indiscriminately from their speeding truck. The soldiers of the colonial reconquest were everywhere.

We traveled mostly by night, sustaining ourselves by chewing sugar cane. On the other side of the river we ran into a group of armed men who detained us. In the morning a big strapping fellow appeared—someone not entirely unknown to me. "Where are you coming from?" he asked me. It was Minh, known as The Swimmer, a veteran militant of Ta Thu Thau's group.* His band of independent guerrillas controlled this meandering stream of water. Minh told me that in October 1945, during the French offensive at Thu Dau Mot, the Vietminh had massacred thirty prisoners in the Ben Suc jungle, including members of the *La Lutte* group. Before he was executed, Tran Van Thach had entrusted his watch, his glasses and a notebook to a young Stalinist guard, who happened to be one of his former students, to be transmitted to his brother. Among those shot were Nguyen Van So and Phan Van Chanh, with whom the Stalinists had collaborated in producing *La Lutte* from 1934 to 1937, as well as Nguyen Van Tien, who had recently come back from a hard labor sentence at Poulo Condore; also Ngon, a worker from the Arsenal; and a woman doctor, Nguyen Ngoc Suong, who had apparently cautioned the executioner to take careful aim at her heart. Devastated by this news, we continued on our way.

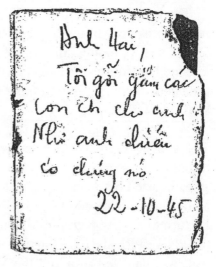

*Tran Van Thach's final note**

At last, one evening at twilight we arrived at the house of a cousin of Nghi's. Nghi took cover elsewhere and arranged for me to stay with this cousin, who took me out every day in his fishing boat. It was the ideal place to hide. I lay flat in the boat under the roofing while my host cast his net. The boat drifted with the tide, keeping near the steep banks. This allowed us to disappear, when necessary, into the little creeks that ran into the river. At times, when we heard the sound of detonations, we went ashore to hide behind the bamboo hedges. My companion constantly plied me with cigarettes to help me tolerate the foul odor of the innumerable corpses floating on the current and edging along the riverbanks—some with no faces, some tied up. Who were they? Where had they come from? Who had killed them?

One day, about noon, Nghi showed up with Nguyen Van Linh! What a delightful sight! He brought news from Saigon . . . and cigarettes. All three of us set off for the city, which was still at war. We passed through a village just after the French had been there. They had lined up all the villagers in squatting positions on the edge of a canal, then machine-gunned them all.

After two days, we reached Saigon.

Chapter 8

TOWARD OTHER SHORES

In Saigon, Nguyen Van Linh took me to the home of one of his relatives, Dzu, a radical lawyer, who would be able to hide me for a while. But the lawyer's bourgeois family was frightened to death by the presence of an "underground resistance fighter." I was confined to a small isolated room in their magnificent house. Dzu was never there. At midday and in the evening a servant came to call me for meals. A strained silence reigned at the table. I would eat, then quickly leave, setting down my chopsticks in the ritual fashion.

One day Sister Two came to visit me, bringing terrible news from our village. She told me that the Vietminh's secret police in Thu Duc, before fleeing the French advance, had taken away an old black man we knew and killed him. He was a native of the Antilles. After having served in the Colonial Infantry, he had settled in our neighborhood, working the land with his Annamite wife.

Then one day at dawn the hamlet had awakened to shouts of *"Tay toi!"* (The French are coming!) and *"Tay di bo!"* (The French and the Terror are here!), followed by rocket blasts. Whole clumps of bamboo and pineapple trees were leveled. Everyone fled or threw themselves to the ground. The uniformed killers ransacked the little straw huts and other dwellings, searching them from top to bottom, breaking open cupboards, upsetting ancestral shrines and smashing the temple of the Guardian Spirit. Women, children and old people were herded to the side of the road. The men found hiding were taken to the Iron Bridge and shot, their bodies thrown into the water. Peasants at work in the ricefields were machine-gunned at point-blank range. Brother Twelve managed to get away, despite a bullet in his knee. That night, one of our neighbors tried to retrieve the body of his brother, who had been murdered in the pumpkin field.

The corpse had been booby-trapped with a grenade, and the unfortunate man was blown to bits.

My sister had also seen severed heads impaled on the railings at the French military post opposite the Go Dua market. Apparently only one inhabitant had resisted the killers, charging at them with his machete. They shot him dead on the spot. Because of this constant terror, my sister urged me not to return to the village.

Eventually I was able to leave the awkward hospitality of the brave lawyer and be concealed in the home of Suu, a new refuge discovered by Nguyen Van Linh. It was a small upstairs room in the very center of the city (which continued to be under curfew). I felt more at ease here, in the company of two other underground activists. Sometimes at a meal our host would surprise us with some cheap red wine that he had obtained on the black market from the local eatery frequented by the French Expeditionary Corps. We had never before drunk any wine whatsoever.

By the beginning of March 1946, masses of French troops had been shipped back to Indochina. We learned from Suu what was happening in the cities. In Saigon, the postwar "new France" lashed out against the small number of French who sympathized with the native Indochinese peoples. Soldiers had beaten the editor of the socialist news-sheet *Justice,* which had denounced the crimes committed by the brutes of the Expeditionary Corps, completely destroying his home as well as the paper's office and printworks. The "Marxist Cultural Group," a semi-clandestine French organization in Saigon, had issued a resolution in favor of the independence of Vietnam. A young French woman, a member of the Women's Auxiliary Army Corps, was forced to walk down Rue Catinat at six in the evening between two paratroopers carrying whips. Her hands were tied behind her back, her head was shaved, and a placard was attached to her back that read: "I signed the Marxist resolution."

At night, Suu would surreptitiously listen to the international news on his secret radio. Someone probably denounced him, because one morning at dawn the police burst into the house. I was getting used to this by now and managed to hide my documents. After turning the place upside down, the cops seized the radio and took us to the Sûreté. We were dumped in the yard along with about fifty others. Toward midday, after having checked our identities, they released us.

I saw Nguyen Van Linh again. He was temporarily staying with his elderly parents, who had escaped from their village after French soldiers murdered their youngest son and destroyed their home. I found shelter for a time with Nguyen Van Nam. This rebel son told me without comment of his father being put to death by the insurgents in September 1945. I was not surprised. His father, the "Tiger of Cho Lach," was a mandarin notorious for having tortured rebellious peasants in the 1930s.

Nguyen Van Nam's hut, set back from the street and surrounded by coconut trees and banana plants, provided us a semi-secret retreat. There I reconnected with Lu Sanh Hanh. He had been locked up by the Vietminh secret police in September and was waiting to be hauled before one of Tran Van Giau's "People's Tribunals" when he got a lucky break: the British seized control of the Central Prison and handed him over to the French Sûreté, which released him a few months later.

Liu Khanh Thinh, a Workers' Militia member newly returned from the Plain of Reeds, told us of the death of our friend Tran Dinh Minh in January 1946, and that our surviving comrades had dispersed after the conditional surrender of the Third Division at Sadec.

Living at the expense of my friends had made me extremely ill at ease. Liu Khanh Thinh rescued me from this situation, getting me a job as an interpreter and clerk with a Chinese merchant who wanted to open an office in Saigon. This Chinese man found me a lodging on Rue Richaud, near my new job. Setting himself up as an import-export firm, my boss managed to obtain a monopoly on the distribution of the salt produced in Phan Thiet, in connivance with the French Resident Administrator of the region. He also trafficked in various rationed goods; by corrupt means, he secured a quasi-monopoly on the transport of foodstuffs from Saigon to Phan Thiet by train (at that time, all trains traveled with military escort); and he colluded with an inspector from the Sûreté, who filched and stored at his place various humanitarian aid shipments, such as sacks of flour and bundles of blankets.

I had never lived so close to the world of the enemy, the world of money and power. Once, when my boss had a meeting with the Adjunct Resident of Phan Thiet, I found myself sitting at the same table as this big shot of the colonial administration. My Chinese boss gave him a sumptuous Swiss watch . . . and received one piaster in return.

Our group was anxious to know what had happened to the "Commune" that the miners had established at Hongai-Campha in Tonkin. Liu Khanh Thinh, a native of the North, managed to receive some information: the movement had remained isolated and thus terribly vulnerable. Troops of Ho Chi Minh's Provisional Government had been sent out under the command of Nguyen Binh to encircle the mining district. Nguyen Binh called on the miners to respect national unity, but eventually, in order to win them over, he promised to more or less maintain the status quo. This pretense did not last long. Not only did he have all the elected workers' delegates arrested (including Lan, Hien and Le), but he also replaced the workers' councils with a new Vietminh hierarchy. After three months of popular self-management and creativity, the militaristic police state of the "Democratic Republic" reigned over the district.

The independent peasant movements in the North suffered a similar fate. In the provinces of Bac Ninh and Thai Binh in Tonkin, and Nghe An and Thanh Hoa in northern Annam, the peasants, under the pressure of an unabated famine and remembering the 1930 ICP slogan, "The land to those who work it!" had rejected the Vietminh's national alliance with the landowners and had pressured the people's committees to confiscate the property of the rich and give the land back to the peasants. In this way, they themselves would be able to make the land productive, and the harvest would not be turned over to speculators. Here, as elsewhere, Ho Chi Minh lost no time in quashing these initiatives. A November 1945 circular to the Provincial Committees decreed that "ricefields and cultivated land should not be divided up." Decree No. 63 on "the organization of popular power" proclaimed the reestablishment of a pyramidal hierarchy conforming to that of the Vietminh: the Executive Committee of each region would be responsible for carrying out government orders, and each level of the pyramid would control the level directly beneath it. In this way the Vietminh hierarchy brought in its police and imposed by military means the restitution of land and property to the landowners.

From the same sources we learned that during this period the Stalinist party had put out a call for us to be murdered. "The Trotskyist gang must be smashed immediately!" screamed *Co Giai Phong* (Banner of Liberation), the Hanoi Communist Party newspaper, in its issue of October 23, 1945. The Party was following the line put forward by Nguyen Ai Quoc (the future Ho Chi Minh) when he was in China in 1939. In three letters to his "cherished comrades" in Hanoi he had, in words reminiscent of the Moscow Trials, "unmasked the ugly face of Trotskyism and of the Trotskyists." And in a report to the Comintern he had stated: "As for the Trotskyists, no alliances, no concessions. They must be unmasked for what they are: the agents of fascism, and they must be politically exterminated."

The activists sympathetic to the Fourth International were being systematically assassinated in the North.

In the South, Duong Bach Mai, the chief of the Vietminh secret police, before fleeing from Bien Hoa upon the arrival of British and Indian troops in October 1945, had ordered the Trotskyist Phan Van Hum to be shot, the same Phan Van Hum who had been his prisonmate in Poulo Condore. Our friend Nguyen Van Vang, who had attempted to form people's committees, and Le Thanh Long, a *La Lutte* correspondent, had also both been shot. Other supporters of the Fourth International had been murdered by Duong Bach Mai's henchmen in the underground resistance in Ben Suc, as I had learned myself when I passed by the site of the massacre.

In Saigon, in order to consolidate his exclusive power, Tran Van Giau had liquidated the nationalists as well as the leaders of the various sects. When the historian Daniel Hémery interviewed Tran Van Giau in 1979 he asked him about Ho Van Nga, the leader of the National United Front, who had been executed by his secret police. Tran Van Giau had the gall to claim that Ho Van Nga was one of his friends. "They were nationalists above all," he said. "They weren't traitors, they were decent men!"

Nguyen Van Chuyen, a Workers' Militia comrade who had returned to Saigon, told me about his dangerous journey across the zones in the Mekong Delta controlled by the Hoa Hao. After

Leclerc's troops had entered Can Tho, the Hoa Hao—regrouped under their leader Nam Lua, whom I had met once by chance when I was working in the Delta—engaged in mass killings and drownings of Vietminh troops, in revenge for Tran Van Giau's repression of the Hoa Hao after his failed attempt to arrest their Master, the Mad Monk, in September 1945. This, however, did not prevent the Hoa Hao from also fighting

Ho Chi Minh toasting the March 1946 treaty with General Leclerc

against the French and organizing ambushes against them. The sect set itself up as the de facto power along the Bassac River, in the regions of Can Tho, Sadec, Long Xuyen and Chau Doc, up to the Cambodian border. But in April 1947, after the Vietminh assassinated the Mad Monk, the Hoa Hao rallied to the occupying power and joined the auxiliaries of the French Expeditionary Corps.

In October 1945, at the moment when the armed groups of the Cao Dai were confronting Leclerc's tanks in the Tay Ninh forests, the Vietminh secret police arrested their leader, Tran Quang Vinh. The number-two man in the Cao Dai hierarchy escaped, then rallied to the colonial regime in May 1946. Shortly afterwards, thousands of his followers, trained in killing by French instructors and organized into "flying columns," took part in the "pacification" operations alongside the French troops.

The Indochina War, which began in September 1945 in Cochinchina, did not spread to the North until December 1946.* The treaty of March 6, 1946, a fool's bargain signed by Ho Chi Minh through which the "new France" recognized Vietnam as a "free state" within the French Union, enabled Leclerc's troops to enter Hanoi "without firing a single shot" and to install themselves at strategic points in the country. As for national unity—the union of Tonkin, Annam and Cochinchina into a single nation—that was supposedly to be decided by a referendum. In reality, the conquerors were maneuvering for the separation of Cochinchina. In Saigon, High Commissioner Thierry d'Argenlieu called together a group of hardened French settlers and bourgeois Annamites and formed them into an Advisory Council charged with designating, from among its members, the head of the provisional government of the "Republic of Cochinchina"—a new façade for the former colony.

We could only follow the events, waiting to learn which sauce we would be eaten with and where the next attack would come from.

In Saigon, now under the tight surveillance of the French Sûreté and policed for the French by the separatist Cochinchinese bourgeoisie, the Vietminh began a campaign of sabotage and terror. In April 1946 the Pyrotechnie explosives factory blew up. For three days an inferno raged along the banks of the Arroyo de l'Avalanche, where four thousand tons of munitions had been stockpiled. The neighboring areas were burned to the ground.

Two members of the Advisory Council were shot down. This did not prevent Dr. Thinh from proclaiming the "Republic of Cochinchina" on June 1, 1946, from the square in front of the cathedral, presenting his government to the bourgeoisie of Cochinchina in the presence of the French officials. Its ministers were an assortment of old guard dogs of the colonial regime: Examining Magistrate Tran Van Ty (my judge in 1936) became Minister of Justice; Nguyen Van Tam, the "Tiger of Cai Lay" and notorious torturer of peasants during the 1930s revolts, was put in charge of Internal Security. The hostility and open contempt by the colonists toward this rump Annamite government with nonexistent powers soon overwhelmed Dr. Thinh. In November 1946 he hanged himself. Another bourgeois, Dr. Le Van Hoach (a Cao Dai dignitary), took his place. For one year this government played the role of backup police support for the reinstalled colonial regime.

In Saigon, day and night, we would often hear the distant sounds of explosions, the rattle of machine-guns, and the muffled echoes of confrontations between guerrillas and the soldiers of the Expeditionary Corps. Neither the police surveillance nor the curfew could prevent grenades from going off from time to time in the hotels, cinemas and cafés used by Europeans.

Police mopping-up operations spread terror in the Saigon-Cholon region. Once, as I was going to Cholon with a convoy of salt, I passed a camp surrounded with barbed wire where the French killers were piling up the prisoners they had captured during these raids. They shot them in batches of ten at a time, like hostages. Among the corpses was a boy, still holding a piece of paper, probably indicating his name and address.

One morning at dawn, near where I worked, I came across a scene of absolute horror: the removal of bloody corpses from an Annamite lodging. The rumor was that these assassinations had been carried out by the commandos of Nguyen Binh, whose real name was Nguyen Phuong Thao, a Vietminh envoy from the North. Having recently rallied to the Vietminh, he was the man assigned by Hanoi to destroy the miners' "Commune" in Hongai-Campha at the end of 1945. Now he was in charge of the resistance in the South.

His mission was to bring into line the armed groups of Binh Xuyen pirates, who, while still holding their own against the Expeditionary Corps, maintained their independence from the Vietminh. Their leader, Ba Duong, had made contact with the nationalist leaders. In 1946, his troops in the underground numbered twelve or thirteen hundred well-armed men organized into seven companies led by Ba Duong, Muoi Tri, Bay Vien, Nam Ha and Tu Ty. In an attempt to bring the Binh Xuyen under his control, Nguyen Binh nominated Bay Vien as second-in-command of the Resistance Army and incorporated Vietminh political commissars into the ranks of the Binh Xuyen. A large part of the Binh Xuyen under Bay Vien soon nevertheless rebelled against Nguyen Binh's authority and retreated into the swampy forests of Rung Sat. Nguyen Binh sent in his troops to annihilate them. The survivors then followed Bay Vien in joining the Expeditionary Corps.

In September 1947, my former boss, the Constitutionalist Nguyen Van Sam, editor of *Le Flambeau d'Annam,* died at the hands of Nguyen Binh's death squads. He had been trying to regroup the nationalist formations that were independent of the Vietminh into a new National United Front.

During this same period I was relieved to learn of the return to Saigon of our friends Ngo Chinh Phen and Anh Gia (Dao Hung Long), who had been exiled to Madagascar since 1941. This news appeared in the *Tranh Dau* news-sheet, which some survivors from the *La Lutte* group were trying to relaunch as an "organ of the proletariat" under the emblem of the Fourth International. In it they published a translation of the *Communist Manifesto* and reported the arrest of Ta Thu Thau in Quang Ngai and the disappearance of other veteran group members in the Thu Dau Mot underground resistance. The new *Tranh Dau* was banned after its second issue.

I brought Chi Nam Thin and her two young boys into my lodging. She was fleeing from Ben Tre, where she had been ordered to live after three years in prison at My Tho. Her sons went to school with my three children, Do, Oanh and Da. I also converted my place into a kind of bookshop, called *Tim Hoc* (Research and Study), which in reality served as a meeting place and a letter drop. Among the books that arrived from France were Jean Malaquais's *Planète sans visa* [World Without Visa]* and a number of subversive pamphlets. As internationalists caught in a crossfire, we survived as an informal group, striving above all not to lose hope.

Liu Khanh Thinh managed to make contact with the Communist League of China in Hong Kong. That was how the communist opponents of Mao Zedong—Peng Shuzi, his very active partner Cheng

Saigon harbor (1997)

Bilan, and Liu Jialiang—would later join the group in Saigon. Peng Shuzi, who was born in 1895, was one of the founders of the Chinese Communist Party; and Liu Jialiang had translated into Chinese Harold Isaacs's book *The Tragedy of the Chinese Revolution.*

One day, I learned that the cops had been snooping around my "bookshop." The next day the gentlemen of the Sûreté paid me a visit. They found nothing to seize, since most of the books and pamphlets had been securely hidden the day before, but they continued to return from time to time. Soon after this, Lu Sanh Hanh and Nguyen Van Nam went into exile in France.

Harassed by the Sûreté in the city and denied refuge in a countryside dominated by two terrors, the French and the Vietminh, I too decided to leave the country. I entrusted my small savings—often realized at the expense of my boss—to the safekeeping of a sympathetic friend, a fish-sauce merchant. He promised to support my family as best he could. Chi Nam Thin would look after them when I had gone. The Sûreté refused to give me a passport for France, but I managed to convince my Chinese boss to falsely declare that he was sending me on a business trip to Paris, which enabled me to obtain a three-month round-trip visa.

Thus it was that in the spring of 1948 I embarked in the hold of an old Messageries Maritimes freighter, heading for Marseilles. Standing on the back deck, my heart gnawed by melancholy, I watched the foam in the wake of the ship disappear, along with my past life. Before me stretched a horizon obscured with fog and clouds. And what would become of those I had left behind?

* * *

Devastating and heart-breaking news. In 1950, Nguyen Van Linh, Liu Khanh Thinh and the Chinese comrade Liu Jialiang were invited to take part in a secret meeting in the Vietminh military zone of Bien Hoa, supposedly organized by Trotskyist sympathizers to discuss the participation of Trotskyists in the resistance. In reality it was a trap set by the Vietminh. Nguyen Van Linh's partner went to look for them, accompanied by Chi Nam Thin, who had fought in the ranks of the Vietminh. The Vietminh in Bien Hoa detained the two young women, tortured them by suspending them from the roof beams, slitting their calves and stuffing flaming gasoline-soaked rags into the wounds in order to extract information about their friends, those "Trotskyist traitors to the Fatherland." Chi Nam Thin was able to write to me later; in this way I also learned that our three comrades had been put to death, and that the Vietminh radio station, the Voice of the Plain of Reeds, had naturally accused them of being "agents of French imperialism."

Of all those who had taken part in the revolutionary opposition movement and who had remained in the country, hardly a one survived.

Chapter 9

AND MY FRIENDS?

Friends are like clouds,
Life scatters us
But only death can separate us.

What happened to my friends, my closest comrades? Underground struggle created a strong bond between us, but the clandestine nature of this struggle meant that we often remained unaware of significant aspects of each other's lives. Despite this, I want to do my best to record what I can of these obscure figures. I'm sorry there are so many gaps in my account.

* * *

VAN VAN KY, the typographer who stole the type that made our underground printshop possible, was the youngest defendant at our trial [the August 1936 trial of members of the League of Internationalist Communists]. As he lay dying of tuberculosis, he sadly confided to a friend, "I thought I would die fighting in the street on a barricade."

VO VAN DON, a coolie who worked with me at Descours & Cabaud, had the courage to keep silent under torture, revealing nothing about our "fraternal association." All he would admit to was having peddled newspapers and having one night strung a banner calling for a general strike across the Giong Ong To road on the far bank of the

Saigon River. He died of tuberculosis. I was deeply moved to learn from his sister how desperately in his last moments he had wanted to see me at his side again, as in the days of our struggles.

VAN VAN BA, a worker and League member who had been arrested along with us, died in January 1939 of typhoid fever. More than two hundred worker and coolie friends accompanied him to his final resting place.

TRINH VAN LAU was one of the founders of the League. He was condemned to eight months in prison at the trial of August 31, 1936. He led underground resistance against the war, was captured by the French, and died on board one of the prison barges where the peasants who had taken part in the November 1940 uprising were held.

NGO CHINH PHEN had also been sentenced to prison at the trial of League members. He was a member of the "Internationalist Workers" group at Gia Dinh who in September 1939 campaigned against the recruitment of Vietnamese into the army and distributed leaflets to the infantrymen of Thu Dau Mot: "Don't shoot your comrade workers in the enemy army—turn your guns on the imperialists in our own country!" Captured in the underground resistance movement at Rach Gia, he was imprisoned in the mountain concentration camp in Ba Ra, then deported to Madagascar from 1941 to 1946. A few years ago he sent me a message of friendship from Houston, Texas, asking me to transmit his "fraternal greetings to comrades." Just before he died, in January 1996, still haunted by the assassinations of Trotskyists half a century earlier, he told his children: "I can still see the *De Tam* (Stalinists) surrounding us . . . *Cac bum, cac bum!*" (Sound of trigger, then shot, trigger, then shot.)

PHAM VAN MUOI was still a high-school student at the time of our trial. I lost contact with him after that. Did he survive?

TRAN THI MUOI was born into a family of small property owners in My Tho in 1914. Her family owned a small estate. Her father was a supporter of the rebel prince Cuong De, her elder brother a Communist who had been trained in Moscow. She became the partner of Anh Gia (Dao Hung Long) and joined the Trotskyist Left Opposition. Arrested in October 1932 and put through the Sûreté torture chambers, she spent six months in prison. In 1935 she helped me circulate League leaflets and papers among Stalinist contacts in the countryside. Her sister **TRAN THI CHIN**, born in 1912, was arrested in October 1929 during the Rue Barbier affair. In 1931, along with her partner Nguyen Van Dai, she joined the Communist League (*Lien Minh Cong San Doan*), the first internal opposition group in the Indochinese Communist Party. She died at Ca Mau in 1932.

VO THI BANG, alias **NGUYEN THI MY** (1915–1934), was a member of the Trotskyist group "Indochinese Communism" (*Dong Duong Cong San*). Arrested in August 1932, she was sentenced on May 1, 1933, to four months in prison. She died less than a year later as the result of the tortures she suffered at the Sûreté.

NGUYEN HUE MINH, born in Binh Dai (Ben Tre) in 1912, was a member of the Communist League, then was active in the "October" group* (Left Opposition). Arrested in August 1932, she was sentenced to three months in prison in May 1933. She became the partner of Ho Huu Tuong. She was the younger sister of Nguyen Trung Nguyet, the "heroine" of the Rue Barbier affair.

VO THI VAN, born in 1913, was originally from Ben Tre. She was a member of the Indochinese Communist Party and was condemned to eight months' prison in September 1933. Passing over to the Left Opposition and becoming the partner of Lu Sanh Hanh, one of the organizers of the League of Internationalist Communists, she participated in the Indochinese Congress movement in 1936 and also in the action committee based in the Cho Quan and Cho Dui neighborhoods of Saigon. She was very active in the underground labor union movement, especially with the railway workers during their strikes. She was imprisoned in May 1937.

LE VAN OANH was born in 1908 in Hai Duong (Tonkin). He worked for the railway, then became a secretary at the Saigon

Arsenal, but was fired during the 1936–1937 strikes. Very active in the underground unions, he was sentenced to two years in prison in November 1937. I saw him for the last time in 1945 during the Saigon insurrection. What became of him?

TA KHAC TRIEM was born in 1912 at Son Tay (Tonkin). From 1927 on he lived in Cochinchina, where he was an accountant at the Charnier Department Store in Saigon, then a clerk at the Arsenal until he was fired during the 1936–1937 strikes. The General Workers Federation, secretly organized by the illegal Trotskyists, held a meeting on May 29, 1937, in the northern suburbs of Saigon. Worker delegates from 44 companies were discussing what statutes to institute for this organization when Sûreté agents burst in and arrested 62 of them, including Ta Khac Triem. After his release he returned to his active role in the organization of strikes. During the strike at the Trans-Indochina Railway Company he helped to set up fraternal groups in Quang Ngai (Annam) and Tonkin. He was arrested in September 1937 and condemned to a year in prison because he was, according to a Sûreté dossier, "the Trotskyist ringleader who played an important part in the general strike on the railways."

VO BUU BINH, born in 1910 at Sadec, belonged to the Communist Left Opposition. He was arrested in August 1932 and spent three months in prison. He was among those arrested at the meeting of worker delegates on May 29, 1937. It was his partner who generously offered me a place to live when I came out of prison in June 1937. I remember that he told my son Do, who was very impressed: "Your father is a rogue who would sell the Heavens without consulting the God of Thunder!" (*Ban Troi khong moi Thien loi,* as the popular saying goes).

* * *

The "biographies" that follow, lamentably incomplete though they are, include some of my closest comrades (Nguyen Van Linh, Lu Sanh Hanh, Nguyen Van Nam, Anh Gia). Some of the others I knew less well, having just crossed paths with them in prison or elsewhere, but they all meant a great deal to me and my companions.

> *Society today overflows with injustice,*
> *Heaven, how can we make you hear our cries?*
> *Those who build the mighty mansions live in rotting huts,*
> *Those who weave silk are clothed in rags.*
> *The educated exploit the ignorant,*
> *Fools reinforce the gangs of oppressors.*
> *When people become conscious of their misfortune*
> *The myriad disasters will be overcome.*
>
> —Phan Van Hum

PHAN VAN HUM (1902–1945) was born on April 9, 1902, in An Thanh (Thu Dau Mot) in Cochinchina. His father was an educated Buddhist and a small landowner. In 1924 Phan Van Hum was admitted to the École des Travaux Publics [School of Civil Engineering] in Hanoi and then worked as a technician in Hue. Appalled by the misery and injustice he saw all around him, he found comfort from visits to the veteran nationalist and anticolonial campaigner Phan Boi Chau,* who was living under house arrest in Hue. He provided as much help as he could to alleviate the older man's destitution. Then, as a result of sheltering some students who had been expelled from their boarding school for taking part in a strike, he lost his job. He left for Saigon, where he became a friend of Nguyen An Ninh. They went all over the countryside together, spreading ideas of liberation among the peasants.

He was arrested in September 1928, and on his release from prison wrote a denunciation of the prison system: *Ngoi Tu Kham Lon* (In the Central Prison). The text was serialized in the paper *Than Chung,* arousing many younger readers.

In September 1929 Phan Van Hum left for France, where he joined the action committee of Indochinese émigrés in Toulouse. On May 22, 1930, he took part in the demonstration outside the Élysée Palace in Paris against the death penalties handed down to the

Phan Van Hum

Yen Bai insurgents. He managed to evade the police, fleeing the country along with Ho Huu Tuong. They took refuge in Brussels, where they produced a duplicated broadsheet *Tien Quan* (Vanguard), which argued against sectarian authoritarianism and warned of the danger of believing, as some did, that you could become an expert on Marx just by spending a few months in Moscow. One night in July, the two of them were successfully smuggled back to Paris by Pierre Naville and Raymond Molinier. Soon after that, together with other émigrés, they formed an Indochinese Group within the Communist League.

Phan Van Hum got a job as a teacher in Toulouse, but was fired for producing subversive propaganda. He returned to Saigon in July 1933, where he once again met Ta Thu Thau and Ho Huu Tuong. He taught Annamite at Paul-Doumer High School, but in June 1935 he was fired due to pressure from the Sûreté political police.

He took part in the *La Lutte* united front while continuing his studies of philosophy. When *La Lutte* split in 1937, he stayed with Ta Thu Thau and wrote for *Tranh Dau* (Struggle), which had become an organ of the Fourth International. In 1939, along with the Trotskyists Ta Thu Thau and Tran Van Thach, he decided to run for election to the Colonial Council (representing the district of Saigon-Cholon, Tan An and My Tho), running against the Constitutionalists and against the Stalinists' "Democratic Front" slate: Nguyen Van Tao, Nguyen An Ninh and Duong Bach Mai. The Trotskyists proclaimed the necessity of a "workers' and peasants' front" against war, and focused their propaganda against a rise in taxes and the imposition of an arms tax, and against forced conscription into the supplementary infantry—all of which were supported by the Stalinists' "Democratic Front." *La Lutte* published the group's electoral platform while at the same time attacking the Constitutionalists for being "indifferent to the exploitation of those who are hungry and thirsty" and reminding its readers that the Stalinists had been responsible for defeats of the proletariat in Germany in 1923 and 1933, in Estonia in 1924, in China in 1925–1927, and in Spain in 1936–1939. It denounced the infamous Moscow Trials and lost no opportunity to show how and why the "defense of Indochina within the framework of French imperialism and national unity" would turn the exploited Indochinese into tools and victims of Russian diplomacy.

Phan Van Hum, Ta Thu Thau and Tran Van Thach were elected despite their meetings having been banned, while the Stalinist "Democratic Front" candidates were all defeated. The discontented electorate had seen the latter as "pro-government," i.e. as part of the status quo. Elected to the Colonial Council on April 30, 1939, Phan Van Hum was arrested on June 28. He was sentenced on October 13 to five years' hard labor and ten years' restricted residence for having campaigned against war loans and war taxes. After his years in the penal colonies, where he contracted beriberi and was physically debilitated, in 1944 he rejoined the *La Lutte* group.

On September 10, 1945, the enlarged Vietminh (Stalinist) government cynically offered him a temporary post (he had been a popular figure ever since the 1929 publication of his book *In the Central Prison*). He refused to take part in what he considered a sinister, pseudodemocratic sham. Meanwhile, the news arrived that the Vietminh had arrested Ta Thu Thau.

After the October 1945 massacre of the Trotskyists at the Thi Nghe bridge by the Anglo-French troops, Phan Van Hum and other survivors—including Tran Van Thach, Phan Van Chanh, Ung Hoa, Le Van Thu and Nguyen Van So—formed a new group in Thu Duc to fight against the troops of colonial reconquest. The Stalinist Duong Bach Mai had Tran Van Thach, Phan Van Chanh and Nguyen Van So arrested. They were shot, along with some thirty other prisoners. Among the latter were Nguyen Van Tien, the former managing editor of *La Lutte* who had just been released from Poulo Condore, and Ngon, a worker at the Arsenal. Later in the same month (October 1945) it was the turn of Phan Van Hum to be arrested in Bien Hoa by Duong Bach Mai's secret police.

One of his co-detainees, who was later freed, was the teacher Truong Minh Hai. He told Tran Nguon Phieu (then also in the Bien Hoa resistance, now a doctor in Texas) about the following exchange, which he heard one evening between Duong Bach Mai and the imprisoned Phan Van Hum. They knew each other well, since they had been comrades in the *La Lutte* group in the 1930s and had been deported to Poulo Condore together in 1940. Duong Bach Mai said to Phan Van Hum:

"At Poulo Condore you put yourself between the warders' blows and the other prisoners, to defend them. But now, we're in the middle of a revolution . . ."

"If you want to kill me," replied Phan Van Hum, "do it here. What's the point of taking me somewhere else?"

Phan Van Hum was murdered along with other Annamite prisoners in Song Long Son, on the Trans-Indochina Railway line between Phan Thiet and Tour Cham, 232 kilometers from Bien Hoa. Their bodies were thrown into the river. (Truong Minh Hai was also killed soon afterwards.)

Publications by Phan Van Hum: *Ngoi Tu Kham Lon* (In the Central Prison), Saigon, 1929. Duong Linh (pseud.), *May Duong To* (A Few Poems). *Sa Da Du Tu* (Journal of a Wanderer: Impressions of Life and Travel in France), published in *Than Chung*. *Bien Chung Phap Pho Thong* (Dialectics Made Easy), Saigon, 1936. Nguyen Phi Hoanh (pseud.), *Tolstoy,* Saigon, 1939. *Phat Giao Triet Hoc* (Buddhist Philosophy), Hanoi, 1942. *Vuong Duong Minh, Than The Va Hoc Thuyet* (The Life and Teaching of Wang Yangming), Hanoi, 1944.

TA THU THAU (1906–1945) was born in Tan Binh (Long Xuyen) in Cochinchina into a family of poor artisans and was obliged to work from an early age. He won a grant to attend high school in Saigon, where he joined the Jeune Annam group, who were "plotting" to drive the French out of Indochina. He came under the influence of Nguyen An Ninh, who had been attacking the colonial regime in his journal *La Cloche Fêlée* since 1923, and who had also been exhorting young people to "leave the homes of your fathers"—only then, he said, could they hope to shake off the "suffocating ignorance" in

which they were trapped by obscu-
rantism. ("Our oppression comes
from France, but so does the spirit
of liberation.") Ta Thu Thau set sail
for France. At the age of 21, he was
studying at the Faculty of Science
in Paris. At first he was active in
the Annamite Independence Party,
assuming the leadership when its
founder, Nguyen The Truyen, returned to Vietnam in early 1928.
Together with two other students,
Huynh Van Phuong and Phan Van
Chanh, Ta Thu Thau published *La*

Nguyen The Truyen

Résurrection, "Journal of Revolutionary Annamite Youth," which
was seized by the police when its third issue appeared.

In January 1929, in the wake of a fight between the extreme
right-wing Jeunesses Patriotes [Patriotic Youth] and Annamites who
supported the Annamite Independence Party, he attacked the French
Communist Party for not supporting the Annamites who had been
arrested, and took it to task for the bad faith of the report in its newspaper *L'Humanité*. He also criticized the "salaried Annamites of the
Colonial Commission of the French Communist Party" who were
infiltrating the ranks of the Annamite Independence Party in order to
turn the latter's members into "puppets carrying out the Communist
Party's dictates." One of his leaflets ended with this desperate appeal: "In our nameless servitude, we call out to the oppressed of the
colonies: Unite against European imperialism—against Red imperialism as well as White—if you want a secure place under the sun."

The Seine Tribunal dissolved the Annamite Independence Party
in March 1929. In July in Frankfurt, Ta Thu Thau took part in the
Second Congress of the Anti-Imperialist League. In Paris, he and
his friends made contact with dissidents in the French Communist
Party—Alfred Rosmer (Left Opposition), Daniel Guérin, Maurice
Paz's *Contre le Courant* [Against the Current] group—and moved
away from a shortsighted nationalist position. They saw that ra-
cial and nationalist oppositions had tended to conceal the opposi-

tions between social classes. Ta Thu Thau began studying Marx and the history of Russia during the twelve years since the October Revolution, and soon arrived at a global vision of revolution and a critical communism that was instinctively internationalist.

After the bloody defeat of the 1930 insurrection at Yen Bai, he expressed his views on the Indochinese revolution in the April, May and June issues of *La Vérité* [The Truth]. Criticizing the Third International, he declared that the choice for him was no longer be-

Ta Thu Thau

tween slavery or independence, but between nationalism or socialism. "Imperialism can be overthrown only by the organized action of a homogeneous mass that is a *social* enemy of imperialism. Independence is inseparable from proletarian socialist revolution."

He was arrested on May 22, 1930, during the Annamite students' demonstration in front of the Élysée Palace against the death sentences imposed after the Yen Bai uprising, and on May 30 he was deported from France along with eighteen compatriots. When they arrived in Saigon on June 24, they were greeted by Stalinist leaflets denouncing them as counterrevolutionaries.

At the end of 1931, Ta Thu Thau cooperated with the underground group Ta Doi Lap (Communist Left Opposition) in Saigon, then organized the Indochinese Communism group (*Dong Duong Cong San*), which was broken up in August 1932 when he and 65 other Trotskyists and sympathizers were arrested. Released on bail the following January, Thau joined the *La Lutte* group and collaborated with the Stalinists in legal struggle against the colonial regime. He was active in the election campaign for the first Workers' Slate in Saigon. In 1934 he wrote *Trois mois à la Sûreté rue Catinat* [Three Months at the Sûreté on Rue Catinat], based on his experiences of interrogation before his trial and denouncing the systematic torture of those charged with political crimes.

He was frequently imprisoned during the strikes of 1936–1937 under the Popular Front government. When major strikes broke out in Indochina in 1936, he relentlessly attacked the Popular Front in *La Lutte* for betraying its promises of reforms in the colonies. The Stalinists distanced themselves from him in an open letter of December 17, 1936. The April 1937 Saigon City Council election brought Ta Thu Thau and the Stalinist Nguyen Van Tao together for the last time (they were both elected). At the end of May the Stalinists, following orders from Moscow transmitted via the French Communist Party, broke the united front with *La Lutte* by bringing out the newspaper *L'Avant-garde,* in which they called the Trotskyists "twin brothers of fascism." (Ta Thu Thau and Nguyen Van Tao were both in prison at that time, and were only temporarily released on June 7.)

Imprisoned yet again later in 1937, Ta Thu Thau was not freed until February 1939. In April 1939 he was elected to the Colonial Council on the platform of the Fourth International, seriously alarming the government. On May 20, Governor Brévié sent a cable to Colonial Minister Mandel denouncing "the Trotskyists under the leadership of Ta Thu Thau," who "want to take advantage of a possible war in order to win total liberation." In the same cable he expressed his appreciation of the Vietnamese Stalinists, who "are following the position of the Communist Party in France" and "who will thus be loyal if war breaks out."

In August 1939 Ta Thu Thau left the country. Arrested in Singapore in October and brought back to Saigon, he suffered more than four years' forced labor at Poulo Condore. After this harsh punishment, he was confined to the town of Long Xuyen in his native province. While there he wrote to Phuong Lan, a woman he had known in his adolescence: "Here I am in the place where a quarter of a century ago I lived without a care in the world. Twenty-four years have passed and the young boy returns with his wings clipped. While I was on Poulo Condore I learned some poems by heart, including the whole of the *Kim Van Kieu*. I want to reread it now to be sure I have fully grasped its meaning." (*Kim Van Kieu* is a long and quite unconventional eighteenth-century love poem very popular in Vietnam.)

During 1945 Ta Thu Thau analyzed and criticized the position of the Vietminh. Their policy of counting on the support of foreign powers to gain independence seemed dubious to him, and in any case it lacked a perspective of liberation for the workers and peasants. He wanted to rebuild a workers' party that would fearlessly confront the nationalist and Stalinist currents. That was what he and other *La Lutte* veterans envisioned when they met together again in Saigon after March 9, 1945.

At the end of April, he secretly traveled to the North. Tonkin and northern Annam were in the grip of famine, and he managed to get an appeal for aid published in the May 14 edition of the daily paper *Saigon:* "The scale of the disaster is such that I feel justified in entreating my brothers in Cochinchina to eat only what you need to stay alive and to send here everything you possibly can, immediately."*

In the North he had the good fortune to encounter a fraternal group that published the Trotskyist bulletin *Chien Dau* (Combat). He met Luong Duc Thiep and many young people who had abandoned their studies and dedicated themselves to arousing the political awareness of the poorest classes. Ta Thu Thau took part with them in clandestine meetings of mine workers and in secret gatherings of peasants. Many of his comrades were uneasy about the smears being spread about them by the Vietminh, which accused them of being "antiworker elements," but he had a seemingly unshakeable confidence in the workers' ability to see through such lies. On August 10, 1945 (just after the dropping of atom bombs on Hiroshima and Nagasaki), Ho Chi Minh called for a general uprising. Ta Thu Thau journeyed south once more. In Hue, to escape surveillance by the Stalinists, he separated from his young companion Do Ba The. In Quang Ngai he fell into the hands of the Vietminh.

On September 7 the *La Lutte* group learned of his arrest and spread the news, which aroused strong emotion among the common people of Saigon. The *La Lutte* group interceded with Tran Van Giau, who responded on September 9 with a communiqué: "The arrest of Ta Thu Thau in Quang Ngai is no concern of the Executive Committee. The People's Committee has the power and the right to pass judgment on Ta Thu Thau." He had probably already been assassinated.

Exactly a year later, in Paris, Ho Chi Minh, when questioned by Daniel Guérin about the death of Ta Thu Thau, declared: "Anyone who does not follow the line determined by me will be smashed."

In addition to his articles in *La Lutte* and *Three Months at the Sûreté on Rue Catinat,* Ta Thu Thau left a Vietnamese translation of Politzer's *Elementary Principles of Philosophy* and the pamphlet *Tu De Nhut Den De Tu Quoc Te* (From the First to the Fourth International).

NGUYEN VAN SO (1905–1945) was born into a poor family in Cholon. A fervent disciple of Nguyen An Ninh, he was expelled from the École Normale in Saigon in 1926 for political agitation. He became a mess-hand on a shipping line, spent some time in Marseilles, then returned to Saigon in 1928, where he worked in a printshop and taught in a private school. An activist in the *La Lutte* group, he was a candidate in the Saigon City Council elections of 1933 and 1935 and in the Colonial Council election in 1939. Arrested in July 1937 for "illegal association" (membership in a labor union organizing committee), he was incarcerated in the Central Prison, where he went on hunger strike. He was acquitted on September 9, 1937. Gravely ill with tuberculosis, he was rearrested and on November 10 sentenced to a year in prison followed by ten years' restricted residence for "subversive activities." He was arrested yet again in September 1939 and deported to Poulo Condore. An active member of the *La Lutte* group in 1945, he was among those shot by the Vietminh in Thu Dau Mot in October 1945.

PHAN VAN CHANH (1906–1945) came originally from a prosperous family in Binh Truoc (Bien Hoa), where his father was a government secretary. He graduated from Chasseloup-Laubat High School and left for France on September 25, 1925, to register at the Faculty of Medicine in Paris. He collaborated on Tran Van Thach's *Journal des Étudiants Annamites* and became an active member of the Annamite Independence Party with Ta Thu Thau. He and Ta Thu Thau joined the (Trotskyist) Left Opposition in 1930. He was one of the nineteen students deported from France on May 30, 1930, after the demonstration against the Yen Bai death sentences.

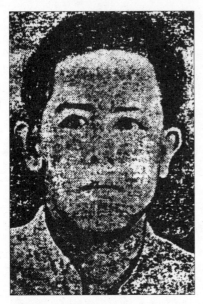

Phan Van Chanh

In Saigon, he taught in private schools and participated in the formation of the underground Communist Left Opposition. In 1932 he and Huynh Van Phuong distributed radical literature to workers, including translations of the *Communist Manifesto* and of Engels's *Socialism: Utopian and Scientific*. He was arrested, and on May 1, 1933, was given a four-year suspended sentence. He was a member of the *La Lutte* group and supported Ta Thu Thau after the break with the Stalinists in June 1937. A *La Lutte* candidate in the Colonial Council election of April 1939, he was arrested on July 13, 1939, and sentenced on March 16, 1940, to three years at Poulo Condore, five years of restricted residence and ten years' loss of civil rights. In October 1945, still active in the *La Lutte* group, he was shot by the Stalinist Tran Van Giau's thugs at Thu Dau Mot.

TRAN VAN THACH (1903–1945) was born at Cholon into a prosperous family, and graduated from Chasseloup-Laubat High School. He went to France in May 1926, studying for a philosophy degree in Toulouse and then in Paris. On March 15, 1927, he launched the *Journal des Étudiants Annamites* [Annamite Students' Newspaper]. In the December 15, 1927, issue of this paper he published a story entitled "Un Rêve Singulier" [A Strange Dream], a visionary account of Saigon in 1955, on the eve of independence, divided between a bourgeois party and its opponent, a workers' party. "The best action program we could possibly adopt would be one that brought together both a solution to the social problem and a solution to the national problem," says an enlightened bourgeois character in this story. In another piece, published in January 1928, Tran Van Thach criticized the conservative nationalists. The same year, in the

Bulletin de la Ligue contre l'oppression coloniale et l'impérialisme [Bulletin of the Anti-Imperialist League] he denounced "the hostile intentions of those who govern us, whose undeclared aim is to mold us in such a way that we will always continue to obey them."

Tran Van Thach met Ta Thu Thau in the Annamite Independence Party. He took part in a protest meeting against the arrest of Nguyen An Ninh on September 28, 1928, and in a *Manifesto of Annamite Students* issued on December 2 declared that the aim of studying abroad should be to liberate one's country. In the January 1929 issue of the *Journal des Étudiants Annamites* he stressed the importance of unity between intellectuals and workers. In May he became president of the Indochinese Mutual Aid Association in Paris, on whose behalf he conveyed protests to the Colonial Minister against the deportation of "undesirable" Annamites.

He returned to Saigon in January 1930. The country was soon to be profoundly shaken by the Yen Bai insurrection and by the powerful peasant movement, which were followed by the bloody repression of 1930–1931. While earning his living teaching French in private schools, he participated in the founding of the *La Lutte* group. Together with others who had visited France and who were now gathered around Nguyen An Ninh, he legally challenged the colonial regime in the Saigon City Council elections of April–May 1933. He was elected, as was the Stalinist Nguyen Van Tao, but the vote was soon annulled. In September 1934, Tran Van Thach was among those who re-formed the *La Lutte* group, which had been disbanded after the elections. In 1935 he was elected once again to the Saigon City Council, along with Ta Thu Thau, Nguyen Van Tao and Duong Bach Mai. He contributed an irreverent satirical column in *La Lutte* called "Petits Clous" [Little Nails].

Tran Van Thach

He was a member of the *La Lutte* action committee in the Indo-chinese Congress movement. The first Moscow Trial caused him to distance himself definitively from the Stalinists, and from then on he supported the Trotskyists.

On February 2, 1937, Tran Van Thach's election to the Saigon City Council was invalidated. A few months later he caused quite a stir with a report in *La Lutte* (June 27 and July 1, 1937) about the scandalous plundering of the peasants of Rach Gia. He was also involved in labor union activity, for which he was imprisoned for two months in September 1937. In June he took the side of Ta Thu Thau when the Stalinists in *La Lutte* broke the unity with the Trotskyists. He was among the Fourth International candidates for the *Tranh Dau/La Lutte* group in the Colonial Council elections of April 1939, and was elected along with Ta Thu Thau and Phan Van Hum. The vote was annulled in October, and he found himself behind bars once more.

On April 16, 1940, he was sentenced again, this time to four years at Poulo Condore and ten years' restricted residence. Released in 1944, he was confined to restricted residence in Can Tho. After the fall of French colonial rule on March 9, 1945, he and other *La Lutte* comrades organized a Revolutionary Workers Party. After the Japanese surrender, they also revived the publication *Tranh Dau*. On September 23, 1945, when the people of Saigon rose up against the reoccupation of the city by the French (who had been rearmed by the British), the Vietminh government of Tran Van Giau fled the city to organize the resistance, while continuing to hunt down the Trotskyists. Tran Van Thach survived the massacre of *La Lutte* fighters by the Anglo-French troops at the Thi Nghe bridge, and along with other survivors withdrew to the Thu Duc region, only to be arrested by Tran Van Giau's secret police.

Tran Van Thach was shot to death by the Vietminh in Thu Dau Mot in October 1945.

NGUYEN VAN TIEN was born in 1916 in Saigon. He worked at the Rubber Manufacturing Company and was a member of the Trotskyist labor union group. Arrested in 1937, he was sentenced to a year in prison and five years' restricted residence. He became the last managing editor of the newspaper *La Lutte*. In 1940 he was sentenced once again and deported to Poulo Condore. On his return from penal servitude, he fell into the hands of the Vietminh, who shot him along with other *La Lutte* members in Thu Dau Mot in October 1945.

HO HUU TUONG (1910–1980) was born into a family of small farmers. In 1926 he was expelled from the Can Tho high school for political agitation and left for France, where he studied mathematics, first at the University of Marseilles, then at Lyons. In May 1930 he met Ta Thu Thau in Paris during the Annamite demonstrations against the death sentences against the Yen Bai insurgents. Escaping arrest, he fled with Phan Van Hum to Brussels, where they produced the publication *Tien Quan* (Vanguard). They returned to Paris shortly after the deportation of Ta Thu Thau, and gathered around Pierre Naville, Raymond Molinier and Pierre Frank to form, along with Nguyen Van Linh, Tran Van Si, La Van Rot, Nguyen Van Nhi, Nguyen Van Nam and Nguyen Van Cu, the Indochinese Group of the Communist League (Opposition).

Ho Huu Tuong returned to Cochinchina at the beginning of 1931 and taught mathematics in private schools. In May of that year, he met Dao Hung Long from the Lien Minh Cong San Doan (Communist League). Dao Hung Long had brought together oppositionists from inside the Indochinese Communist Party after the peasant soviets of Nghe-Tinh had been crushed, and had won them over to the Left Opposition.

In August 1931, Ho Huu Tuong and Dao Hung Long started a clandestine duplicated journal, *Thang Muoi* (October). In November, all the Oppositionists united in the Ta Doi Lap (Left Opposition) and adopted *Thang Muoi* as their theoretical organ. Ho Huu Tuong was arrested in Saigon in October 1932, and received a three-year suspended sentence at the trial of the 21 Trotskyists on May 1, 1933. His partner Nguyen Hue Minh got three months. He campaigned with the first *La Lutte* group in the Saigon City Council elections of April 1933, and from 1934 to 1937 was continuously in touch with the second *La Lutte* group. He was active in developing anti-Stalinist theory.

Ho Huu Tuong was the "secret advisor" of the League of Internationalist Communists for the Construction of the Fourth International (formed by Lu Sanh Hanh in 1935). He also edited the sole issue of the journal *Cach Mang Thuong Truc* (Permanent Revolution), the first printed* clandestine Trotskyist publication. In it, he predicted that a powerful workers' movement would sweep France after the victory of the Popular Front, and that the workers and poor peasants of Indochina would then be caught up in this tremendous wave of hope. Why shouldn't other Lenins

Ho Huu Tuong

and Trotskys arise here, too? (Despite everything that had happened, he was still thinking in terms of "leaders"!) He did, however, envision a "mass-based party," not a party of professional revolutionaries as advocated by the Stalinists. Such a party, he said, must arise out of the real struggle of the proletariat of the cities and countryside and prepare a general strike together with the French proletariat, since it was impossible to build socialism within national boundaries.

In September 1936 he brought out *Le Militant,* the first legal Trotskyist weekly paper. In it he denounced *La Lutte*'s collaboration with the bourgeois Constitutionalists, the repressive measures of the Popular Front government, and the bloody farce of the first Moscow Trial. He also brought together underground militants to form the Bolshevik-Leninist Group for the Construction of the Fourth International, which published the illegal bulletin *Tho Thuyen Tranh Dau* (Workers' Struggle).

After the second Moscow Trial in March 1937, he revived *Le Militant,* which was supported by a growing number of sympathizers, and published Trotsky's article *Whither France? The Decisive Stage* and, most importantly, Lenin's *Testament,* with its warnings about Stalin.

In September 1938, taking advantage of the relative freedom that French Prime Minister Daladier granted to the native Vietnamese-language press, Ho Huu Tuong and Dao Hung Long launched the

Saigon Insurrection 1945

Children in the Rain

Boats at Cape Saint-Jacques

Donkey Hauling a Barrel

Red Boats

Hedge

Cambo

Nive River at Cambo

60 Rue Nationale

Rue des Chiffonniers

Two Homeless People

Dog

Tao

The Spirit of Tea

Sophie

agitational bulletin *Thay Tho* (Wage and Salary Workers). They also revived the theoretical journal *Thang Muoi,* of which five issues appeared up to March 1939. In this journal, Ho Huu Tuong criticized the "four years of mistakes involving the tactic of a united front" between Stalinists and Trotskyists. In January 1939, he printed the statutes of the Fourth International and explained how the theory of permanent revolution applied to Indochina.

Like all the other opponents of the colonial regime, Ho Huu Tuong was arrested at the start of the war and sent to Poulo Condore. When he was released in 1944 he broke with revolutionary communism, to the great dismay of his comrades in struggle.

His signature, along with those of two important Vietminh figures, appears on a telegram of August 1945 sent to Emperor Bao Dai from the People's Revolutionary Committee in Hanoi, demanding Bao Dai's abdication. Returning to Cochinchina after the partition of the country in 1954, Ho Huu Tuong became the advisor to Bay Vien, leader of the Binh Xuyen pirates. In 1957 the American puppet Ngo Dinh Diem sentenced him to death, but after the intercession of Nehru and Albert Camus he was instead deported again to Poulo Condore. After the fall of Diem, Ho Huu Tuong became a deputy in the farcical "opposition" under the military regime of Nguyen Van Thieu.

In 1977, two years after North Vietnamese troops had captured Saigon, Ho Huu Tuong was interned in a "reeducation camp." He was released in 1980, but collapsed and died on the doorstep of his home. Four years later his short autobiography, *41 Nam Lam Bao, Hoi Ky* (Memories of 41 Years of Journalism), was published in Paris.

DAO HUNG LONG, alias **ANH GIA**, came from a peasant family of Long Tri (Rach Gia). He was born in 1905 and became a member of the Thanh Nien (Revolutionary Youth League) in 1926. As part of the latter's communist wing, in 1929 he became a "special delegate" of the Indochinese Communist Party* in western Cochinchina. The defeat of the peasant movement in 1930–1931—including the suppression of the soviets in Nghe-Tinh and of the peasant uprisings in Annam and Cochinchina—made him rethink the politics of the

Stalinist party and he denounced its leadership, noting that it was composed mostly of petty-bourgeois intellectuals and peasants.

At the beginning of 1931 he organized the Communist League group at Bac Lieu, with a *ban mao hiem* (death-defying) committee responsible for obtaining money to finance its projects. In May 1931, Ho Huu Tuong won him over to the Left Opposition. Arrested in 1933, Anh Gia was sentenced to a year in prison and was sent to do forced labor in the quarries of Chau Doc. There he convinced the nonpolitical prisoners to refuse to work, then led a hunger strike. After this struggle was harshly repressed, he was separated from the other prisoners and sent back to the Central Prison in Saigon.

In 1934 Anh Gia began working as a sign painter. In 1936 he wrote the pamphlet *Action Committee Tactics*. For his work in the labor union movement, which had been outlawed by the Popular Front, he was sentenced in 1937 to two months in prison. At the end of 1938 he launched a legal Vietnamese-language bulletin, *Thay Tho* (Wage and Salary Workers). He was also one of the editors of *Tia Sang* (The Spark), which first appeared in January 1939, denouncing war and the imposition of loans and taxes for the "defense of Indochina." In October 1939 he was condemned to two years in prison and ten years of restricted residence. During the war he was interned in camps at Ta Lai and Ba Ra, then deported to Madagascar, from which he was not released until the end of 1946. He ended up by abandoning class struggle, following Ho Huu Tuong down the path toward a neutralist nationalism.

LU SANH HANH (1912–1982) was born at Ben Tre into a prosperous family. He studied at the My Tho high school. In 1932 he was a member of the Saigon committee of the Indochinese Communist Party, but, shaken by reading the theses of the Left Opposition, he tried to reorganize his party on a critical basis. He launched the paper *Lao Cong* (The Worker). Arrested on October 9, 1932, he was sentenced to 15 months in prison. Assigned to push wagons along with the nonpolitical prisoners at the Cape Saint-Jacques quarries, he led them in striking. Punished with solitary confinement, he started a long hunger strike and was sent back to the Central Prison in Saigon.

After his release he decided to "devote his life to making revolution." Selling off his family inheritance, he set himself up as a traveling barber in order to spread revolutionary propaganda, then became a reporter for the Constitutionalist newspaper *Duoc Nha Nam* (The Torch of Annam). In July 1935 he was one of the founders of the underground League of Internationalist Communists for the Construction of the Fourth International. It was broken up by the Sûreté the following year when it called for the formation of action committees to prepare a general strike. In August 1936 he was sentenced to 18 months in prison. Upon his release, he resumed his life of political action and in January 1939 collaborated in the publication of *Tia Sang,* which was edited by Ho Huu Tuong and Dao Hung Long. He escaped the arrests of September 1939 and took refuge in western Cochinchina, then returned to Saigon in 1945 to secretly reconstitute the League, whose March 24 *Manifesto* called on workers and peasants to prepare for an imminent revolution.

After the Japanese surrender, the League, which had continued to operate underground, came out openly with radical slogans that glaringly contrasted with those of the Stalinists. The de facto Stalinist government of Tran Van Giau, feeling threatened by the growth of the League-dominated people's committees, sent troops to arrest the thirty-odd delegates who were attending a meeting on September 14, 1945. Lu Sanh Hanh was one of them. They were disarmed and thrown into prison. On September 22, the British took control of the Central Prison and handed over the prisoners to the French Sûreté. Paradoxically, that was how Lu Sanh Hanh and his comrades escaped certain death.

He emigrated to France in 1947, where he was active among the Annamites who had been "imported" to work in the munitions factories during the war, and also contributed to the journal *Quatrième In-*

Lu Sanh Hanh

ternationale [Fourth International] under the name of Lucien. In 1954 he returned to his native country. He died of tuberculosis in Saigon on November 2, 1982.

NGUYEN VAN NAM, alias **ANTONY**, was born on May 26, 1912, at Ben Tre, into an old established Catholic family who had amassed their immense fortune in the early days of French colonization. He was the son of the *doc phu* (Administrative Delegate) Michel My, who became known as the "Tiger of Cho Lach" and was infamous for his savage repression of rebellious peasants in 1930. Michel My embezzled vast amounts of public money, then had a church built at Cho Lach dedicated to St. Michael to expiate his sins. He was killed by insurgents at Gia Dinh in September 1945.

As a high-school student at the Catholic Taberd Institute in Saigon, where his brother was a "teaching brother," Nguyen Van Nam, the rebellious son, was active in the strikes of 1926 that broke out at the funeral of the pioneering nationalist Phan Chau Trinh. Leaving for France in 1928, he continued his studies at the Lycée Lakanal in Sceaux, where he joined the Left Opposition, and in 1932 participated in the Paris-based Annamite Trotskyist group [i.e. the Indochinese Group of the Communist League] along with Tran Van Si, La Van Rot and Nguyen Van Linh.

He returned to Saigon in 1935 and made contact with the Trotskyists of the *La Lutte* group, publishing articles in their paper on strikes and on Algeria. In 1938 he collaborated with Ho Huu Tuong on the semi-legal journal *Thang Muoi* and in February 1939 he became the administrator responsible for the paper *Tia Sang*. The latter publication was banned and he was arrested, along with Edgar Ganofsky (the managing editor), Dao Hung Long and others. He remained in prison until early 1940.

After the collapse of France in May 1940, Nguyen Van Nam was sought along with many other "dangerous individuals" on the "wanted" list, but he eluded the Sûreté and hid out with various comrades in Ben Suc, Tra Vinh, Phnom Penh, Hanoi and Quang Ngai. He returned to Saigon in 1943.

In August 1945, when Saigon was in turmoil following the surrender of the Japanese, he resumed his activity in the reconstituted

League of Internationalist Communists. He wrote the leaflet that called for the formation of people's committees and for the arming of the people, positions that were to be widely adopted during the huge demonstration of August 21, 1945.

Managing to escape the systematic liquidation of the Trotskyists by the Stalinist Communists and the Vietminh, Nguyen Van Nam emigrated to France in early 1948. In late 1949 he broke with Leninism-Trotskyism and began widening his circle of contacts in order to develop new revolutionary perspectives. As he put it: "The so-called workers' parties—particularly those of the Leninist type—are embryos of a state. Faced with the power of the bourgeois state, these parties advocate a 'counterpower.' But this is just juggling with words in order to deceive people: all power is coercive and oppressive. Once in power, these parties become the nucleus of a new exploiting class which installs a new system of exploitation. The state is always the state of the exploiters. Talk of the 'withering away' of the state only serves to mystify the masses. To arrive at a 'nonstate,' we have to envision a 'nonpower.' Workers councils could represent such 'nonpower'."

My friend Nguyen Van Nam worked in a factory until 1961, then as a bookkeeper, while continuing his studies. He graduated in English, and wrote a dissertation on immigration in England.

NGUYEN VAN LINH, alias **RENÉ** (1909–1950), was born at Ben Suc (Thu Dau Mot) into a wealthy family. He went to France in 1926, studying first at the Lycée Michelet in Vanves, then at the Sorbonne in Paris. In 1931 he and Tran Van Si organized the Indochinese Left Opposition group [i.e. the Indochinese Group of the Communist League]. In a speech at the International Antiwar Congress in Amsterdam, he stressed that the proletariat should not be deluded into thinking that war could be prevented without destroying its foundation, capitalism. He took part in the Indochinese Mutual Aid Association and in the Social Studies Circle set up in 1934, where he met people who had been expelled from the French Communist Party.

He criticized the Popular Front for its repression of the Indochinese Congress movement in 1936. In 1937, in the bulletin *Quoc*

Nguyen Van Linh

Te IV (Fourth International) he denounced the dictatorship over the proletariat by the party in power in the USSR and criticized the French Communist Party, which, since the Laval-Stalin Pact of 1935, "was urging the Annamite masses to support the democratic imperialisms" and which was seeking "peace at any price in the three French colonies in North Africa."

He returned to Cochinchina at the outbreak of the war, and taught at a school in Can Tho. In August 1945 he joined the League of Internationalist Communists in Saigon, concentrating on the political training of the Workers' Militia of the Go Vap streetcar workers and on maintaining communication between the comrades in the countryside and in the city. In July 1947 he renewed contact with the Internationalist Communist Party in France. He wrote to Molinier and Craipeau: "Having survived the savage repression of the Stalinists, our group intends to continue the struggle," and added that he did not understand "the purely intellectualistic approach of Naville and Rousset."*

In 1950 he received an invitation to a secret conference ostensibly organized by Trotskyist sympathizers in the Vietminh military zone in Bien Hoa to discuss the participation of Trotskyists in the resistance. It was a trap, and on May 13, 1950, Nguyen Van Linh fell into it, along with Liu Khanh Thinh and the Chinese comrade Liu Jialiang. They were assassinated. The Vietminh radio station accused them of having been "agents of French imperialism."

TRAN VAN SI (1907–1941) was born at Tan Thanh Dong (Gia Dinh). After studying in Hanoi, he worked as a technician, then left for France in July 1929. In Paris, he and Nguyen Van Linh were at the heart of the Indochinese Left Opposition group, which an-

alyzed the mistakes of the Indochinese Communist Party in the
same spirit as the Left Opposition
that had supported Trotsky in his
struggle against the bureaucracy
in power in Russia. With Maurice
Nadeau, he was active in the Communist League cell in the 13th Arrondissement of Paris.

Beginning in February 1932, the
Indochinese Left Opposition group
published the theses of the Left Opposition on the Indochinese revolution in the mimeo bulletin *Duoc Vo
San* (The Torch of the Proletariat).
They were violently attacked for
this by Annamites in the Colonial
Section of the French Communist

Tran Van Si

Party. In October 1933, finally realizing that they would never be
accepted as an opposition within the Indochinese Communist Party,
they decided to try to build a new communist party. In 1935 Tran
Van Si was one of the founders of the Indochinese Section for the
Fourth International. The group took an active part in anti-imperialist meetings and demonstrations and remained in contact with Annamite dissidents in the French Communist Party.

After returning to Cochinchina on September 13, 1937, Tran Van
Si joined Ta Thu Thau in the *La Lutte* group, which had by then be-
come Trotskyist, and in April 1939 his name appeared on the Fourth
International slate of candidates for the Colonial Council election.
Arrested on July 13, 1939, for campaigning against a national de-
fense fund, he was sentenced on April 16, 1940, to three years at
Poulo Condore. He died there after only a year.

LIU JIALIANG (1911–1950) was originally from Guangdong in
China. His political awakening came at the age of 14 during the sec-
ond Chinese revolution (1925–1927). In 1931 he went to study in
Beijing and joined the Trotskyist movement there. When he went

to Shanghai in 1933 he was arrested and imprisoned until 1937. After his release at the outbreak of the Sino-Japanese war, he went to Hong Kong to train young Trotskyists in southern China. It was during this period that he translated into Chinese Harold Isaacs's book *The Tragedy of the Chinese Revolution*. He was arrested, then deported to Shanghai by the British. Though seriously ill, he continued his political activity. He returned to Hong Kong in March 1949. Hunted by the police, he fled to Saigon in January 1950. In May of that year he and two Vietnamese comrades from the League of Internationalist Communists were ambushed by the Vietminh at Bien Hoa, north of Saigon, and he was tortured to death.

TRAN DINH MINH, alias **NGUYEN HAI AU** (1912–1946), was a poet, and author of the novel *Nguoi Con Gai Cam* (The Silent Girl), whose young heroine, poor, ugly and mute, regains her beauty and the power of speech when she is loved—a metaphor for the enslaved masses who will be born into a real life through social revolution. He also wrote books on the economy: *Kinh Te Hoc Pho Thong* (Political Economy Made Easy) (Hanoi, 1944) and *Kinh Te The Gioi 1929–1934* (The World Economy 1929–1934) (Hanoi, 1945). He left teaching to become a typographer at the Le Van Tan Printworks in Hanoi, where in 1944–1945 he and other comrades put together the clandestine bulletin *Co Do* (Red Flag). He joined the League of Internationalist Communists in Saigon in 1945.

He was accepted into the Go Vap Workers' Militia, and he and Nguyen Van Thuong were elected to lead this militia during the uprising in Saigon. He was killed at the front on January 13, 1946, in My Loi, near Cao Lanh (Sadec), under fire from indigenous auxiliaries in the French army who were disguised as resistance fighters. The villagers of My Tay erected a tomb for him.

EDGAR GANOFSKY (1880–1943) was a Frenchman born on the Indian Ocean island of Réunion. He was fired from his teaching post for political reasons. Fervently anticolonialist, he published *La Voix Libre* [The Free Voice] in Saigon from 1923 to 1932. A modest and free-spirited man, he lived as an Annamite, lodging with a coolie family in a run-down apartment in Da Kao. In 1933 he helped the *La*

Lutte group by taking advantage of his French citizenship to assume the official managerial responsibility for the *La Lutte* newspaper. In 1936 he took part in the Indochinese Congress movement, whose aim was to present the demands of the Annamite people to the Popular Front government. In 1939 he once again became an official publishing manager, this time of the Trotskyist paper *Tia Sang*. He was sentenced to one year in prison and five years of restricted residence—terms which were increased in June 1940 to three years and ten years. During the war he was forced to live in Can Tho, and died there in poverty in 1943.

Edgar Ganofsky

THAI VAN TAM, one of the founders of the Hanoi newspaper *Ban Dan* (The People's Friend), broke with the Stalinists in 1937 after the Popular Front banned the Indochinese Congress movement. In Tonkin he started the *Tia Sang* (The Spark) group and also put out the weekly *Thoi Dam* (Chronicles), which in August 1938 called on workers and peasants to set up "unified people's committees in a joint struggle for rice, freedom and democracy"—committees which the process of revolutionary struggle would tend to transform into workers' and peasants' councils. When this publication was banned, Thai Van Tam started *Chanh Tri Tuan Bao* (The Political Weekly) in November 1938 and published a translation of Trotsky's book about his son, *Leon Sedov*. Prosecuted for his antiwar articles in *Thoi Dam,* he was sentenced in April 1939 to five months in prison, as were his companions Bui Duy Tu and Nguyen Uyen Diem. During the war, he died in a prison in central Annam.

LE QUANG LUONG, alias **BICH KHE** (1915–1946), was a primary school teacher and a popular poet. He originally came from Thu Xa, in the Quang Ngai province of Annam. When André Gide's book *Retour de l'URSS* [Return from the USSR] was published in 1936, he quickly translated it. As a result, the Stalinist party identified him as the inspiration behind the Du Tu (Fourth International) group in that region. He died of tuberculosis in 1946 at the age of thirty-one. The local population gave his name to the street leading from the bus station to the east gate of Quang Ngai, though "Rue Bich-Khe" never appeared on official maps of the town. His tomb was neglected and overrun with weeds—just as in his own poem, *Nam Mo* (The Tomb):

> *Day co xanh xao may lop phu,*
> *Tren mo con qua dung yem hoi.*

[Lush green weeds smother the tomb, a crow perches there silently.]

In 1991, the young bureaucrat Bon, Secretary of the local People's Committee, refused to give his family permission to take his remains back to his birthplace, on the pretext that the bones of a man who died of tuberculosis might infect the village; and besides, Bich Khe had been "a Trotskyist" and "according to our local veteran revolutionaries, Trotskyism is completely reactionary." (This anecdote is drawn from a report by the journalist Tran Dang, published in *Lao Dong,* official newspaper of the Vietnam General Confederation of Labor, on January 20, 1994.)

LUONG DUC THIEP (?–1945) was born in Thanh Hoa in northern Annam. He was expelled from the Nam Dinh high school after protest strikes against the brutality of "Paul Rednose," a French teacher who called his pupils "bastards, pigs, filthy Annamites." Luong Duc Thiep tried to flee the country but was arrested at Bangkok and sent back to Thanh Hoa where, after a year in prison, he was put under house arrest. In 1937 and 1938 he was one of the leaders of the clandestine Typographers Trade Union Federation in Hanoi. In 1941 he participated in the critical historical journal *Han Thuyen,* which questioned the ideology of national heroism. In 1945 he founded the Socialist Workers Party of North Vietnam (*Dang Tho Thuyen Xa Hoi Viet Bac*), which supported the Fourth International and brought together large numbers of workers and students, including many women. This group published the newspaper *Chien Dau* (Combat) and many pamphlets, and set up Marxist education classes. By means of posters and leaflets the group called for the arming of the people, workers' control of the factories and redistribution of land to the peasants, as in the South. The group prepared for armed resistance to the return of the French, and its revolutionary program was welcomed with enthusiasm at huge rallies, notably in Bach Mai.

Faced with the autonomous development of a revolutionary movement of workers and peasants outside the control of the Vietminh, Ho Chi Minh ordered the arrest of members of the group. Luong Duc Thiep and Quan Thuong Hao, who had just been released from the Son La penal colony, were rounded up along with many others and executed. The murder of Luong Duc Thiep in 1945 is documented by the writer To Hoai in his memoirs, *Cat Bui Chan Ai* (published in California in 1993). Luong Duc Thiep's militant political activity in 1945 is described by Do Ba The in *Thim Bay Gioi* (cited by Phuong Lan in her book *Nha Cach Mang Ta Thu Thau 1906–1945* [The Revolutionary Ta Thu Thau]) and in a letter of 1947 from a North Vietnamese militant, discovered in the archives of Pierre Frank in Paris.

* * *

This book is dedicated to all these friends and comrades, and to so many others; to all those who have dreamed of a new world liberated from oppression and exploitation; to the serfs of the ricefields, the slaves of the plantations, the miners, coolies, farm laborers, workers and peasants who died anonymously, "combatants who fell in the struggle with no one to tell their story, no one to evoke their spirit" (*tu si may nguoi, nao ai mac mat, nao ai goi hon*);* and to the memory of my mother.

Paris, September 8, 2000

Part II

IN THE LAND OF HÉLOÏSE

Chapter 1

WORKER IN THE PROMISED LAND

I had left my country in the spring of 1948. The heartrending pain of a loving mother silently enduring the permanent departure of her prodigal son! . . . The tears of a 12-year-old girl holding her little brother in her arms!

The old tree drifting down the river can never return to its native land—this image flitted around in my head as the Messageries Maritimes freighter raised anchor in the Saigon harbor in that sad late afternoon.

It took more than four weeks to lug us from Saigon to Marseilles.

I traveled fourth class, in the hold with a dozen young men hoping to study in France. We slept in bunks. At one end of the hold were coffins bearing the remains of officers of the French Expeditionary Corps who had been killed in the ambush at Da Lat. The specters of the Indochina War followed us.

And so that spring of 1948 I set foot once again in the ancient Mediterranean city of Marseilles, gateway to the promised land. Fourteen years earlier, working as a launderer on the *Aramis,* I had arrived at the same port and roamed around the city for three weeks during the drydocking of the ship, then returned to Vietnam. I had intended to go to Paris and stay there, but it turned out that I would not get my sailor's pay until the end of the return trip, so I didn't even have the money for a Paris train ticket.

This time I was here for good. Some Vietnamese students came to the dock to help new arrivals—a tradition of solidarity dating from the first student emigrations in the 1920s. They advised me to stay in Marseilles, pointing out that, if nothing else, it was warm all the time. For me this was out of the question: it was Paris or bust.

They put us up in a cheap hotel. The next morning we had our first practical lesson in urban life. The chambermaid, coming to our room to change the sheets, was astonished to see that the bedding had not been disturbed. She asked us:

"Where did you sleep last night?"

"On the beds!"

"You're supposed to sleep *in* the beds!" she explained, drawing back the covers to show us how it was done.

In Vietnam, where it's warm all the time, we were used to sleeping on bundled branches and covering ourselves with grass mats. We had never heard the phrase "getting into bed."

Our guides put us on the night train, and the following morning we arrived at the Gare de Lyon [train station] in Paris. The clock on the tower with its sinister-looking hands made a strong impression on me, as if it was proclaiming: "Now you're in for it, my boy! You're in my power!"

I settled into the Saint-Sulpice neighborhood. My friend Luc [Lu Sanh Hanh], who had arrived in France the previous year, had reserved a room for me in the little Hôtel de la Principauté on Rue Servandoni, right around the corner from Rue Vaugirard where he lived. Another Saigon refugee, a radical student named Phuc, lived there too.

That winter was my first experience of ice—in the basin in front of the Saint-Sulpice church. I touched it, fascinated.

During the first few months my Saigon friends and relatives would periodically send me two or three kilos of rice, which I sold on the black market—postwar rationing was still in effect, and rice was extremely hard to come by. Later, I got by with other scams while in the process of learning a trade and finding some regular work. I sent used cameras to a photographer friend in My Tho (who was sheltering my son Do) and radio parts to an old Saigon radio-repairman friend (who was taking care of my other son, Da).*

In exchange for the rice I brought, I was able to eat freely at La Baie d'Along, a restaurant on Rue Grégoire-de-Tours.

Dang Van Long

That was also where I made my first contacts with the Vietnamese diaspora and developed friendly relations with Vietnamese who had been forcibly conscripted to fight or work in France during World War II. They had been among the 20,000 Vietnamese soldiers (of whom 6000 had been killed in the fighting) and the 20,000 civilians deported from Vietnam to France to work in dangerous war production. They had been penned up in camps under military discipline. Many died in the prisons established within those camps to stamp out rebellion; others succumbed to starvation or disease. Despite numerous revolts, these camps continued well beyond the war years, the majority until 1948, a few as late as 1952. This amounted to a double exploitation: by the state, which acted as the intermediary with the enterprises, levying its tithes in the process, and by the bosses in textile factories, construction, salt production, etc., to whom these captive workers had been delivered. In 1948 I thus came to know those who had deserted or had been demobilized thousands of miles from their country. Some, like Dang Van Long, became close friends.*

Their meeting place, which also served as a haven for unemployed people, was just down the street from the Baie d'Along restaurant. It also functioned as a schoolroom where a few students gave free lessons to their compatriots in French, arithmetic, etc. I joined in, helping to teach Vietnamese illiterates how to read and write their own language.

* * *

Nanterre [an industrial suburb west of Paris]. November 1951. It's still dark. The Simca auto factory rises before me, an immense wall of illumined dirty windows, its sinister geometrical silhouette standing out against the dawning sky. At the workers' entryway on the right side of the factory, across the street from a jam-packed café-bar, I merge with the dense crowd waiting for the gate to open and swallow us up. I've joined the working class.

Two uniformed guards control the entry. Each worker presents his identity card. I show them the notification inviting me for a test. They direct me to the hiring office.

The personnel chief is M. Bouygues. I'm applying for work as an electrician. "You're 38 and you've never worked before?" He gives me a strange look, as if to say, "These Orientals, you never can tell their age . . ." After examining my diploma in industrial electricity from the Conservatoire des Arts et Métiers [National School of Engineering and Technology], he directs me to the electrical repair and maintenance department on the third floor, to take a test.

An energetic foreman sets me up on an empty work bench, beside another one where an old worker is busy with some small task. The old man gives me a sidelong glance over his glasses, then returns to his work.

The foreman sets a bunch of equipment in front of me.

"These are the parts from the control mechanism of a welding machine. You have to reassemble it according to this blueprint."

Then he spreads out the schematic diagram next to a pile of electrical parts—resistors, capacitors, rectifiers, coils, etc.—along with solder, pliers, and a few other tools.

Deafened by the clashing noises from the assembly line, I put the parts together, then start the wiring. I become so wrapped up in this that the noises bother me less and less.

Making sure that the foreman is no longer present, the old worker beside me whispers, "How are you doing with that?" He avoids looking in my direction—if he's caught helping me, he'll be fired. He continues to watch me out of the corner of his eye while pretending to be busy with his own task. Another whisper: "No, not that way! You've got the rectifier upside down!" He looks relieved when he sees me redo it correctly.

At noon, everyone stops for lunch. The assembly-line noise ceases all at once, as if by magic. The old man, whose name is Guillaume, introduces me to a congenial younger guy who has come in from the workshop. He was hired two weeks ago, having passed the same test I'm doing. He goes to wash his hands, then takes me to the cafeteria.

We have 45 minutes to chow down and have a coffee. Then he says, "Come with me," and we leave a bit early. He leads me to the locker room in the basement. Making sure that no one else is there, he takes a pencil and a piece of paper from his pocket and quickly sketches a diagram: "This is how the wiring of the heat relay goes. It's the trick part of the test." I sigh in relief, touched by this spontaneous help.

The following afternoon I finished the wiring. The foreman brought in his boss Gaido, an Italian engineer who had learned the ropes at Fiat during the Fascist era, to check my work. The rebuilt machine seemed satisfactory to both of them. Gaido picked it up and put it on the testing chassis. My heart was beating—this was the moment of truth! He turned on the switch and it worked! But just to make sure, he retested it by rapidly turning the machine on and off at irregular intervals. It still passed—no leaking solder, no bad connections.

"Okay, you're hired."

The employment contract included all the internal factory regulations, all the rules of industrial servitude. They had me go through an identification screening and I was photographed. It reminded me of being run through the judicial identity laboratory on Rue Filippini in Saigon, across from the Central Prison, during my first arrest in 1936. Now I had my plastic-covered identity card with an administrative number and photo—my passport into the factory. I was part of the impersonal flock of Simca personnel.

I had the right to speak with labor union representatives, and was given a free choice among the three unions present in the factory: the CGT [the Stalinist union], the CFTC [the Christian union], and an "independent" union organized by the company, which consisted mostly of Indochina veterans. I chose not to join any of them.

During my medical exam, the old doctor, seeing the dilapidated state of my lungs, ordered an additional exam. The social worker, sensing my anxiety, kindly took me aside: "Don't worry. I'm going to drag this out so that you will have worked long enough to get Social Security in case you have to stop working."

At the medical laboratory, near Rue Ampère, a pretty lab assistant in white hospital garb did an intubation. I practically suffocated as she forced the rubber tubing down my esophagus, all the way to my stomach. Then she sucked some gastric juice into the tube and put it in a culture fluid. If tubercular bacillus developed within the next three months, I'd be in trouble.

My job, which I shared with one other guy, was to watch over the electric switch boxes of the welding machines, which were installed on the chassis assembly line on the same floor where I'd done the test. Inexorably, the assembly line advanced after each pause, leaving just enough time for the worker to make the required number of welds. The assembly line must not be allowed to stop, the welding machines must not be allowed to break down. In case of any mechanical failure, our role as maintenance electricians was to immediately repair it during the regular pauses of the line. I spent most of my time in the midst of this deafening atmosphere doing nothing but watching the welders, who were working frantically to "keep in time" at each pause of the line. From time to time they would call on us to regulate the current of the welding machines or to adjust their hydraulic pliers.

What was in the minds of these companions, slaves riveted to the assembly line? I have no idea. All that constant striving to work harder and faster so as to make a little extra. We were expected to produce 350 cars per day; anything over that and each worker got a proportionate share of the bonus.

The bosses control our time. Time eats away our life. We proletarians are nothing but the bosses' "variable capital." I'm still haunted by the huge hands of that clock in the Gare de Lyon—a giant cross to crucify the world—which loomed up before me when I first arrived in Paris that spring morning in 1948.

> Horloge! dieu sinistre, effrayant, impassible . . .
> Le gouffre a toujours soif; la clepsydre se vide.
> (Baudelaire)

[Clock! Sinister, terrifying, inscrutable god . . . The thirst of the abyss is unquenchable; the water clock runs dry.]*

From then on clock faces spiked with pointed hands pursued me endlessly in the city. As Marx wrote in *The Poverty of Philosophy:* "Time is everything, man is nothing; he is at most the carcass of time."*

* * *

I lived in a shabby hotel in the Chalons quarter, next to the Gare de Lyon. A room rented by the week, with a tiny sink. The single light bulb gave out a pale, gloomy light that was insufficient for reading. Strange little cheap Chinese restaurants crowded both sides of the meagerly lit street. Puddles of household waste water glittered here and there on the lower end of the roadway like a urinal that never drained away. Drug dealing and black market trafficking of every kind took place late into the night.

I crossed this dismal little street early each morning to catch the first subway at 5:30, so as to arrive on time in the industrial suburb west of Paris. It took me more than an hour and a half to get from the Gare de Lyon to Nanterre. During this commute I tried to keep my eyes open and read Engels's *The Origin of the Family, Private Property and the State* in the old Costes edition. I read and reread the same pages in the subway till it reached the Pont de Neuilly, then transferred to a bus. Then a quick coffee in the bistrot across from the factory gate.

The guards closed the gate at the beginning of the shift. If I was late, they phoned the chief foreman before letting me in. One day my foreman said sarcastically, "It looks like we're going to have to give you an alarm clock."

Ngo Van in the 1950s

I continued my studies at the Conservatoire des Arts et Métiers. When I obtained diplomas for three years of industrial electricity theory, I qualified for hands-on lab work. There were only a dozen places in the school's laboratory, and they were reserved for the students with the best exam scores. Leaving the factory on the evening of the test, I arrived a bit late at the school. But somehow I managed to worm my way through the packed room to be one of the first to hand in my papers. It sometimes happened that among those who had the same scores, whoever handed his in first was selected. With relief, I learned that I was admitted. I slipped away quickly. In the crowd behind me I heard someone whisper: "That Chink pulled a fast one!"

I was confused and I was ashamed. For my own survival, I had sunk to struggling against my fellow creatures. But if I got through the lab courses, I would perhaps be able to find a less painful way to make ends meet.

Then the tuberculosis bacilli played me a dirty trick. The factory doctor called me in one day after work. "Your test was positive. We can't keep you at work. You have to go get cured."

The social worker, sympathetic as before, showed me the procedures I needed to follow to get unemployment and health benefits. It was understood that I could get my job back once I was cured.

I took advantage of this time free from the brutalizing routine of the factory to try to clarify my ideas and commitments, past and future. During the same period I continued to take technical classes in electricity at the Conservatoire des Arts et Métiers.

After a couple months of rest, it was back to the daily grind. This time I was on the night shift. A deathly silence reigned on all the floors. The motionless assembly lines, machines, and presses slept an iron sleep, seeming to be renewing their energy so as to be ready to extract the next day's living labor.

The first few nights were the hardest. I found it impossible to recuperate on daytime sleep, and this upside-down life left me constantly exhausted. After two weeks on the night shift, I asked to return to my former day crew.

I was put back on the assembly line, still in charge of maintaining the electrical controls for the welding machines, but this time for fenders and doors rather than chassis. The sheet metal parts, suspended from an overhead belt, twisted about like a venomous caterpillar above my head. As they advanced, the worker had to apply the weld at the precise instant that each piece arrived. One piece passes, another arrives. Man himself becomes a part of the machinery.

Once when I had to replace a pair of worn electrodes on a suspended welding machine, I cut the current and the line stopped. The repair took me about twenty minutes. Then I reconnected the current, but it took the assembly line another ten minutes to start moving again. This was extremely upsetting to the managers, who were all breathing down my neck. As I was calmly replacing my tools, Gaido shouted:

"That interruption of the line cost the company five million francs! Don't you understand? You can't just cut the current like that!"

"At school I was warned never to work with the power on," I replied.

This incident did not cause me any further trouble, but the welders were annoyed because of the bonus they forfeited. Other members of my team, French workers who were stronger than I, could have done the same repair in five or ten minutes, and they would not have cut off the current. But I was following the correct rule of the trade, without taking into account the bosses' measure of time. I hadn't forgotten the old electrician who was electrocuted in the basement while changing a fuse without cutting off the electricity.

From then on I was assigned to do repair work in the shop. The pace of work was less frantic than on the assembly line, but repairing the machines required considerable strength. It strained my back to drag heavy cast-iron machine parts to the work bench or to secure them between the mastodon jaws of the vise.

"Is that how you do it in your country?" Gaido snarled at me once when he saw me make an awkward move.

I felt his remark to be a racist slur, but at the moment I couldn't think of any good retort to the fascist. I fumed over it for a week.

Then, in April 1954, I resigned.

"Where else are you going?" Gaido asked.

"I don't know."

"Don't kid me, you must have already found something else."

"No, nothing."

"Well, think it over."

When the period for giving notice had passed, Gaido and my team boss kept insisting that I reconsider my decision. But I was sick of the whole scene. My fellow workers seemed uninterested in anything outside the daily grind of "Commute, work, commute, sleep . . ." There didn't seem to be any point in trying to make them aware of their slavish condition.

Do what must be done, come what may! Finally in May 1954 I returned my tools. Goodbye, Simca!

The next day I applied for work at Hispano-Suiza, a well-known brand of luxury cars, in Bois-Colombes [a suburb northwest of Paris]. I had an unusual reception: after registering my identity, the secretary took my fingerprints.

"It's for National Defense," she explained before leading me to the employment office.

Upon looking over my certificates from the Conservatoire des Arts et Métiers and noting my past experience as a repair electrician, the engineer proposed to hire me as a technician. The work consisted of measuring airplane wing vibrations when the attached machine-gun was fired. But the idea of contributing to the fine-tuning of engines of death repelled me, and I turned down their job offer.

* * *

After five weeks of being unemployed, I finally found a job as a technician at Mors in Clichy [a working-class suburb north of Paris]. The factory produced railroad signal relays, but also worked for the Navy. It was there that I met Paco Gómez, a survivor of the Spanish Civil War who became my lifelong friend.

Born in 1917, Paco was brought up in Madrid by his seamstress mother. After a period in the Communist Youth and then in the Trotskyist Left Opposition, he joined the POUM. In June 1937, while a delegate at a POUM congress in Barcelona, he was arrested by the Stalinists, who had taken over the Republican Police. After spending a year in various Spanish Republican prisons, he was released and fought on the Pyrenees front in a troop composed mainly of members of the CNT. Upon the victory of Franco's forces in January 1939, he joined the mass exodus to France and was taken to a refugee concentration camp at Argelès-sur-Mer in Pyrénées-Orientales. French Trotskyists got him out of the camp and brought him to Paris, but he was reinterned in the same camp when he was caught while searching in the south of France for his refugee comrades. Suzanne, a teacher whom he had met in Paris, recontacted him and married him, thereby enabling him to leave the camp and return to Paris.

Paco Gómez

At Mors, I was assigned to the team of "relay regulators," and worked sitting down. The work was less arduous than at Simca, but nevertheless very tedious, demanding more dexterity than technical knowledge.

One afternoon at work, I suddenly felt sick. After an X-ray, the factory doctor exclaimed, "You must go to the hospital immediately!"

Once I was in the hospital, they wouldn't let me leave. A nurse made me wash in a bathtub, then I was confined in a bed for tubercular pleurisy.

What would become of my son Da, whom I had succeeded in bringing over from Saigon just a few months earlier? He had arrived on May 17, 1956. He was twelve years old and did not know a word of French. There I was, "a rooster bringing up a chick," as the Vietnamese put it. I had enrolled him in the local school just a few steps from our room at 60 Rue Nationale. He had a delightful and very devoted teacher who cut out pictures of objects and pasted them in a copy book to facilitate his learning the new language. Da and I only saw each other in the evening, but were able to spend the weekends together.

While I was hospitalized, Paco and Suzanne took Da to live with them. Suzanne placed him in the school where she herself taught, where he formed a close attachment to three other classmates. They called themselves "the Four Musketeers," and are still friends.

One time Suzanne brought Da to visit me in the hospital, but he was not allowed to enter the room. Sitting on a bench just outside, he told me about his new life. The white hairs on his head reflected the terrifying night he had spent during the previous year (1955), bullets whistling over his head as he crouched under the bed during the battle between the Binh Xuyen pirates and Ngo Dinh Diem's mercenaries in the straw hut neighborhood between Saigon and Cholon.

Among the friends from the factory who came to see me in the hospital was old man Guyot.

"Don't worry! I'll take care of your son," he said to me as he placed some oranges on my bed. "I'll return him to you as good as new!"

Vandenstein, a cable maker at the plant, made the same warm-hearted offer.

* * *

After two and a half months at the hospital, I was granted a long rest in the Pyrenees. At the beginning of December I entered a sanatorium in Cambo-les-Bains, not far from the Spanish border. It was called "Les Terrasses" [The Terraces] and consisted of a group of multistoried buildings and pavilions built on wooded terraces overlooking the Nive River. In front of the sanatorium, beyond the curtain of autumn-colored trees that hid the river, rose the rounded peaks of the Lower Pyrenees. I was finally seeing that blue sky country of the South that Brassens's companion dreamed of in the film *Porte des Lilas,* full of the drifting clouds I so loved. I started to paint.

One of the paradoxes of my life: In prison or in a hospital I have felt free, freed from worrying about how to get my daily rice. At the Central Prison in Saigon we were able to meet and discuss things without worrying about being spied on by the cops, whose surveillance was so prevalent everywhere else. In the hospital or the sanatorium, apart from the periods of treatment, I was able to breathe freely, living outside the realm of time to gain and time to lose.

Ngo Van in the sanatorium with his paintings (1957)

The smell of turpentine and paint disturbed my roommate, so the doctor gave me a room of my own in the neighboring pavilion. My window opened onto a splendid view of Mt. Ursuya and the poetic banks of the Nive.

In the factory, time dominated me, devouring the moments of my life. Here, I was intoxicated with space, with the poetry of the trees, the song of the river, the melodious silence of the mountains.

I drew and painted like a bird sings, like one of those prehistoric men drawing, painting, carving, or leaving impressions of his hands on the walls of caves. It was an internal necessity, like the silkworm:

> *Même si, dit-on, le fleuve se dessèche et la montagne s'use,*
> *Le ver à soie jusqu'à sa mort continuera à cracher sa soie.*

[Even if, as the saying goes, the river dries up and the mountain wears away, the silkworm will continue all its life to spit forth its silk.]*

My previous paintings, *60 Rue Nationale* and *Rue des Chiffon-niers,* portraying the poor neighborhoods in the 13th Arrondisse-ment, had been painted in the evenings after my factory work. Now here was the magnificent silhouette of Mt. Ursuya, disappearing and reappearing behind the white patches of fog rising from the valley of the Nive River beyond the rows of autumn-colored trees. I was enthralled by the charm of this landscape, and devoted a whole se-ries of paintings to it.

Chapter 2

NEW RADICAL PERSPECTIVES

In 1948 my friend Nguyen Van Nam had told me that when I got to Paris I should contact Sania Gontarbert. Sania ran the tiny Camée Bookshop near the Carrefour des Gobelins in the 13th Arrondissement. In his memoirs he later described our first meeting: "The shop door opened and in came a tall, thin Indochinese man who had just arrived from Saigon and who, amazingly enough, had my address. This was the beginning of my long friendship with Van." It was he who received for me the packages of rice sent from Saigon.

Rereading Marx (illuminated by the work of Maximilien Rubel), discovering the existence of the Councilist Republic of Bavaria (1918–1919) and of the Kronstadt revolt in Russia (1921), and then seeing the resurgence of workers councils in Hungary in 1956, led me to investigate new revolutionary perspectives and permanently distanced me from Bolshevism-Leninism-Trotskyism. I developed a total distrust of anything that might turn into a "machine." The so-called "workers' parties" (Leninist parties in particular) are embryonic forms of the state. Once in power, these parties form the nucleus of a new ruling class and bring about nothing more than a new system of exploitation.

In France I found new allies in the factories and elsewhere, among French people, colonized people, and refugees from the Spanish Civil War of 1936–1939—anarchists and Poumistas who had gone through a parallel experience to ours. In Vietnam, as in Spain, we had been engaged in a simultaneous battle on two fronts: against a reactionary power and against a Stalinist party struggling for power.

Since arriving in France I had stopped taking anything for granted. Rather than meekly following those who preceded us, I felt that we needed to go beyond them, to stand on their shoulders so we could scan more distant horizons. But how to do this? This and so many other questions that had continually gnawed at me were now finally answered in the lively and fruitful discussions with my new friend Sania. Until then, in Paris I had sometimes felt the isolation of a lone survivor as I looked back on my past in Indochina. My friends and I had not only fought against the colonial regime, we had striven for a radical social revolution, and in so doing we had come up against other enemies. Most of our comrades in that struggle, if they were not massacred, imprisoned or sent to the penal colonies by the French colonial regime, or forced into exile, ended up being murdered by Ho Chi Minh's "Communist" Party. My encounter with Sania helped me to understand and reassess my previous history.

Scarcely ten years had elapsed since the October 1917 revolution in Russia when, in 1927, at the age of 14, I had gone to Saigon to work and had become directly aware of the oppressive reality of Indochinese society. For me, like so many others, the Russian Revolution was a sign full of hope for a possible liberation. Yet even then, during those early years of my apprenticeship in life and revolt, the rare news that reached us from Russia sometimes contained disturbing features. There, too, oppositionist revolutionaries were being hunted down and Trotsky had just been forced into exile. Through the Third International, Stalin was imposing a totalitarian policy that seemed to my friends and me to betray the most precious aspect of our revolutionary engagement: a fraternal internationalism among all the exploited of the world. Under those circumstances, confronted with the emergence of a regime whose full horror became glaringly evident with the Moscow Trials, it was natural that our critique of Stalinism was initially oriented around the ideas and partisans of Trotsky.

But since my recent departure from Indochina in 1948, if the hope and conviction of the necessity of overthrowing the despicable world order never left me, they were nourished by new reflections on Bolshevism and revolution.

It was thus with great joy and relief that I met people who had passed
through diverse experiences yet had
ended up asking the same questions.
Sania introduced me to the Union Ouvrière Internationale (UOI) [Interna-
tional Workers' Association], a group
formed in 1948 by militants who had
broken with Trotskyism following the
split of the Internationalist Communist
Party just after the war.

Sania Gontarbert

Sania and I took part in regular
meetings of this group in Edgar Pesch's
small room at 5 Rue Clavel in the 19th
Arrondissement. At these meetings I came to know Jacques Gallienne, Sophie Moen, Lambert Dornier, Benjamin Péret and Manuel
Munis. There were other group members, such as Marcel Pennetier,
Mangano and Bilbao, whom I never met. Some other people later
joined the group, including two refugees from the Spanish Civil
War, Agustín Rodríguez and Jaime Fernández, and two of my Indochinese friends, Luc and Phuc.

Edgar Pesch gave me copies of his *Cahiers de la Pensée,* a journal that he published dealing with issues such as existentialism,
Marxism, and the psychoanalytical interpretation of magic, as well
as his book *Freud et la Psychanalyse* (Bordas, 1948).

In issue #2 of its bulletin *La Bataille Internationale* [The Inter-
national Battle] (October 1951) the UOI criticized the Vietnamese
Trotskyists in France for their slogan "Defend the government of
Ho Chi Minh against the attacks of imperialism," which they had
adopted despite the assassination of almost all their comrades in
Vietnam by Ho Chi Minh's hired thugs.

The Trotskyists who supported Ho Chi Minh were acting like
a hanged man clinging to his rope. In the "Opinion" section of the
Trotskyist paper *Tieng Tho* (Workers' Voice), October 30, 1951, I
scandalized the Trotskyists with my article on the Indochina War
(signed Dong Vu): "Prolétaires et paysans, retournez vos fusils!"
[Workers and Peasants, Turn Your Guns in the Other Direction!].

I was aware that most of the Trotskyists would pay no attention to what I said, but I couldn't resist telling them what I thought. Which could be summed up as follows: The dynamic of the war against the colonizers had enabled Ho Chi Minh to develop a superior military force, which he used to crush the other groups struggling against colonial reconquest, along with any other opposition, and to exert an absolute hegemony over the conduct of the resistance. His underground government had become integrated into the Sino-Russian bloc that was struggling against the Western bloc, so that the Indochina War was taking place in the context of the Cold War between the two imperialist blocs.

I thought that the workers and peasants who had guns in their hands should fight for their own emancipation, following the example of the Russian workers, peasants and soldiers who formed soviets in 1917, or the German workers' and soldiers' councils of 1918–1919. In the cities, which were dominated by the French Expeditionary Corps and its lackey, the Bao Dai government, the soldiers should be urged to turn their weapons against their own generals. In the countryside, where Ho Chi Minh and his Vietminh were keeping the poor peasants under the yoke of the landowners, those peasants should revolt in order to realize their old dreams of liberation, exemplified in the 1930–1931 peasant soviets of Nghe-Tinh.

The indispensable first condition for this utopia to become reality was an awakening consciousness among those who had been recruited to fight for the Bao Dai government or for Ho Chi Minh's underground forces; they had to realize that the soldiers on both sides were being duped. It was obvious that if Bao Dai triumphed they would remain slaves of the bourgeoisie and the landowners. If Ho Chi Minh won, the workers and peasants would simply have changed masters, being at the mercy of a rapacious state-capitalist bureaucracy, as in Russia and China.

The second essential condition for such a utopian realization was that the social transformation in the Southeast Asian corner of the world would have to spark a chain reaction among other proletarians all over the planet.

To this the Trotskyists in France replied: "While we have certain political differences with the Ho Chi Minh government, we support it in the current stage of resistance against imperialism." They should have added: ". . . as long as Ho Chi Minh leaves our head on our shoulders."

* * *

The UOI broke up in 1952. Soon afterwards Sophie, Sania, Lambert, Agustín, Pesch, Guy Perrard and I gathered into a new, less formal group around Maximilien Rubel.*

I had already been familiar with Maxime's writings. In the Saigon underground in the 1930s I had struggled to understand the first volume of *Capital* in the Costes edition—a study that was interrupted in 1936 when the Sûreté confiscated my books. In France I had discovered *Pages choisies de Karl Marx, pour une éthique socialiste* [Selected Passages of Karl Marx: For a Socialist Ethic], edited by Maximilien Rubel (1948). For an epigraph, Maxime had chosen an astonishing quotation by Marx himself: "One thing for sure: I am not a Marxist." This inspired me to reexplore Marx during my first years in Paris, which helped me to get over my feelings of confusion and helplessness following the tragic events of 1945 in Saigon. I had thus already had a certain connection with Maxime even before I met him.

Maxime noted that in the nineteenth century there were other thinkers contemporary with Marx, "incorruptible and pitiless judges of their era" such as Soren Kierkegaard or Friedrich Nietzsche. (Nguyen An Ninh, the revolutionary who had awakened my own consciousness in 1926–1929, had been strongly influenced by Nietzsche.) These thinkers had espoused "new sets of values, new reasons for living, new norms for acting, a new ethic."

But Maxime stressed that it was Marx who had truly embodied the Promethean faith ("I

Maximilien Rubel

hate all gods") and who had conceived of life as a project of building a genuine human community here on earth. The Marxian ethic is characterized by its amoralism and by its essentially pragmatic approach. Like Spinoza, Marx brought man into the eternal cycle of infinite nature and assigned him the ideal of fulfilling his own total human potential.

Marx also brought the utopian future into the present struggle. By becoming conscious of their own alienation, the workers become capable both of destroying capitalist society and of building a utopia—a society without a state, without classes, and without money.

In the process of criticizing Hegel's political philosophy, Marx took an increasingly radical direction, to the point of transforming this critique into a pure and simple negation of the state. Although Marx never used the term, at its deepest level his critique essentially amounts to anarchism. In his later book, *Marx critique du marxisme* [Marx as a Critic of Marxism] (1975), Maxime quotes the following passage from Marx: "All socialists recognize that 'anarchy' is the goal of the proletarian movement; that once classes have been abolished, state power, whose purpose is to keep the great majority of producers in bondage to a small exploiter minority, will disappear and governmental functions will be transformed into simple administrative functions" (*Fictitious Splits in the International,* 1872). Maxime repeatedly stressed and illustrated this essential sentence of Marx: "The existence of the state and the existence of slavery are inseparable."

Maxime also stressed that we needed to become more familiar with the groupings that had been eliminated by the large, official political and labor-union organizations. Their ideas and actions had been completely smothered. It would be good to bring those positions back into view, if only to demonstrate that our own positions were part of a tradition and that what certain groups seemed to be discovering today was in no way new. We needed to translate texts of the IWW comrades (in particular, Daniel De Leon) and of revolutionary syndicalists all over the world (Spain, Italy, Netherlands, Russia, etc.), as well as the libertarian and anarchist documents of ancient China (cited by Étienne Balazs in *Chinese Civilization and Bureaucracy*).

Sophie Moen and Maximilien Rubel

* * *

In 1958 our study and discussion group—which later adopted the name Council Communist Group—began to collaborate closely with ICO (*Informations et Correspondance Ouvrières*) [Workers' News and Letters],* which was facilitating a *"regroupement inter-entreprises"* [a linkup of workers from different companies]. This new formation aimed to "bring together workers who no longer have any confidence in the traditional working-class organizations, namely the parties and labor unions," which have become "elements of stabilization and conservation of the exploitive regime. ICO seeks to create actual direct linkups between workers, to inform each other about what is going on in different workplaces, to denounce labor-union maneuvers, to discuss our desires and demands, and to mutually aid each other. This process of dealing with particular current problems inevitably leads us to call into question the present regime and to discuss general problems such as capitalist property, war or racism. Each participant is free to express his views and remains free to act as he wishes within his own workplace."

We took part in these reunions as ICO correspondents—Guy at the Post Office, Agustín in a photoengraving company, Lambert at the Chausson bus factory, and I at Jeumont-Schneider, a company that manufactured electrical machines.

* * *

On the night of May 10, 1968, a social tornado swept through Paris. Paving stones were hurled at the CRS [national riot police]. Students built barricades on Rue Gay-Lussac and around the Sorbonne. As Sophie and I passed the knocked-down trees near the Saint-Germain subway exit and along Boulevard Saint-Michel, we felt that a new force had emerged, rejecting authority, the current regime, and the state itself. Panic-stricken, de Gaulle denounced the "filthy rioters" before secretly flying off to the army base at Baden-Baden, the headquarters of the French-occupied sector of Germany, where he prepared for the possibility of crushing the May 1968 insurgents with military force.

The Maoists from the École des Beaux-Arts carried banners proclaiming: "Good weather comes after the rain." I shouted out: "How pathetic can you get! Here we are in the land of the Paris Commune and you can think of nothing but reciting the Hunan peasant's *Little Red Book*!"* From then on I was *persona non grata* in the local action centers—they practically treated me and my friends as cops.

I was working at the Jeumont-Schneider factory. Students were calling for a general strike and coming to the factories in order to make contact with the workers. The CGT prevented the workers from meeting them, keeping the workers isolated in their factories and driving away the students. . . .

[*See the following article.*]

ARTICLES

A FACTORY OCCUPATION
IN MAY 1968

Now that everything is back to "normal," it may not seem very interesting to recall the very different sort of normality that briefly prevailed at the end of last spring. Moreover, what happened at this particular factory (Jeumont-Schneider) was not all that different from what was happening elsewhere, which everyone is already familiar with. Nevertheless, looking into the tarnished mirror of the past may help us to better understand ourselves.

On the afternoon of Friday, May 17, there were rumors in the workshops that the labor unions were cooking something up to deal with the rising wave. But over the weekend nothing happened.

Monday morning, the workers walked down the street, which was decorated with red flags, and gathered in front of the gates, not knowing whether they were supposed to go in or stay outside. They waited for an order. The union representative gave it: "Go on in, we'll decide what needs to be done." As usual the heavy iron gates closed again after everyone, like robots, had clocked in. But in the nearby Sifa antibiotics factory something had already happened. The red flag waved over their iron gates, which were sealed with handwritten white posters calling for a strike of indefinite duration, for things to change, for work to be transformed into a part of life rather than the destruction of life. . . .

"Something's going to happen here, soon," I was alerted by a young friend in the CFDT.*

And in fact in the workshops everyone had practically stopped working, with some showing impatience as they waited for that "something" to happen. At about nine o'clock the union representatives went around with a duplicated questionnaire to be filled in:

"Are you for or against the following demands: minimum wage of 800 francs, 40-hour week without wage reductions, retirement at 60, repeal of the Social Security regulations, company recognition of labor-union rights? Are you for or against a general assembly of all the workers?" What responsibility were we going to have to take on, we the perennial signers of petitions, demands, requests, all destined for the wastebaskets?

At ten o'clock the workshops emptied and we gathered in the packing workshop. There were about 500 of us, mostly blue-collar workers, but also, this time, the foremen and a few white-collar workers. Over the years this particular workshop had been used for routine union-called meetings lasting half an hour or an hour, but there had never been nearly as many participants as this Monday morning (May 20). But routine had not ceased to rule—the same people managed the game and the rest only played along.

The union representatives were on the platform and the crowd, as usual, was almost totally silent. The first to speak was a CFDT representative, a middle-aged lathe operator with deep, shining eyes and a determined, passionate air. He praised the students' courage and said that it was time for the workers to enter the struggle, so as to "open the eyes of the employers and the government, who have for ages refused to negotiate with the unions." Shyly, a small red flag was unfurled and then raised behind the group of speakers. "I am not a Communist," he said, "but I am for the red flag." Then he recalled how the emblem had originated: during the barricades of 1848 someone had picked up a shirt steeped in a worker's blood. This had served as a flag, and the shirt is said to be still preserved in a museum in Moscow. Even so, this red flag was a bit startling. In the past, collections for striking coal-miners or for Vietnam had always been conducted with the national tricolor flag. It was spread out at the factory exit and everybody showed their "active solidarity" by casting their contribution onto this sacred rag of the fatherland. But in fact we would have looked pretty lame to those students on the barricades, with their red flags and black flags, if we had brought out nothing but the old blue-white-red.

After the CFDT representative, the one from the CGT* confessed that he didn't have much to add, and proposed to support the

demands put forward by the unions by launching a strike of indefinite duration plus occupation of the factory. The younger workers
seemed eager for action, while the older ones appeared cautious.
The decision was taken by ballot. Everyone wrote their yes or no
on a little piece of paper. The result was two-thirds for the strike,
one-third against, with about twenty voting for a strike without an
occupation.

With a tone of official authority, the CGT representative declared:
"We call on you to put away your tools and leave the benches clean."

The everyday routine was broken. Everyone was shaken and to a
greater or lesser degree jolted out of their apathy. The problem was
posed, and each saw it in their own way.

"Now we have to discuss what we're going to do," said G., a
foreman. "Some of you want to overthrow the government. But if
we do that, we need to know where we go from there. Tomorrow
there will be no more milk for the babies . . ."

After lunch we gathered in the lunch room and elected a strike
committee. Most of the candidates put forward for approval by our
assembly were union representatives or other members of the CGT
or CFDT, but a few unaffiliated young workers were also allowed in.
A strike picket of forty volunteers was set up to ensure that the factory stayed occupied day and night. The committee invited everyone
to come every day to take part in the factory occupation; but in reality this was just to protect the access to the factory, since only the
strike picketers were allowed to freely move about inside the workshops. "Why do we need to occupy the factory? So that the boss
doesn't lock us out. Because once before he played that dirty trick
on us, and then called back one by one only those workers he was
willing to take on again." The younger members of the committee
were given the job of "organizing" our "leisure activities," so as to
counteract the boredom that would be suffered by the occupiers, a
boredom that might be as unlimited as the strike itself.

Among the younger workers (a very small minority) a vague
feeling developed that a profound change in our way of life was
needed—one so profound that it would imply a change in the structures of society as a whole. To some of them who went to the Latin
Quarter during the nights of the barricades, it seemed that the leaden

lid of the Old World had been half-opened above our heads and that the time had come to blow it completely off. But the majority experienced the events passively, as though letting themselves be carried a little way into the unknown by the wave. Those over fifty had experienced the strike movement of 1936, and thus had no illusions: they remembered that the union bureaucrats had "known how to end a strike."*

During the first week many of us came to the factory, and meetings organized by the strike committee for information and discussion took place frequently.

After the Grenelle Accords,* the CGT and CFDT showed less enthusiasm for strike committee meetings and general assemblies, using the inter-union meetings that were held nearly every day as the excuse for calling the larger meetings as infrequently as possible. Or else they briskly hurried through the meetings of the strike committee, with talk only about the lunch room or the nighttime guard, and nothing more.

On Tuesday, May 21, the young workers suggested that discussion groups be formed in order to consider our demands and other problems. After the assembly meeting, about thirty workers who liked this idea gathered in the conference room (which in normal times was open only to the managerial staff). A very good discussion developed about our demands, and about their contradictions and inadequacies. This led to the question of the relation between labor unions and political parties, but the discussion was brought to a sudden halt when the CGT representatives intervened, speaking aggressively and interrupting everyone.

On the first day of the strike the red flag flew alone over the factory gate, which was sealed with a big red poster expressing our demands. From the next day on, however, the tricolor was also there, side by side with the red flag. We later realized what this meant when the Communist Party proclaimed itself a party of order, "the first to denounce the sects of extremists and provocateurs," and declared that it had been able to unite "the flag of the French Revolution" with "the flag of the working class." Monsieur Waldeck-Rochet was really going too far. The flag of the Communards should not be associated with the flag of Versailles.* The tricolor is the flag of today's bourgeoisie and bourgeois state. Since 1789 it has been under those colors that the bourgeoisie has exploited the workers and sent them to die on the field of honor; under those colors that it has enslaved the peoples of Africa and Asia.

In reality, of course, our CGT comrades were the Communist Party's cell in the factory, just as Comrade Séguy, the leader of the CGT, was also a member of the Communist Party's Political Bureau.

In the assemblies the workers said little, expressing themselves with difficulty. I will mention at random a few things that I recall. Someone proposed that we discuss the demands we had formulated, reminding us that we had already supposedly won the 40-hour week in 1936, yet since then we had continued to work between 48 and 56 hours. And now here we were, thirty-two years later, back at the same point.

"In those thirty-two years technology has evolved and production has increased," said an old worker. "Why demand 40 hours and not 35?" In any case, even if tomorrow the bosses and the government were to agree to 40 hours, what would prevent them from double-crossing us just like they did before? Retirement at 60 would enable the older workers to enjoy some rest and the young to find work. This proposal did not arouse much interest among those present, and the committee closed the debate when it had scarcely begun.

Later, after Grenelle, there was no more talk in the strike committee about the 40-hour week or retirement at 60, only about a gradual reduction of working hours and lowering of the age of retirement.

Some comrades spoke of unity in struggle between the universities and the factories, and proposed that we invite the students of the UNEF and of the March 22nd Movement* to come to our factory and tell us about their actions. When the strike committee rejected this, they asked for their proposal to be put to a vote in the general assembly, but this proposal was ignored. Although a certain number of comrades favored the idea, nobody insisted. The representatives and younger members of the CFDT were in favor of such communication between workers and students, but they did not want to oppose the CGT representatives, for fear of "breaking unity of action."

A group of young workers went to the "Communist" town hall of Saint-Denis seeking a venue outside the factory where they would be able to meet and talk with the students. At first they met with refusal, on the pretext that there were some suspicious elements in the Jeumont-Schneider factory. But then, to satisfy these young workers, a CGT representative intervened and they were given a room at 120 Avenue Wilson, a few hundred meters from the factory. The intended meeting did not take place, however, because the UNEF students did not show up.

* * *

On the day of the demonstration at the Saint-Lazare railroad station—which was organized by the CGT in favor of a democratic government that would include Communist ministers—at the factory general assembly the strike committee, or rather the CGT representatives, invited those present to take part in that demonstration in order to "support the negotiations between the bosses and the metalworkers' union." Somebody responded: "You're trying to politicize the strike. Who do you think you're kidding? The demonstration is aimed at supporting your policy, Séguy said so last night on television, and you're trying to make us believe it's only to support our demands." Then the CFDT representative proposed supporting a government headed by Mendès-France.

At about one o'clock, four or five young men and women from the March 22nd Movement showed up outside the factory and tried to engage in conversation with the strikers. The CGT representatives intervened at once. One of them challenged the intruders: "What do you want? What is your program?" "Madame, we are not a political party, we don't want to take power and we have no program. We just want to make contact in order to learn what is going on."

In the discussion with the workers, one of the young men mentioned Séguy disdainfully. An enraged CGT representative sprang to grab him by the throat, as though he had blasphemed. One of the women workers, indignant at this representative's fanaticism, broke in: "You have no right to stop him talking. Let him talk. I belong to the CGT, too, but everybody should be allowed to speak. Even the Trotskyists who came to hand out leaflets. You have no right to bully them." Then she went on: "We can win improvements. Why make a revolution? Why cause bloodshed?"

Little by little, people began to speak out, especially outside the general assemblies and during the nighttime pickets. As a workmate put it, "If nothing else, this strike will at least have served to get the workers talking." We discussed the events, the students, fascism, and all sorts of other issues. Some went in the evening to the Sorbonne, the Odéon or the École des Beaux-Arts, and when they returned the next day they brought back the ideas and the liberating atmosphere of those scenes.

Very often, in reaction against the farcical bread-and-butter demands presented at Grenelle, the idea of workers' self-management was brought up. Responses were not hostile, but the workers generally thought themselves incapable of carrying out such a task effectively. They felt that this was a worldwide problem, something that could not be carried out within an individual factory, or even within a single country. They also sensed that the labor unions were not in favor of putting an end to the existing social order.

The entertainment committee invited some Portuguese musicians to come and perform *fado* songs. On May 21, when they arrived at the gate of the factory, these Portuguese friends contrasted the breadth and depth of the movement with the paltry content of our factory's demands, and this had the effect of arousing the distrust of one of the CGT representatives. After the songs were over, a CFDT representative asked the performers, "Why are you on strike, and what are *your* demands?"

One of them answered: "Capitalist society exploits us through the impresarios, the record companies and the radio, just as it exploits the workers through the bosses. We are not demanding a 40-hour week (which we were supposed to have had since 1936) nor a minimum wage of 800 francs (because one needs more than 800 francs to live decently)—and in any case, why 800 francs here, 600 francs there, and 1000 francs somewhere else? We are also striking out of solidarity with the workers and the students. We are going into the factories to start a dialogue between workers and artists, which helps us to see more clearly that we all have the same problem: challenging the existing social system." He concluded by saying that we must not let ourselves be hoodwinked.

This latter remark produced a violent reaction from the CGT representative: "You are here to sing, so sing! As for the workers, they are our concern." The dialogue continued nevertheless, but soon these friends were asked to leave the factory and were ushered out by the union guards. Some of us left with them, and passed the rest of the afternoon with them in a café, away from the reactions of the union representatives.

Apart from a few such incidents, the union bureaucracy maintained its control in the factory. The tools were left intact; there was no smashing of machines by the students. No conflict, no hostile behavior of any sort by the young radicals or the older "anarchistic" workers. The manager was there every day, in his office. He signed for the release of funds for the lunch room, arranged advances of wages for the strikers, had occasional talks with the union representatives, and took no decision on his own. He, too, was waiting and following instructions.

An important event: the engineers came out on strike. On the first day, they held their meetings separately. Four days had to pass before, by a small majority, they decided on a solidarity strike. They held out for three weeks, meeting every day to discuss and work out their own statement of demands. Then they called for a secret ballot of the entire workforce, for or against going back to work. The majority of the workers were opposed to secret voting, and the engineers went back to work. Since the factory was closed and guarded by the strike pickets, the engineers worked on sites outside it.

In the middle of the last week of the strike, the big boss agreed to talk with the union representatives. Events speeded up. At the general assembly of Thursday, June 13, the CGT representative said that we should recognize that we had no choice but to go back to work. He then proposed a secret ballot on this question. The following day we proceeded to vote on the issue. The polling booths were brought out, just as for the routine elections when we had to choose a factory committee or other workforce representatives. The majority of the workers were discouraged and thought that one week more or less would make no difference, considering that the other branches of industry were already back at work, the workers' front had been broken, and the metalworkers were almost alone in continuing to fight.

The lunch room was full when the result was announced: 423 votes for going back to work, 135 for continuing the strike, 3 invalid votes. The meeting erupted. Those who wanted to "continue the struggle" were at least pleased to find that they were still so numerous.

The management and the union representatives hurried to bring the affair to a close. They proposed that work be resumed that very afternoon, and the management would generously pay wages for the whole day. On every side the workers called out: "Monday, Monday!" A clear majority seemed to reject the bargain offered. At 1:00 p.m. we witnessed an astonishing spectacle, which could only have happened because the bureaucrats were under such intense pressure. The entire leadership of the CGT and the CFDT appeared at the factory gates, which were wide open. Two union representatives carrying the flags, the red one and the tricolor, made their way into the factory, followed hesitantly by a minority of the workers. Once inside, they sang the "Internationale."

Monday morning, everyone was present at work and things were "back to normal."

* * *

P.S. On Wednesday, May 22, two days after the beginning of our strike, the unions announced their readiness to negotiate with the bosses and the government. At the news of the opening of talks with Pompidou, everyone thought that, given the paralysis the country was in and the constant insurrectionary agitation by the students (which had aroused the workers in the first place), there was a good chance that the bosses and the capitalist state would make significant concessions. The hopes of some went further still, imagining that they were going to surrender quickly and that we would probably resume work within a week.

However, as soon as the famous Grenelle Accords of May 26 had been announced, and Séguy and Company had been booed at the Renault works, everyone felt that they had been double-crossed and realized that the struggle would get harder. At the general assembly on Tuesday, after telling the strikers the terms of the agreement, the union representatives themselves, as though gripped by the general dissatisfaction, simply proposed a continuation of the strike.

The feeling that we had been swindled was strengthened when the government broke the movement by granting advantageous conditions to the key sectors (electricity, the subway, the railways, the postal service, etc.) and the unions celebrated this as a victory.

[*Informations et Correspondance Ouvrières* #76, December 1968]

ON THIRD WORLD STRUGGLES

What does "national liberation" mean for workers and peasants? The imperialist powers speak of "the right of peoples to self-determination," and this phrase is adopted by the parties striving for power in colonial and semicolonial countries. We propose to banish the word "people" from our vocabulary: it implies an equality of right between the exploiting classes and the exploited masses. Who "self-determines" whom in the new national "peasant" states? In countries within the Western sphere of influence, national independence hands power over to the local bourgeoisie, which exploits the proletariat, and to the landowning class, which exploits the peasantry; in countries within the so-called "Communist" bloc, the state-capitalist bureaucracy exploits proletariat and peasantry alike. For workers and peasants, national liberation means nothing more than a change of masters.

Needless to say, in countries like India, where imperialism has handed power over to the local bourgeoisie, peasants die of hunger or live on the verge of starvation, at the mercy of greedy landowners. In countries where immense peasant uprisings have brought "Communist" parties to power, bureaucratic-military states have emerged that have introduced agrarian reform for their own ends: they abolish land ownership, eliminate the landowning classes, and redistribute land to the peasants in order to secure their support during the initial phase of their rule; but once state capitalism is established, the superexploitation of the peasants forms the basis of primitive accumulation for industrialization.

We live in an era of permanent war. The major powers confront each other, either directly or through the states under their dominion, and, as in the past, they each lay the responsibility on the other side.

Whatever the country, the victims are always the workers and peasants. "A people that oppresses another people is itself oppressed." We have no country to defend, even if that country claims to be "communist." For all the exploited, the struggle for self-emancipation means the duty to fight against their own exploiters, and war is nothing other than the most extreme form of that exploitation. The peace or war promoted by our masters, be they bourgeois, landowners, generals or "Communist" bureaucrats, is no concern of ours. We have no interest in the defense of the "Free World" or the defense of a "workers' and peasants' government." No matter where we live, we must struggle directly against those who send us to slaughter by refusing to manufacture or to bear arms; and that struggle is an integral part of our struggle for self-emancipation, across all borders.

[*Cahiers de discussion pour le Socialisme des conseils* #8, April 1968]

REFLECTIONS ON THE
VIETNAM WAR

Since the Tet Offensive,* propaganda has been churning out deceit
with ever greater intensity. While the killing game goes on 10,000
kilometers away, newspapers and television the world over revel in
sensationalistic images of an intolerable carnage to which the public
is becoming increasingly habituated. This two-way brainwashing
helps people to die, or to watch the dying, if their sensitivity has
not already been completely dulled by the relentlessly deepening
quagmire.

Young Americans go off to defend the "Free World" of the dollar
and of military bases in the Pacific, and end up rotting under Russian or Chinese rocket fire in the ricefields and hillsides of Vietnam.
Young Vietnamese in one camp or the other are sent to slaughter,
willingly or not, in the name of "national independence," "national
liberation," or "socialism." Sooner or later the killing will cease,
when "peace" is declared by the masters of the contending states.
The American survivors will head back to their country's factories,
offices, and farms; the invalid veterans, those left armless or leg-
less, will drag out the remainder of their decorated existence. On the
other side of the globe, the "heroes of the resistance"—Vietnamese
peasants and workers—will return to their ricefields or find themselves cast into industrialization's new factories, soon to lose whatever illusions they may have had. Neither the American-style capitalist regime nor Ho Chi Minh's state capitalism will put an end to
their exploitation under a police-state dictatorship. If the bourgeoisie and the landowners are driven out, the bureaucracy will carry on
the same exploitation with even greater efficiency.

The Vietnam War is part of the permanent war opposing two capitalist blocs in today's society. The stake is fundamentally the same
as in the World Wars of 1914–1918 and 1939–1945—world domi-

nation. What obscures that fundamental aspect is the cooption and manipulation of the anti-imperialist peasant revolts that erupted in Vietnam and elsewhere when the colonial structures collapsed following World War II. The bourgeois nationalist or "Communist" parties brought to power by those "peasant wars," with the major powers' direct or indirect acquiescence, took over as ruling bureaucracies and converted the rebel peasantry into hierarchical troops whose struggle ultimately benefited one bloc or the other. The so-called wars of "national liberation" enable the two opposing Cold War powers to test their respective strengths without going to war directly against each other. The newly formed states amount to nothing more than a change in the form of exploitation.

The United States, engaged in a policy of coexistence with Russia and its satellites, tacitly accepts the fact that Russia is neutralizing China's influence by delivering prescribed doses of arms to Ho Chi Minh and the NLF. The Russians, for their part, have no reason to fear a prolonged war that unremittingly bleeds America dry. This bloodbath also presents a favorable opportunity for China, which is striving to become a great power: the two larger vultures' fight over the carrion gives China time to develop its atomic weaponry and to prepare for its entry into the Southeast Asian free-for-all.

As for the working class, as long as its existence is not directly threatened it remains indifferent to the destructive designs of its masters. The experience of the last two World Wars is tragic but instructive: the majority of workers, like most other people, marched behind the flag of their exploiters in each camp, despite the heroic resistance of a handful of revolutionary workers and intellectuals.

In the United States, the active participation of students, intellectuals and hippies in the antiwar movement, however significant, is powerless without working-class support. As for the American labor unions, they are accomplices to Johnson's policies.

In Europe, intellectuals swallow and regurgitate the lies of the "Communist" camp. When people like Sartre and Bertrand Russell parrot the Nuremburg Trials to denounce American "aggression" and "war crimes,"* they are not condemning the war as such. They avoid challenging the social content of a conflict which, far from liberating workers and peasants, can lead to nothing but a change of masters; they employ the legalistic jargon in fashion since the last war, lending it new credibility rather than exposing it as a lie. In reality, the slaves sent to their death are the dupes and victims of the barbarism of both camps. What do words like "aggression" and "war crimes" mean to them, when peace and war are decided exclusively by their masters? Are we to believe that those gentlemen who call for resistance by others to the point of total extermination would be satisfied if the war was fought with bayonets and rifles instead of napalm and cluster bombs, or if the blankets of bombs from B52s were dropped on combatants alone instead of razing villages and blowing women and children to pieces?

Everyone is receptive to the image disseminated by the Stalinist-orchestrated leftwing propaganda, which depicts the North as David bringing down Goliath; everyone is revolted by the destruction; everyone sympathizes with the sufferings of a population cruelly afflicted for the past twenty-eight years; and everyone naïvely applauds the heroism of the combatants without realizing that warmongering heroism can mask every type of enslavement and every type of tyranny. Hence the widespread tendency to think that victory by Ho Chi Minh and the NLF over America would restore an "equitable" peace in the world. The French Communist Party has taken full advantage of this popular sentiment, especially after the latest developments: in Hanoi, Waldeck-Rochet loyally parroted the Russian line, thereby incidentally serving de Gaulle's policy.*

The only way to really stop the killing and prevent any possibility of further genocides is through an awakening awareness by the workers of the world. The antiwar struggle has to come from the workers of the United States and from the workers and peasants of Vietnam, and it must be integrally connected with a struggle for emancipation from capital, whether "democratic" or "Communist." Although we must regretfully admit that we currently see no such prospect emerging, we should let nothing prevent us from fighting the mystifications that shroud the true face of this war, a war whose victims are, as always, the workers and peasants.

[*Cahiers de discussion pour le Socialisme des conseils* #8, April 1968]

TRANSLATORS' NOTES

Page viii. Some Web sources give the misleading impression that there was a significant anarchist influence in early Vietnamese struggles. Closer examination usually reveals that the supposed connection is extremely flimsy. The pioneering anticolonial leader Phan Boi Chau, for example, is sometimes referred to as "a proponent of anarchism" merely because "his thinking reflected certain distinctly anarchist themes, notably anti-imperialism and direct action," and because he was on good terms with a few anarchists he met in Japan and China—though he was on equally good terms with monarchists, nationalists, socialists and militarists, and the organizations he founded advocated nothing more radical than a constitutional monarchy or a democratic republic. His overriding goal was to drive out the French; political groups and ideologies interested him only insofar as they might contribute to that goal. Until late in his life he scarcely manifested any interest even in socialism, let alone anarchism. (For more on Phan Boi Chau, see Note 155.)

Nguyen An Ninh is a different matter. His eclectic and romantic perspective did indeed reflect some anarchist influence (picked up from his years in Paris). This anarchism was blended with a variety of other European philosophical and cultural currents from Rousseau to Nietzsche, and since Ninh was a very popular and charismatic figure, those themes undoubtedly had some influence during the 1920s, particularly among the more educated urban youth. Hue-Tam Ho Tai's *Radicalism and the Origins of the Vietnamese Revolution* gives a good account of the cultural ferment of that period, which served as a prelude to the more directly social and political struggles of the 1930s.

The only explicit Vietnamese anarchist mentioned in the present book is Trinh Hung Ngau. (Other sources describe him as a "nationalist with anarchist leanings.") According to Ngo Van, he participated in the Jeune Annam movement (1926) and in the newspaper *L'Annam* (1926–1928) and was one of the founders of *La Lutte* (1933); but he withdrew from the latter after the third issue "because he was unable to express his anarchist ideal within it" (*Vietnam 1920–1945,* p. 212). He later took part in the Indochinese Congress movement (1936–1937).

xiii. Allusion to Orwell: "Who controls the past controls the future: who controls the present controls the past" (*Nineteen Eighty-Four,* Part 1, Chapter 3).

xiv. Here is Baudelaire's poem (1851), followed by a translation:

LA CLOCHE FÊLÉE

Il est amer et doux, pendant les nuits d'hiver,
D'écouter, près du feu qui palpite et qui fume,
Les souvenirs lointains lentement s'élever
Au bruit des carillons qui chantent dans la brume.

Bienheureuse la cloche au gosier vigoureux
Qui, malgré sa vieillesse, alerte et bien portante,
Jette fidèlement son cri religieux,
Ainsi qu'un vieux soldat qui veille sous la tente!

Moi, mon âme est fêlée, et lorsqu'en ses ennuis
Elle veut de ses chants peupler l'air froid des nuits,
Il arrive souvent que sa voix affaiblie

Semble le râle épais d'un blessé qu'on oublie
Au bord d'un lac de sang, sous un grand tas de morts,
Et qui meurt, sans bouger, dans d'immenses efforts.

THE CRACKED BELL

It is bitter and sweet, during the winter nights,
to listen, beside the quivering, smoking fire,
to distant memories slowly rising
at the sound of the bells chiming in the fog.

Blessed is the strong-throated bell,
alert and healthy despite its old age,
which faithfully sends forth its pious tones,
like an old soldier keeping watch under his tent!

But I—my soul is cracked, and when in its distress
it wants to fill the cold night air with its songs,
it often happens that its enfeebled voice

seems like the thick death-rattle of a wounded man,
     forgotten
beside a lake of blood, lying beneath a mass of corpses,
dying but unable to move despite immense efforts.

That is a fairly literal translation. For some
more poetic attempts (none very satisfactory), see http://fleursdumal.org/poem/157.
xvii. *"Hundred Flowers" movement* (1956–
1957): a campaign initiated by the Chinese
Communist government, encouraging people to freely express their views on national
policy questions. When millions of letters
were received, most of them highly critical
of the Maoist regime, the movement was
brought to a prompt halt and the most critical authors were rounded up and interned in
"reeducation" camps.
xix. Lines from Brassens's song "Les Fu-
nérailles d'antan" (The Funerals of Long
Ago), ca. 1956.
1. The quote is from Pascal's *Pensées* #593
(note that the numbering is different in
some editions).
2. *Spanish Civil War* (1936–1939): In
July 1936 the fascistic general Francisco
Franco (supported by Hitler and Mussolini) launched a military uprising against
the recently elected Popular Front government. The latter, fearing genuine popular
autonomy, had refused to arm the people,
thereby enabling Franco's forces to rapidly take over half of the country. Seeing
no alternative, the anarchist-oriented workers and peasants bypassed the government,
seized arms, and themselves took up the
fight against Franco—a process that rapidly
overflowed into a widespread and very radical social revolution. The Spanish Communist Party did everything in its power to
crush this revolution, in the name of unity
in the struggle against Franco (who ultimately prevailed anyway, in part due to the
demoralization resulting from the Stalinists' vicious attacks on the popular revolution). The best general history is Burnett
Bolloten's *The Spanish Civil War*. See also

Sam Dolgoff (ed.), *The Anarchist Collectives: Workers' Self-Management in the
Spanish Revolution 1936–1939.*
   Poumistas: members of the POUM
(*Partido Obrero de Unificación Marxista/*
Workers Party for Marxist Unification),
a revolutionary Marxist party allied with
the anarchists, opposed to Stalinism, and
somewhat at odds with Trotskyism. During
the Spanish Civil War the Poumistas were
hunted down and killed or imprisoned by
the Stalinists. George Orwell's *Homage to
Catalonia* is an account of his experiences
fighting in the POUM militia.
   workers councils: The council form was
invented by striking workers during the
1905 Russian revolution (*soviet* is the Russian word for "council"). When soviets reappeared in 1917, they were successively
supported, manipulated, dominated and
coopted by the Bolsheviks, who soon succeeded in transforming them into parodies
of themselves: rubber stamps of the "Soviet
State." Workers councils have nevertheless continued to reappear spontaneously
at the most radical moments in subsequent
history, in Germany, Italy, Spain, Hungary
and elsewhere (including the 1945 Hongai-
Campha "Commune" in Vietnam), because
they represent the obvious solution to the
need for a practical form of nonhierarchical
popular self-organization. The classic work
on the subject is Anton Pannekoek's *Workers' Councils.*
   Bavaria: Following the surrender of Germany at the end of World War I (November 1918), the Bavarian region of Germany
overthrew its local monarchy and declared
itself an independent state, with independent socialist Kurt Eisner as Prime Minister supported by councils of workers and
soldiers. Eisner's assassination in February
1919 was followed by a chaotic and rapidly
changing succession of more or less radical regimes, including a short-lived "Councilist Republic" whose leaders included anarchists Erich Mühsam, Gustav Landauer,
Ernst Toller and Ret Marut (B. Traven). It
was militarily crushed in May 1919 by the

German "Socialist" government.

Kronstadt: In March 1921 the sailors of Kronstadt, who had been among the most ardent participants in the 1917 Russian revolution, revolted against the Communist government, calling for a genuine power of popular democratic soviets as opposed to the rule of the "Soviet State." Denounced as reactionaries, they were crushed by the Communist regime. See Ida Mett's *The Kronstadt Uprising* and Paul Avrich's *Kronstadt 1921.*

Hungary: In 1956 the people of Hungary revolted against the Russian-imposed Stalinist regime. Though the movement was nominally in favor of a reform government under Imre Nagy, a nationwide network of workers councils was the real power in the country, until it was crushed by the invading Russian army. See Andy Anderson's *Hungary '56.*

The Marx quote is from "Critical Notes on the Article 'The King of Prussia and Social Reform' " (1844).

3. *Sûreté:* French colonial Security Police, in charge of investigating criminal and political offenses.

coolie: Roughly equivalent to "day laborer," "coolie" was the common term, used by the Chinese and Vietnamese as well as their colonial rulers, for the lowest-level workers. Unskilled and illiterate, they were paid the bare minimum for hard physical labor.

Annamite: Following the tradition of the previous Chinese rulers, the French referred to the entire indigenous Vietnamese population as "Annamites," although Annam was only one of three Vietnam regions in French Indochina (see p. 239). The term was still widely used during the period described in this book, although it was tending to be replaced by "Vietnamese" during the 1930s and 1940s.

4. Of the confiscated books, Paul Gentizon's *Mustapha Kémal ou l'Orient en marche* (Mustafa Kemal, or The Orient on the Move) (1929) is about the Turkish nationalist leader Kemal Ataturk. Georges

Garros's *Forceries humaines* (Human Hothouses) (1926) is about early anticolonial struggles in Vietnam. Marx and Engels's *Communist Manifesto* (1847) is a crucial historical document that has little connection with the "Communist" parties of the twentieth century. Leon Trotsky's *The Permanent Revolution* (1929) expounded his view that the bourgeoisie in Russia, and in other even more underdeveloped countries, would be unable (or unwilling) to carry out a "bourgeois democratic revolution," and that therefore the proletariat would need to take the lead to accomplish such a goal; and that in so doing, it would push things beyond the bourgeois stage. Louis Roubaud's *Vietnam: la tragédie indochinoise* (Vietnam: The Indochinese Tragedy) (1931) is a denunciation of colonial repression. John Reed's *Ten Days That Shook the World* (1922) is a firsthand account of the Russian Revolution. The Marx biography is probably David Riazanov's *Karl Marx and Friedrich Engels: An Introduction to Their Lives and Works* (1927). Sun Yat-sen (1866–1925) was a leader of the Chinese revolution of 1911 and the founder of the Guomindang (Chinese Nationalist Party). Erich Maria Remarque's *All Quiet on the Western Front* (1928) is an antiwar novel about World War I. Silvio Pellico's *My Prisons* (1833) is an account of ten years in Italian prisons.

5. *Central Prison* (*Maison Centrale,* literally "Central House"): the main Saigon prison.

9. Lines from Victor Hugo's poem "Dicté après juillet 1830" (Dictated After July 1830), about the 1830 revolution.

10. Ngo Van was very big by Vietnamese standards (six feet tall), so average-size clothes would not fit him.

11. Unless otherwise indicated, "League" always refers to the League of Internationalist Communists, the Trotskyist group founded by Lu Sanh Hanh, Ngo Van and Trinh Van Lau in 1935, destroyed in 1939, and revived in 1945. In contrast to the "legal Trotskyists" of the *La Lutte* group, who took part in elections and registered their publications, the LIC was an illegal group which focused on underground organizing and clandestine publications.

12. In May 1936 a Popular Front government (an alliance of Socialist, Communist, and other more or less center-left parties) was elected in France. Its inception was accompanied by a nationwide wave of strikes and factory occupations.

17. *notables:* wealthy, literate or respected local "worthies." Councils of notables were the administrative power in the peasant communities under the old imperial regime and continued under the French colonial regime to serve as the lowest rung of the administration, collecting taxes, rounding up conscripts, dispensing justice for minor crimes, etc.

18. *Poulo Condore* (a.k.a. Con Son Island): an island lying off the coast of southern Vietnam. In 1861 the French colonial government built a penal colony there to hold political prisoners. In 1954 it was turned over to the South Vietnamese government, which continued to use it for the same purpose. It attained international notoriety in July 1970 when American congressional representatives, following a map drawn by a former inmate, broke away from the official guided tour and uncovered horrendous ill-treatment of prisoners. Photographs of some of the horrors ("tiger cages," torture-caused mutilations, etc.) appeared in *Life* magazine and contributed to the growing American opposition to the Vietnam War.

20. In traditional Vietnamese families the first child is referred to as number Two, to fool the evil spirits who would like to make off with the firstborn. Ngo Van's narrative mentions Sister Two, Sister Five, Brother Seven (all from a previous marriage), Brother Ten, Brother Twelve and Brother Thirteen (Van himself, the youngest), so there were a total of twelve children in his family. The ones not mentioned had either died young or grown up and moved away (as had Sister Two and Sister Five). Brother Ten was tortured to death by the French in 1946.

26. *vu:* short for *vu et approuvé* (seen and approved). The French word would seem "cabalistic" (mysterious) to the Vietnamese children.

27. *capitation tax:* a personal tax imposed on each adult individual, regardless of income. Though trivial for the rich or middle classes, it amounted to a significant portion of a poor person's wages and a virtual impossibility for peasants living largely outside the money economy.

30. Lady Hieu's banyan tree, planted in memory of a generous rich lady who lived near Ngo Van's village, provided shade for women returning from the market under the hot sun. See Ngo Van and Hélène Fleury's *Contes d'autrefois du Vietnam,* pp. 80–81.

40. Slightly abridged passage from Baudelaire's Preface to Pierre Dupont's *Chants et chansons* (1849).

41. *Constitutionalist Party:* a very moderate reformist tendency that began in 1917 as a loose interest group of merchants, landowners, bureaucrats and journalists, and that became an officially recognized political party ca. 1923. It sought liberalization of certain laws and increased status for a small elite of Vietnamese bourgeois and officials under French rule, but opposed demands for national independence or significant social reforms. Its main leader, Bui Quang Chieu, had a horror of mass democracy, to say nothing of mass action. The notion of granting voting rights and access to French citizenship to a somewhat larger segment of the population caused him to "shudder at the thought of admitting undesirables into the great French family: people without means of livelihood and without culture. . . . I cannot help being seriously disturbed when I think that if, by some extraordinary measures, mass naturalization was decreed in Cochinchina, the result of a legislative election could depend on the vote of our cooks and rickshaw boys." The fact that the colonists (for whom De La Chevrotière was one of the leading spokesmen) could view such timid reformists as dangerously radical gives some measure of how reactionary the French colonial system was.

Phan Chau Trinh: On Phan Chau Trinh and the other early anticolonial leader, Phan Boi Chau, see Note 155.

43. The quote is from Jean-Jacques Rousseau's *Discourse on the Origin of Inequality* (1754).

Richepin's *La Chanson des Gueux* (1876) was considered so immoral and obscene that the author, publisher and printer were each sentenced to a month in prison. The *gueux* were not only tramps but the down-and-out in general—beggars, pickpockets, vagabonds, homeless street people, etc.

44. Phan Van Truong's *Une histoire de conspirateurs annamites à Paris* (1928) was reprinted with an Introduction by Ngo Van (L'Insomniaque, 2003). The quotation is from pp. 20–21 of that edition.

45. *"Nguyen An Ninh Secret Society":* The existence of this supposed secret society remains doubtful. Most of the "evidence" for it (stories of bizarre initiation rites, etc.) was concocted by the Sûreté and produced by torture, and even most of the peasants who were tortured denied any such affiliation. On the other hand, it is hard to imagine that Nguyen An Ninh's wanderings through the countryside did not have some subversive aims. In 1926 he had made public statements to the effect that he was inclining toward a more spiritual path and had expressed interest in the recently formed Cao Dai sect. In early 1928 he shaved his head like a Buddhist monk and began traveling by bicycle from village to village selling a medicinal balm that he had concocted. Though he himself does not seem to have done any "organizing," his comrades may have done so among the peasants who gathered around to meet him and listen to his talks; or other underground groups may have used his name as a rallying symbol to enhance their own appeal; or there may simply have been loose associations among people who shared a sympathy with him and his "teachings." After refuting most of the evidence for the existence of such a se-

cret society, Ngo Van noted that "Ninh inspired the peasants with a quasi-mystical confidence; many of them felt ready to follow him without knowing exactly where or how. . . . He had succeeded in creating a virtual peasant movement, though one far removed from a disciplined and structured organization" (*Vietnam 1920–1945*, p. 95). See also Hue-Tam Ho Tai's *Radicalism and the Origins of the Vietnamese Revolution*, pp. 186–195.

Bazin: A detailed account of the assassination (Hoang Van Dao's *Viet Nam Quoc Dan Dang: A Contemporary History of a National Struggle, 1927–1954*, pp. 35–41) gives the name as René Bazin. Most Web references give Hervé Bazin, but this may be simply a case of an erroneous mention in Wikipedia being endlessly repeated.

46. *40% death rate:* Although this may seem improbably high, official sources confirm that very high death rates were common. For example, the Phu Rieng plantation supervisors informed the French Colonial Minister that 17 percent of their workers died in 1927, and this was undoubtedly a conservative figure since the supervisors had an interest in covering up as many of the deaths as possible. Reliable studies indicate that many of the plantations had an *average* annual death rate of over 20 percent.

Yen Bai revolt (1930): This revolt was instigated by the Viet Nam Quoc Dan Dang (National Party of Vietnam), a radical nationalist organization founded in Hanoi in 1927 by the young teacher Nguyen Thai Hoc. By the following year it had 1500 members organized into 120 clandestine cells. Its violent audacity alarmed the colonial regime, but soon brought about its downfall. The 1929 assassination of Bazin by a renegade VNQDD member led to numerous arrests; the defeat of the Yen Bai revolt a year later led to the group's virtual annihilation. Nguyen Thai Hoc and twelve other leaders were guillotined and hundreds of other members were captured and given heavy sentences. The VNQDD never really

Nguyen Thai Hoc

recovered from this blow, though remnants of the group escaped to southern China and returned to Vietnam fifteen years later in the aftermath of World War II, fighting in the ranks of the "Third Division" that appears in Chapter 7.

48. Names in parentheses usually refer to provinces. "Hanh Lam (Thanh Chuong)" thus means the town or village of Hanh Lam in the province of Thanh Chuong. Note also that most of the events described in this book took place in Cochinchina (the southern region of Vietnam) unless it is specifically indicated that they took place in Annam (the central region) or Tonkin (the northern region).

50. *Indochinese Communist Party:* This name was imposed by the Comintern in the hope of eventually including insurgent groups from Laos and Cambodia, but in reality the ICP was always almost exclusively Vietnamese.

52. *"Moscow trainees" (retours de Moscou,* literally "returnees from Moscow"): radicals who had spent time in Moscow being trained as cadres for the Communist Party.

55. *restricted residence (interdiction de séjour):* an order specifying that someone had to live in a particular place or was banned from particular places.

56. *Saigon City Council:* In order to create the appearance of democracy in Cochinchina, the French colonial regime established a few "representative" bodies such as municipal and colonial councils. These bodies had very limited powers, and in any case only a tiny percentage of property-owning natives were allowed to vote, so the allotted portion of indigenous representatives tended to be fairly conservative.

60. *invitation au voyage* (invitation to travel): title of a Baudelaire poem (1854).

67. Line from Baudelaire's poem "Moesta et errabunda" (Sad and Restless) (1855).

77. *Moscow Trials* (1936–1938): notorious frameups, now universally discredited, in which many of the original leaders of the Bolshevik Party gave false and often obviously absurd "confessions" and were then shot. Trotsky (then in exile) was considered the arch villain and was tried in absentia. The other old Bolsheviks confessed to conspiring with him and with Wall Street or the Nazis or the Japanese imperial government to assassinate Stalin, sabotage Russian production, etc. The trials helped Stalin get rid of potential rivals and discourage any resistance to his power; but the idea that the majority of the original leaders of the October revolution had been plotting against the "Soviet regime" for years was so obviously absurd that it disillusioned countless Communist Party members and sympathizers around the world.

Indochinese Congress movement (1936–1937): an attempt to take advantage of the election of the Popular Front government in France by organizing popular action committees throughout Indochina, which would send delegates to meet in a congress in Saigon to present demands for improving conditions in Indochina. The idea turned out to be very popular and hundreds of committees were organized, but the colonial regime suppressed the movement before any congress could convene.

79. *Auprès de ma blonde:* popular French song dating from the seventeenth century.

Le Temps du mépris (Days of Contempt): 1935 novel about a Communist militant imprisoned in a Nazi concentration camp.

81. Céline's *Voyage au bout de la nuit* was published in 1932. The passages quoted are from Ralph Manheim's translation (*Journey to the End of the Night,* New Directions, 1983, pp. 56–57, 193–194, 345) with a few slight modifications. The last two lines are from a 1913 popular song.

86. *Lenin's "Testament":* letter written during Lenin's last illness in December 1922 to the Russian Communist Party, stating his views on how the regime should proceed following his death. The letter featured a sharp attack on Stalin's brutality and deceitfulness and urged his removal from the position of General Secretary of the Party. It also criticized Trotsky's bureaucratic tendencies. The "Testament" was suppressed by the Stalinists and officially acknowledged only in 1956 by Khrushchev.

90. The renowned writer André Gide had sympathized with Communism, but following a visit to the USSR in 1936 he expressed his disillusionment in *Return from the USSR* (1936) and *Afterthoughts on the USSR* (1937).

101. Quotation from Victor Hugo's play *Ruy Blas* (1838).

112. *Vichy government* (1940–1944): a fascistic puppet state in the southeastern area of France which remained nominally independent after the defeat of French forces by Nazi Germany. Marshal Philippe Pétain was head of state, and his government cooperated with the Nazis who had occupied the rest of the country.

116. The Indochina colonial administration was pro-Vichy, so the Japanese occupation forces had felt comfortable leaving it in place. After the defeat of the Vichy regime in France (August 1944), the colonial administration's loyalty to Japan became much more doubtful, particularly in the event of an Allied invasion. The Japanese thus felt obliged to take over the direct administration of Indochina and to preempt a potential French rebellion.

Bao Dai: the last emperor of Vietnam. During the Japanese occupation he "ruled" as a Japanese puppet. In 1945 he went into exile, then returned in 1949 to rule as a French puppet during the Indochina War. In 1955 he was ousted by his prime minister, Ngo Dinh Diem, and emigrated to France.

122. *Nam Bo* ("South Country"): another name for Cochinchina, the southern part of Vietnam.

124. *"Third Division":* an independent nationalist anticolonialist army including surviving members of the VNQDD and led by Nguyen Hoa Hiep. The Division sometimes had as many as 15,000 men and successfully fought both the French and the Vietminh from late 1945 to early 1946. It was eventually forced to disband and disperse into the population, in part because the Vietminh had begun providing the French with information on its locations and movements.

127. *Gurkhas:* Nepalese soldiers serving in the British colonial army.

138. *"Ta Thu Thau's group":* It is unclear what group this refers to.

Tran Van Thach's final note: This photocopy was sent to Ngo Van by Tran Van Thach's son. It reads: "Brother Two: I leave my children in your hands. Please take care of them. 22–10–45."

145. The Indochina War—the war between the Vietnamese (primarily the Vietminh once it had destroyed all the rival opposition forces) and the French—is usually considered to have begun in December 1946, but there were preliminary maneuvers and skirmishes during the previous year. The Vietminh received aid from Russia and China (after the Chinese Stalinists' victory in 1949), and the French were largely supported by the United States. The war ended in 1954 with the defeat of the French at Dien Bien Phu. At the Geneva Conference in July 1954, Vietnam, Cambodia and Laos were granted independence. Vietnam was temporarily partitioned between the North (ruled by the Vietminh) and the South (ruled by Emperor Bao Dai) pending a nationwide election that would unify the country. After deposing Bao Dai, South Vietnam president Ngo Dinh Diem refused to go through with such an election, being aware that the Vietminh would easily win it. When the Vietcong (a new incarnation of the Vietminh) began attacking Diem's dictatorship in the late 1950s, the United States backed Diem with money, arms, advisors, and eventually hundreds of thousands of troops. This Second Indochina War (1960–1975), more commonly known as the Vietnam War, was ultimately won by the guerrilla forces of the Vietcong and the regular army of North Vietnam.

148. *World Without Visa* (1947): novel about an international group of exiles stuck in Vichy France during World War II. The author, Jean Malaquais, later took part in the Council Communist Group mentioned on p. 203.

153. *"October" group:* So called from its 1931–1932 journal *Thang Muoi* (October). Although this is the only use of this term in the present book, in other accounts (particularly Trotskyist ones concerned with retrospectively distinguishing the correct or incorrect lines of different groups) "the October group" or "the October tendency" is often used in a loose general way to refer to the ongoing tendency around Ho Huu Tuong, which is contrasted with the *La Lutte* group. In this broad sense, the "October" tendency is seen as including the League of Internationalist Communists for the Construction of the Fourth International (1935–1939), the Bolshevik-Leninists for the Construction of the Fourth International (1936), the journal *Le Militant* (1936–1937), the revived journal *Thang Muoi* (1938–1939), the bulletin *Thay Tho* (1938), the Saigon paper *Tia Sang* (1939), and the revived League of Internationalist Communists (1945–1946). These groups and publications criticized the *La Lutte* group for its accommodations with the Stalinists and tended to put more stress on underground grassroots agitation; but the two tendencies also overlapped and collaborated in many

regards. This is probably why Ngo Van, though pointing out particular tactical differences in particular circumstances, did not use the "October group" label, so as not to present the history as a simplistic stuggle between two distinct rival currents.

155. *Phan Boi Chau* (1867–1940): pioneering anticolonial leader. In 1904 he founded the Vietnam Modernization Society, whose goal was to drive the French from Indochina and establish a constitutional monarchy under the rebel prince Cuong De. The following year he and Cuong De slipped out of the country and went to Japan, which was at that time seen as a possible model for East Asian independence (it had achieved an impressive modernization during the Meiji Era and had just won the Russo-Japanese war of 1904–1905). The Japanese authorities did not offer any direct aid for Phan Boi Chau's military schemes, but tentatively allowed him to organize an "Eastern Study Movement," which brought more than two hundred Vietnamese students to Japan to learn about modern developments there and elsewhere in the outside world, to meet insurgents from China and other Asian countries, and to be able to discuss anticolonial strategies without censorship or fear of arrest. Under French diplomatic pressure they were all expelled from Japan in 1909. Phan Boi Chau relocated to Siam and then to China. The 1911 Chinese revolution influenced him to go beyond monarchism and in 1912 he formed the Vietnam Restoration Society, dedicated to establishing a democratic republic by means of armed struggle. Over the next few years this organization carried out or inspired a number of assassinations and abortive revolts in Vietnam, and Phan Boi Chau was sentenced to death in absentia. In 1925 he was kidnapped in Shanghai, brought back to Vietnam and sentenced to hard labor for life. Pardoned by Governor-General Varenne, he lived under house arrest in Hue until his death.

Phan Boi Chau had made some significant breaks from previous anticolonial revolts, which had generally been limited to

Phan Boi Chau

reactionary nativist perspectives (appeals for loyalty to the Emperor and for the restoration of the Confucian feudal system). But his social awareness was minimal, his foreign-based organizations failed to generate any sustained movement within Vietnam, and his schemes to elicit support from other countries invariably fell through. His influence was primarily as an inspiring symbol of perseverance in the struggle for national independence.

He can be contrasted in many ways with his slightly younger contemporary *Phan Chau Trinh* (1872–1926). While Phan Boi Chau focused exclusively on driving out the French without paying much attention to social questions and was until late in his life quite willing to use monarchism as a rallying point, Phan Chau Trinh was sharply opposed to monarchism and to the whole mandarin feudal system and wished to use certain aspects of French culture to challenge that system and revolutionize traditional Vietnamese society (he was a great admirer of Rousseau and Montesquieu). Phan Chau Trinh was also dubious about the advisability of violent struggle against the far superior French forces, and

favored a more gradual strategy centered on education and cultural issues. Phan Boi Chau pointed out that despite France's pretense of "civilizing" the natives, its colonial system brutally repressed any potentially subversive education, resisting even rather minimal attempts to foster literacy, let alone any dissemination of the values of the French Enlightenment. Phan Chau Trinh was all too aware of that brutality (he had done time at Poulo Condore), but he noted that the scattered attempts at violent resistance encouraged by Phan Boi Chau's groups had led to nothing but horrendous repression and demoralization.

It should be noted, however, that the two leaders' strategies were complementary as well as contradictory. Phan Boi Chau's organizations had close connections with "free schools" and "culture centers" within Vietnam, which spread knowledge of modern subjects such as science, geography and history to thousands of ordinary people and which also served as centers for public discussion and popular drama and as libraries and publishers, disseminating subversive poems, songs, satires, and translations of Western works. The most popular speaker at these centers was Phan Chau Trinh (before he was imprisoned and then exiled to France).

Phan Chau Trinh's challenging of traditional values undoubtedly had a significant influence on the multifaceted cultural ferment of the 1920s; yet his death in 1926 ironically served as a catalyst for more direct political confrontations of the sort that he had tried to avoid—confrontations which were at the same time far more socially complex than the militaristic attacks that had been envisaged by Phan Boi Chau.

For an informative account of this early period, see David Marr's *Vietnamese Anticolonialism 1885–1925*.

162. *famine:* In 1944 and 1945 between one and two million people died of starvation in Tonkin and northern Annam. This was partly due to bad weather and to the war, but also to the fact that Governor-General

Decoux had hoarded over 500,000 barrels of rice for profitable export.

168. *"the first printed . . . publication":* a reminder of the difficulties of radical publication under the colonial regime. Most leaflets, newsletters, etc., were secretly produced by various crude forms of mimeographing.

169. *1929 . . . Indochinese Communist Party:* In 1929 several different "communist" groups or tendencies existed in various regions of Vietnam, including the Thanh Nien, an "Annam Communist Party" and an "Indochinese Communist Party." In 1930 most of these groups merged to form the Vietnam Communist Party. On Comintern orders, this name was changed to Indochinese Communist Party (see Note 50). The 1929 Indochinese Communist Party referred to here was the earlier group.

174. Naville and Rousset had abandoned the Trotskyist party on the grounds that the Stalinists were carrying out the revolution through their postwar takeover of East Europe and had thereby undermined the basis of the Trotskyist positions. Nguyen Van Linh implied that he and his comrades had not endured the brutal struggles against the Stalinists only to capitulate to them on such a bizarre and flimsy "theoretical" basis.

179. Quotation from *Chinh Phu Ngam* (Lament of a Soldier's Wife), an eighteenth-century poem by Dang Tran Con.

184. For reasons both personal and political, Ngo Van said very little about his family in his published writings. By the time he emigrated to France he had become estranged from the partner mentioned on p. 108. He had three children: son Do (born 1932), daughter Oanh (born 1935), and son Da (born 1943). Da joined Van in France in 1956. Do was among the "boat people" who escaped from Vietnam during the late 1970s (he too came to France). Oanh stayed in Vietnam and did not see her father again until 1997, during the trip mentioned in Hélène Fleury's introductory essay.

185. *Au pays d'Héloïse* consists of several fragmentary chapters. The excerpts translated in the present book have been rearranged and in a few cases condensed. This paragraph, for example, is a very brief summary of a several-page account in the original book about the tribulations of Vietnamese drafted into European service during World War II. Ngo Van's friend Dang Van Long later wrote a whole book on the topic: *Nguoi Viet o Phap 1940–1954* (The Vietnamese in France, 1940–1954) (Paris: TS Nghien Cuu, 1997).

188. Lines from Baudelaire's poem "L'Horloge" (The Clock) (1860).

189. Quotation from Marx's *The Poverty of Philosophy* (1847), Chapter 1, Part 2.

195. Source of quotation unknown.

201. *Maximilien Rubel* (1905–1996): Born in what is now Ukraine, Rubel emigrated to Vienna, then to France in 1931. He was noted for his numerous works reexamining Marx's actual writings and positions, as opposed to those of the various movements claiming to be "Marxist." In articles such as "Marx as a Theorist of Anarchism," he showed how the state-socialist currents (Leninism, Trotskyism, Stalinism, social democracy, etc.) are inconsistent with Marx's perspective, and in particular how the Bolshevik seizure of state power in 1917 was quite the contrary of the autonomous activity of the working class envisaged by Marx. After Rubel's death, Ngo Van published a small book in memory of their years of friendship and shared struggles: *Avec Maximilien Rubel, une amitié, une lutte 1954–1996.*

203. *ICO:* Founded in 1958 (originally under the name *Informations et Liaisons Ouvrières*), ICO stemmed from a split in the *Socialisme ou Barbarie* group. After the dissolution of ICO in 1973, some of its participants, including Ngo Van, carried on similar activities and publications in the "Échanges et Mouvement" network, which was formed in 1975 and is still active.

204. *"Little Red Book": Quotations from Chairman Mao.* Ngo Van later wrote a critique of this collection and of Maoism in general (see Bibliography, p. 248).

207. CFDT (*Confédération Française Démocratique du Travail*/French Democratic Confederation of Labor): socialist-leaning national labor union.

208. CGT (*Confédération Générale du Travail*/General Confederation of Labor): national labor union dominated by the French Communist Party.

210. *"know how to end a strike":* In 1936, during the strikes accompanying the election of the Popular Front, Communist Party leader Maurice Thorez declared, "We must recognize when it's time to terminate a strike if our demands are met, and when it's time to consent to a compromise if not all of them are won." The French expression, *"Il faut savoir terminer une grève,"* can also be understood as "We must know how to end a strike," and ever since that time this accidental confession of union bureaucrats' actual conservative role has been sarcastically evoked by radical workers.

Grenelle Accords: an agreement negotiated May 25–27, 1968, at the Ministry of Social Affairs on Rue de Grenelle in Paris by Jacques Chirac (representing the government), Georges Séguy (representing the labor unions), and the French Confederation of Business Enterprises (representing the bosses). The agreement, which called for a 25% increase in the minimum wage, a 10% increase in average real wages, and some other benefits, was rejected by the rank-and-file workers.

Waldeck-Rochet: head of the French Communist Party.

Communards: partisans of the Paris Commune (1871). *Versailles:* seat of the French Third Republic government that massacred the Communards.

211. *UNEF (Union Nationale des Étudiants de France):* French National Student Union.

March 22nd Movement: eclectic radical student organization created on March 22, 1968. The anarchist Daniel Cohn-Bendit was its most famous spokesperson, but it also included Trotskyists, Maoists, etc.

219. *Tet Offensive:* A nationally coordinated military campaign launched by the Vietcong on January 30, 1968 (Vietnamese New Year). Although the campaign was very costly in Vietcong lives, it succeeded in shocking and demoralizing the American public, making it more difficult for the American government to claim that victory was just around the corner.

220. Allusion to the International War Crimes Tribunal (1966–1967) organized by Bertrand Russell and Jean-Paul Sartre.

221. The "popular sentiment" was a widespread anti-Americanism, not only on the part of French Communist Party supporters but also by President de Gaulle, who was striving to carve out an independent position (e.g. by withdrawing France from NATO) and in the process aligning France closer to the Communist bloc.

NOTE ON STALINISM
AND TROTSKYISM

For those who are not familiar with the international political background of Ngo Van's story, it may be helpful to make a few remarks about Stalinism and Trotskyism and to outline some of the twists and turns of the Third International under Stalin's control.

The Russian Revolution of 1917 consisted of two relatively distinct stages. The "February revolution" was a series of largely spontaneous popular struggles beginning in February and continuing over the next several months; the "October revolution" was essentially a coup d'état carried out by the Bolshevik Party under the leadership of Lenin and Trotsky. The Bolsheviks had a reputation as radical revolutionaries, due in part to their having been one of the few leftist groups to oppose World War I; but once in power they repressed grassroots radical tendencies and morphed into a new ruling class. Although they changed their name to "Communist Party" in 1918, the system they created had nothing to do with communism in the true sense of the word; it was simply a cruder and more concentrated version of capitalism. Private ownership was replaced by state ownership, but capitalism itself (the system of commodified social relations) was in no way eliminated. The workers who were formerly exploited by a multitude of private capitalists were now exploited by a single all-owning capitalist enterprise: the state. Although this process was complex and gradual, the transformation had become pretty clear by 1921 when the revolutionary Kronstadt sailors were crushed by the "Communist" regime under the direct leadership of Trotsky. (See Voline's *The Unknown Revolution* and Maurice Brinton's *The Bolsheviks and Workers' Control: 1917–1921*.)

Following Lenin's death in 1924, the Communist Party faction led by Stalin became increasingly powerful, to the point that Trotsky was put on the defensive and eventually expelled from the Party and forced into exile. Stalin then imposed the various internal totalitarian developments which will not be discussed here since they are generally well known—police-state dictatorship, forced collectivization, Gulag labor camps, show trials, etc. (Good accounts of this process include Boris Souvarine's *Stalin: A Critical Survey of Bolshevism,* Ante Ciliga's *The Russian Enigma,* and Victor Serge's *Memoirs of a Revolutionary.*)

234

The Stalinist regime also exerted a malignant influence on radical movements in other countries all over the world. The Third International (a.k.a. Communist International or Comintern) had been formed in Moscow in 1919 to unite revolutionary communist parties around the world, after most of the socialist parties of the Second International had betrayed their socialist and internationalist principles by rallying to their respective governments during World War I. Under Stalin's control, the Comintern became increasingly centered on the goal of defending Stalin's regime at all costs. To this end, over the next two decades it imposed a succession of zigzagging policies on the subservient Communist parties in other countries, most of which worked out disastrously.

Following some "adventurist" debacles in the early 1920s (Germany 1923, Estonia 1924, etc.), the Comintern shifted to a defensive policy of compromises and alliances with various bourgeois forces around the world. The most dramatic failure of this policy was in China in 1925–1927. At the very moment when radical workers were attaining significant victories in the major cities of China, Stalin insisted that the Chinese Communist Party subordinate itself to the Guomindang, the nationalist party led by General Chiang Kai-shek. When the workers of Shanghai had taken over the city in April 1927, the Communist leaders thus urged them to welcome Chiang Kai-shek's army and to turn in all their weapons. When they did so, Chiang's army entered the city and massacred the radical workers by the thousands. (See Harold Isaacs's *The Tragedy of the Chinese Revolution*.) This catastrophic result of Stalin's policy, which Trotsky had accurately predicted and sought to prevent, was undoubtedly an important factor in accounting for the readiness of Vietnamese radicals to rally to Trotskyist positions in the following years.

In 1928 Stalin imposed another policy change, arguing that, after the initial post-World War I period of revolutionary upsurges (1917–1923) and then the ebbing, defensive period (1924–1928), the international workers' movement had entered a new "Third Period" in which radical revolutions were once again on the agenda. The primary enemy was now supposedly the socialist parties, which the Stalinists referred to as "social-fascists." Following this policy, the German Communist Party focused on attacking the German socialists while largely ignoring the Nazis, thereby helping pave the way for the Nazis' seizure of power in 1933 (which soon led to the destruction of both the socialists and Communists in Germany).

In 1935 the Comintern line flipped to an opposite extreme. Now it was supposedly necessary to ally with the socialists, and in fact with just about anyone who wasn't outrightly fascist, including centrist and even conservative parties, to form a "united front against fascism." This policy led to the victory of Popular Front governments in Spain and France in 1936. But the radical currents that had supported those fronts now found themselves compromised, their hands tied due to their alliances with more centrist forces. On the Spanish Popular Front, see Note 2. In France, the Popular Front government, pressured by a nationwide wave of strikes and factory occupations, passed some progressive legislation (40-hour week, paid vacations, right to strike, etc.), but did nothing to eliminate French colonialism and scarcely anything even to improve conditions in the colonies beyond a few minor reforms that were mostly not implemented. This put the Vietnamese Stalinists in the awkward position of having to defend the French colonial regime that they had been fighting so desperately for so long.

Then the Hitler-Stalin Pact of 1939 caused yet another zigzag. Now the focus was once again on the struggle against France, while the menace of fascism was played down (although Nazi Germany was on the verge of invading France and Japan was on the verge of invading Indochina).

Then, when Hitler double-crossed Stalin by invading Russia in 1941, it was once again a "war against fascism." The Vietnamese Stalinists thus once again found themselves allied with their French colonial masters (although the colonial regime in Indochina was pro-Vichy and thus more or less allied with the fascists).

Then, in the power vacuum following the defeat of the Japanese in 1945, at a time when the Vietnamese people were in a position to prevent any significant French forces from reentering the country (France was recovering from years of Nazi occupation and demoralized by the Vichy regime's collaboration with the Nazis, and most of its armed forces were half way around the world), the Stalinist leader Ho Chi Minh made a succession of compromises with the Americans, the British, the Chinese and the French, which enabled him to augment his power, destroy the Trotskyists and other potential rivals, and assume total control over the nationalist forces, but which at the same time enabled the French forces to reenter the country, thereby leading to thirty more years of war to obtain the national independence that might well have been won in 1945. Only in 1975 was the country finally liberated from its foreign masters—while remaining subject to an indigenous Stalinist dictatorship.

Most of these Stalinist policies had been sharply criticized by Trotsky. From around 1923–1934 Trotsky and his followers referred to themselves as the "Left Opposition," meaning an opposition within the Russian Communist Party, attempting to recapture power from the Stalinist faction so as to turn the party back into a revolutionary and internationalist direction. After being expelled from the Russian party in 1928, they turned their attention to Communist parties in other countries and to the Third International. This strategy proved equally unsuccessful as Trotskyist tendencies were systematically eliminated from the Stalin-dominated parties around the world. By 1933 or 1934 most Trotskyists had concluded that the Third International had gone hopelessly astray and that it was necessary to form a Fourth International. This took place in 1938 (which is why some interim groups such as Ngo Van's League of Internationalist Communists referred to themselves as "for the Construction of the Fourth International").

It would be far too tedious to discuss the complex differences among the numerous Trotskyist groups and tendencies from the 1930s to the present day. Suffice it to say that since Trotsky was himself directly implicated in the process of the Communist Party becoming a counterrevolutionary force within Russia, and since he never recognized that that party had evolved into a new bureaucratic ruling class, his attempts to push the party to resume a revolutionary international policy were bound to fail. "Trotsky was doomed by his basic perspective, because once the bureaucracy became aware that it had evolved into a counterrevolutionary class on the domestic front, it was bound to opt for a *similarly counterrevolutionary role* in other countries" (Guy Debord, *The Society of the Spectacle* #112). This is why Trotskyist polemics, however radical they may seem in some regards, always end up floundering back into the same lame conclusion: Stalinism is criticized in many ways, but in the final analysis it is still considered to be "progressive." Stalinist regimes are referred to as "degenerated workers' states" or "deformed workers' states," implying that the socio-economic system is basically fine, it's just that it is poorly guided by a faulty political leadership which needs to be replaced by a correct leadership à la Lenin and Trotsky. Trotskyists fail to recognize the origins of Stalinism in the earlier authoritarian practices of Lenin and Trotsky and in the hierarchical structure of the Bolshevik Party, which had already inaugurated the new state-capitalist system well before Stalin came to power.

It should be noted that none of these political tendencies have much connection with Marx, despite the fact that they all claim to be Marxist. One of the reasons that Ngo Van appreciated Maximilien Rubel was that he convincingly showed how Leninism and Trotskyism (to say nothing of Stalinism) diverge significantly from Marx's actual views. While Marx had well-known differences with some of the anarchists of his time, his perspective was in reality much closer to anarchism than to any of the varieties of state socialism. The prevalence of statist "Marxism" during the last century has tended to drown out other currents of Marxism that are closer to Marx (and to the more coherent strands of anarchism), such as Rosa Luxemburg, Anton Pannekoek, Karl Korsch, *Socialisme ou Barbarie,* and the Situationist International.

CHRONOLOGY

It is no exaggeration to say that a colonial war began the moment French troops landed in Indochina in 1859 and never stopped. Once established, the colonial regime engaged in an ongoing battle against the peasant and worker masses, who remained in open or latent revolt until the French and then the Americans were finally driven out more than a century later. The following chronology (mostly drawn from Ngo Van's *Vietnam 1920–1945* and from the British edition of an earlier text by Ngo Van, *Revolutionaries They Could Not Break*) mentions only a few of the more significant events in order to help orient the reader.

* * *

1615. Jesuit missionaries first set foot in Indochina. In order to facilitate the introduction of Christianity they create *quoc ngu,* a Romanized transcription of Vietnamese, to replace *chu nom,* the traditional Vietnamese writing system which used Chinese-style ideograms and which had not been generally accessible to the common people. As in many other regions, Christianity and trade prepare the way for eventual colonial conquest.

1857–1870. French emperor Napoleon III launches a "Catholic Crusade" on the pretext of protecting the Catholics persecuted by the Emperor of Vietnam, Tu Duc. Saigon is taken in 1859 and the port is opened to French merchant ships. Tu Duc calls on the people to resist the foreign invaders. Revolts spread throughout Cochinchina. The French respond with massacres and the process of annexation continues.

1870–1893. After the fall of Napoleon III (July 1870) and the crushing of the Paris Commune (May 1871), the French Third Republic resumes the conquest. In 1874 Tu Duc is forced to sign a treaty of "peace, friendship and perpetual alliance between France and the Kingdom of Annam" that obliges him to recognize French sovereignty over Cochinchina, to open the Red River for French commerce with China, and to open the ports of Qui Nhon, Haiphong and Hanoi.

Tonkin, however, is not yet subdued, and its conquest continues under the government of Jules Ferry (1880–1885). Ferry, one of the butchers of the Paris Commune, declares: "The superior races have the duty to civilize the

238

inferior races." He also notes that by a fortunate coincidence this noble duty will also generate some more mundane benefits: "Europe today can be considered as a commercial enterprise that is facing declining profits. European consumption is saturated; new sectors of consumers must be cultivated. . . . Colonies are the most advantageous investment opportunities for the capital of rich countries."

1893. France has now conquered all of what becomes known as French Indochina, consisting of Vietnam, Cambodia and Laos. The colonizers divide Vietnam into three regions: Tonkin in the north (capital: Hanoi), Annam in the center (capital: Hue), and Cochinchina in the south (capital: Saigon). Tonkin and Annam are protectorates (as are Cambodia and Laos); Cochinchina is a colony.

The "French-protected" Tonkinites and Annamites are formally left under the administration of the native rulers and subjected to feudal judicial regimes whose punishments include a whole range of tortures. The Cochinchinese, referred to as "French subjects," are under direct French administration and officially governed according to a modified version of the French Penal Code. In reality, however, they are subjected to the same sorts of arbitrary brutalities as those in the protectorates.

French profits are based on the exploitation of natural resources (coal, minerals, rubber, rice, cotton) and cheap labor. The country also serves as a monopoly market for industrial products manufactured in France.

In addition to the "normal" functioning of the economy, an incredible level of corruption prevails. Among numerous other schemes involving land purchases, construction contracts, etc., the colonial administrators often grant monopolies on particular products to themselves or their cronies, then impose consumption quotas on local populations to increase their profits.

The colonial domination undermines the feudal agrarian economy based on the so-called "Asiatic mode of production" by introducing capitalist production, thereby engendering new social classes comparable to those of the ruling country, though with certain different characteristics:

- The peasantry, which comprises the immense majority of the population, is exploited by the large landowners. Constantly on the verge of starvation, the mass of peasants are bled dry not only by native landowners but by the various taxes imposed by the colonial regime, especially the personal "capitation" tax.

- An agricultural proletariat develops in the ricefields, the domains allotted to large enterprises, rubber plantations, etc., and in the lands belonging to the Catholic Mission, working under contract-labor conditions that often verge on slavery. "The workers wake up at 3:00 a.m., assemble at 4:00 a.m., and work till nightfall. The worker is tied to a plantation for three years by a drastic contract that forbids him to work for any other employer during that period. Signing on at 0.40 piasters per day, he is unaware that after paying for his ration of rice, reimbursing his advances, and paying various fines, his net earnings at the end of the month turn out to be far less than the sum of his daily wages" (official report on the Mimot rubber plantation by Labor Inspector Delamarre, March 1928). The masters have the right of life and death over the workers, and the plantations generally have their own private prisons and dungeons.

- Alongside, there develops a totally new industrial proletariat in the mines and in the large companies of public works, electricity, cement, distilleries and transport. These workers have no organizations and no political experience, but gradually become radicalized, especially in the cities.

- The European and Chinese bourgeoisie lead and dominate the native bourgeoisie.

- The native bourgeoisie and landowners support the colonial regime, to which they owe their prosperity.

- A large part of the native petty bourgeoisie is incorporated into the administrative and military apparatus.

1904. Phan Boi Chau founds the Vietnam Modernization Society, aimed at expelling the French and establishing a constitutional monarchy under the rebel prince Cuong De. The following year he and Cuong De escape to Japan, where they unsuccessfully attempt to enlist Japanese aid.

1912. Phan Boi Chau, now in exile in China, founds the Vietnam Restoration Society, which incites several assassinations and abortive revolts in Vietnam.

1920s. A group of Vietnamese emigrants in Paris are referred to by their compatriots as "The Five Dragons": Phan Chau Trinh, Phan Van Truong, Nguyen The Truyen, Nguyen An Ninh and Nguyen Ai Quoc (hereafter referred to as "Ho Chi Minh," the name he adopted in 1942). Though of diverse backgrounds and perspectives, their denunciations of colonial subjugation and their determination to liberate their country lay the groundwork for the "Indochinese revolution" of the 1930s.

All of them return to Vietnam and openly defy the colonial regime except for Ho Chi Minh, who remains outside the country, shuttling between Moscow and China (he does not return until 1941). Meanwhile, the French Communist Party sends a number of other emigrant Vietnamese students to Moscow to be trained as professional revolutionaries. They will become the Stalinist cadres of the future Indochinese Communist Party.

1923–1926. In Cochinchina, Nguyen An Ninh publishes *La Cloche Fêlée,* with the ironic subtitle: "Journal for the Propagation of French Ideas." Seeing Vietnam as smothered by oppressive surveillance, he urges those who can to visit France or at least to become familiar with its best traditions, so as to enlarge their horizons. In his view, although France is the source of colonial oppression, there is also a spirit of liberation to be found in the land of the Enlightenment, the Revolution and the Paris Commune.

1925. In Canton, China, under the patronage of the Third International, Ho Chi Minh founds the Thanh Nien Cach Mang Dong Chi Hoi (Revolutionary Youth League). Members are given rigorous ideological and practical training in China, then sent back to Vietnam. The Thanh Nien takes root primarily among the peasantry, spreading from the North to the South.

1927. In Hanoi a group of radical teachers and students form the Viet Nam Quoc Dan Dang (VNQDD/National Party of Vietnam), whose goal is to expel the French from Indochina, overthrow the native feudal system and set up a democratic republic. As means, they advocate conspiracy, military plots and terrorism.

February 1930. Revolt of the infantry of Yen Bai (in Tonkin), instigated by the VNQDD. The revolt is drowned in blood and the VNQDD is virtually annihilated.

The Thanh Nien merges with other similar groupings to form the Indochinese Communist Party (ICP).

May 1930 through early 1931. Thousands of peasants march to administrative centers to demand the lowering of the capitation tax and the abolition of forced labor. The colonial regime responds by firing into the unarmed crowds. The peasants shift to more insurrectionary actions, attacking military posts and police stations, releasing prisoners, looting markets, destroying tax records and executing particularly hated notables. In the Nghe An and Ha Tinh provinces of Annam, they organize themselves into "soviets," seizing land and distributing stockpiled food. These movements are largely spontaneous, but many involve significant ICP participation and influence. In the repression that follows, thousands of peasants are massacred, thousands more are imprisoned, and the ICP is severely damaged.

1930–1932. Inside the ICP various oppositional tendencies criticize the constantly shifting Moscow-directed policies in which the Party's popular base serves only as pawns for mass actions. These tendencies rally to the "Left Opposition" positions of Trotsky and his followers, demanding independence and social revolution, land to the peasants and factories to the workers; whereas the ICP calls for independence first, with socialism to follow at some later stage. Among these oppositional currents is a group formed in Saigon in 1931 by Vietnamese students expelled from France. It is this group that Ngo Van joins in 1932.

April–May 1933. The trials of 21 activists of the Left Opposition and of 121 members of the ICP bring a temporary halt to the underground movement, most of the leaders being in prison or deported to forced-labor sites.

On the occasion of the Saigon City Council election, the Stalinists and Trotskyists still at liberty come together to create the weekly newspaper *La Lutte,* agreeing to refrain from mutual criticism in order to jointly confront the colonial regime on the legal terrain. This astonishing and unprecedented alliance (considering that in Russia and everywhere else in the world the Stalinist parties are calling for the extermination of Trotskyists) comes about in part because Ho Chi Minh and the upper Stalinist bureaucracy remain outside the country with little possibility of directly controlling the rank-and-file party members within it; in part because the Vietnamese Trotskyists have stronger roots among the workers than do the Stalinists, making it difficult for the latter to employ their usual tactics; and in part because the partisans on both sides have shared extremely difficult conditions of struggle and are anxious to create some breathing room for themselves.

1935. After the Laval-Stalin Pact allying France and Russia, the ICP, following in the footsteps of the French Communist Party, no longer speaks of class struggle or of combating French imperialism. The Trotskyists in the *La Lutte* group, bound by their united-front agreement with the Stalinists, remain silent. In protest against this surrender of principle, Lu Sanh Hanh, Ngo Van and Trinh Van Lau found the League of Internationalist Communists for the Construction of the Fourth International, and in a clandestine paper, *Tien Dao,* denounce *La Lutte*'s accommodation with the Stalinist betrayal.

1936–1937. The Popular Front takes power in France, but declares its intention to maintain France's colonial empire. In Vietnam, widespread action committees strive to convene an "Indochinese Congress" that will present their demands to the Popular Front. These committees are soon repressed. A massive wave of strikes follows and is also repressed.

On orders from Moscow, the French Communist Party pressures the Vietnamese Stalinists to break with the Trotskyists. The Stalinists quit *La Lutte* and immediately found another paper, *L'Avant-garde,* in which they denounce their recent Trotskyist allies as "twin brothers of fascism."

1938–1939. The ICP adopts a fervently patriotic position, supporting the colonial government's campaign for the defense of French Indochina against the Japanese threat by taking part in the launching of a War Loan drive and by approving the regime's conscription of an additional 20,000 Vietnamese soldiers. As a result of this unpopular position, the ICP, which has made an alliance with the bourgeois Constitutionalist Party in the Colonial Council election, is defeated in April 1939. The Trotskyists, on the other hand, get three delegates elected despite an explicitly radical platform.

Ho Chi Minh is infuriated by the Trotskyist victory. In May 1939, from Guilin, China, he writes a series of letters to his comrades in Vietnam vilifying the Trotskyists and parroting the delirious and murderous propaganda accompanying the recent Moscow Trials, letters which are published in the Stalinists' Hanoi paper *Notre Voix*. Some excerpts:

> The Trotskyists of China and other countries . . . are nothing but a band of evildoers, the lapdogs of international fascism. . . . In collusion with the police and their Japanese masters, the Trotskyists infiltrate workers' strikes in Shanghai and use every possible means to sabotage the movement. . . . In Spain they call themselves the Partido Obrero de Unificación Marxista (POUM). . . . It is they who constitute the nests of spies in Madrid and Barcelona and other places, in the service of Franco. It is they who organize the famous Fifth Column, the espionage organization of the Italian and German fascist army. The French Trotskyists are plotting to sabotage the Popular Front. Have you read the accusations against the Trotskyists at their trial in the Soviet Union? Doing so will help you see the true repugnant face of Trotskyism and the Trotskyists. . . . They must be politically exterminated.

1940. The Hitler-Stalin Pact (August 1939) leads to a new about-face of the ICP. The Stalinists' focus is once again on the struggle against French imperialism, while the menace of fascism is played down, although Nazi Germany is on the verge of invading France and Japan is on the verge of invading Indochina. The ICP accordingly launches a peasant insurrection in Cochinchina, which is drowned in blood: thousands are killed or imprisoned and hundreds of others are condemned to death.

1940–1945. The Japanese occupy Indochina, but allow the pro-Vichy French colonial administration to continue to maintain order (leaving the Japanese free to invade Siam, Burma, Malaysia, etc.).

1941. Ho Chi Minh puts aside the Communist label and creates the Vietminh (*Viet Nam Doc Lap Dong Minh Hoi*/Front for the Independence of Vietnam). He eliminates class struggle and agrarian revolution from his program so as not to upset the bourgeoisie and landowners whom he hopes to include in this front. Despite the new label, the Vietminh is effectively a continuation of the ICP.

1941–1944. Following Hitler's invasion of Russia (June 1941), Ho Chi Minh once again focuses on the "war against fascism" and seeks alliances with the Allies, including the "Free French" forces under General de Gaulle and the American Office of Strategic Services (OSS, the predecessor of the CIA), which provides him with arms and advisors.

March–August 1945. The Japanese take over the administration of Indochina, shunting aside the previously tolerated French colonial regime and presenting themselves as liberators from Western domination.

August 1945. The Japanese surrender. The Allies decide that Vietnam will be occupied by the Chinese troops of Chiang Kai-shek in the North and by the Anglo-Indian troops of General Gracey in the South, with the understanding that the country will be handed back to the French as soon as possible.

Before the arrival of the occupation troops, Ho Chi Minh's Vietminh, profiting from the political vacuum, takes power in Hanoi, organizes a hunt-down of Trotskyists ("traitors to the Homeland"), destroys the workers councils formed by the miners of Hongai-Campha, and prevents the famine-stricken peasants from seizing and redistributing land.

Meanwhile, Saigon enters into a state of effervescence. Amid a variety of popular networks and new or revived radical or nationalist groupings, the Stalinist leader Tran Van Giau appoints himself the head of a "Provisional Executive Committee." Several nationalist groups rally to this Vietminh-dominated government.

On August 25, a huge demonstration takes place in the center of Saigon. Ngo Van and other members of the League of Internationalist Communists take part, demanding "all power to the people's committees"—popular committees that have been spontaneously springing up in the city, challenging the authority of Tran Van Giau and his political police and armed gangs.

September 1945. In Hanoi, Ho Chi Minh proclaims the independence of Vietnam, while in Saigon the Vietminh organizes a military parade and calls on the population to welcome the Allied troops of General Gracey. Once in the city, Gracey contemptuously kicks the Vietminh's "Provisional Executive Committee" out of the Governor's Palace and rearms the French colonists. The Vietminh forces abandon the city and establish themselves in the neighboring countryside, urging the people to "remain calm" while their provisional government seeks to negotiate with the invading forces.

Meanwhile, the masses of ordinary people of Saigon, refusing to accept the return of the detested colonizers, seek in every possible way to arm themselves so as to drive them out of the city. Ngo Van and his comrades are of exactly the same mind.

September 23, 1945. Insurrection in Saigon. The people of Saigon set up barricades all over the city against the French. After several days of street fighting the French gain control of the city, but the insurgents control all the surrounding areas.

Pursued both by vengeful French colonists and by the Stalinists, Ngo Van and his League comrades regroup outside Saigon and join the Workers' Militia, a fighting unit created by the streetcar workers to combat the French while remaining independent of the Stalinists and nationalists.

1945–1946. In the South, the Vietminh kill every Trotskyist they can get their hands on, then attack the Cao Dai and Hoa Hao religious sects and other independent armed groups who are opposing the return of the French.

In the North, Ho Chi Minh allies himself with the Chinese occupation troops in order to maintain his power, then welcomes the return of French troops in order to get rid of the Chinese. After killing virtually all the Trotskyists, he destroys all the other nationalist movements and radical tendencies, thereby establishing his total political power in the North and his total control over the resistance in the South.

Thus it stands on the eve of the Thirty Year War.

BIBLIOGRAPHY

Works by Ngo Van
(published in Paris unless otherwise indicated)

Vu an Moscou, Nha xuat ban Chang trao luu (Saigon: Chong Trao Luu [Countercurrent Publications], 1937). Pamphlet denouncing the Moscow Trials.

Divination, magie et politique dans la Chine ancienne [Divination, Magic and Politics in Ancient China]. Presses Universitaires de France, 1976; reprinted by You-Feng, 2002.

Viêt-nam 1920–1945: révolution et contre-révolution sous la domination coloniale [Vietnam 1920–1945: Revolution and Counterrevolution Under Colonial Domination]. L'Insomniaque, 1995; reprinted by Nautilus, 2000. Translated into Vietnamese as *Viet nam 1920–1945, cach mang va phan cach mang thoi do ho thuc dan* (Chuong Re/L'Insomniaque, 2000).

Avec Maximilien Rubel, une amitié, une lutte 1954–1996 [With Maximilien Rubel in Friendship and Struggle, 1954–1996]. Les amis de Maximilien Rubel/L'Insomniaque, 1997. Translated into Italian by Paolo Casciola as *Con Maximilien Rubel 1954–1996: un'amicizia, una lotta comune* (Florence: Quaderni Pieto Tresso, 2003). Excerpts reprinted in *Au pays d'Héloïse*.

Au pays de la Cloche fêlée: Tribulations d'un Cochinchinois à l'époque coloniale [In the Land of the Cracked Bell: Tribulations of a South Vietnamese During the Colonial Era]. L'Insomniaque, 2000. Translated into Spanish by Mercè Artigas as *Memoria Escueta, de Cochinchina a Vietnam* (Barcelona: Octaedro, 2004). Translated into Vietnamese as *Tai Xu Chuong Re* (Gex-la-Ville: Le Chat qui Pêche, 2006). Translated into English by Hélène Fleury, Hilary Horrocks, Ken Knabb and Naomi Sager as *In the Land of the Cracked Bell* and included in the present volume.

Contes d'autrefois du Viêt-nam/Chuyen doi xu Viet [Folktales of Vietnam]. French-Vietnamese bilingual edition in collaboration with Hélène Fleury. You-Feng, 2001. Translated into Spanish by Magali Sirera as *Cuentos populares de Vietnam* (Barcelona: Octaedro, 2004).

Utopie antique et guerre des paysans en Chine [Ancient Utopias and Peasant Revolts in China]. Gex-la-Ville: Le Chat qui Pêche, 2004. Translated into Spanish by Magali Sirera as *Utopia antigua y revueltas campesinas en China* (Barcelona: Etcetera, 2005).

246

Le Joueur de flûte et l'Oncle Hô: Viêtnam 1945–2005 [The Flute Player and Uncle Ho: Vietnam 1945–2005]. Paris-Méditerranée, 2005.

Au Pays d'Héloïse [In the Land of Héloïse]. L'Insomniaque, 2005. Memorial volume including fragmentary chapters from the continuation of Ngo Van's auto-biography plus several articles and photographs and a selection of his paintings. English translations by Ken Knabb of excerpts from the autobiographical material and of three of the articles are included in the present volume.

Articles and Other Short Pieces

Bien Ca Chieu Hom. Poem published in a Vietnamese paper, along with some short pieces about peasant life (ca. 1931–1932).

Some articles on movements in the plantations, etc., published in *La Lutte* (Saigon, ca. 1933–1935).

"Ta Thu Thau and Bolshevik-Leninist Politics," in *Tia Sang* (Saigon, April 1939).

An article on the Cao Dai sect, published in *Dien Tin* (1939 or 1940).

"Prolétaires et paysans, retournez vos fusils!" in *Tieng Tho* (France, October 31, 1951). Appeal for resistance on both sides to the Indochina War.

"M. Étiemble, commis-pèlerin suppôt de Mao Tsé-toung," in *La Révolution prolé-tarienne, revue syndicaliste révolutionnaire* #441 (July–August 1959). Critique of René Étiemble's gullible account of Mao's China.

"À propos de la Commune chinoise," in *Défense de l'homme* #154 (August 1961). On the "communes" in China's "Great Leap Forward."

"Introduction à la causerie sur la révolte des Turbans Jaunes" (June 25, 1966). Introductory remarks at a discussion of the Chinese "Yellow Turban Rebellion" (184 AD).

"Sur la paupérisation," in *Cahiers de discussion sur le Socialisme de conseils* #7 (November 1966). On economic poverty, dehumanization and alienation.

"Sur le Viêt-nam," in *Informations et correspondance ouvrières* ##51–69 (1967–1968). Series of articles on Vietnamese history 1900–1945.

"Sur la réforme agraire," in *Cahiers de discussion sur le Socialisme de conseils* #8 (April 1968). Reprinted in *Au pays d'Héloïse.* Translated in the present volume as "On Third World Struggles."

"Réflexions préliminaires sur la guerre au Viêt-nam," in *Cahiers de discussion sur le Socialisme de conseils* #8 (April 1968). Reprinted in *Au pays d'Héloïse.* Trans-lated in the present volume as "Reflections on the Vietnam War."

"Chez Jeumont-Schneider, impressions de mai," in *Informations et correspondance ouvrières* #76 (December 1968). Reprinted in *Au pays d'Héloïse*. Translated by Brian Pearce as "Impressions of May" as part of a series on "1968: Its Causes and Its Consequences" in *Critique 45: Journal of Socialist Theory*, vol. 36, #2 (New York, August 2008). Translated by Ken Knabb in the present volume as "A Factory Occupation in May 1968."

"Ceux qui meurent dans les rizières," in *Informations et correspondance ouvrières* (ca. 1969; issue # unknown). More on the Vietnam war.

"Viêt-nam, Grève généralisée à Saigon, le 7 janvier 1970" (1970; publication unknown). Accounts of strikes in South Vietnam.

"Notes de Lecture: *La Bureaucratie céleste* de Étienne Balazs," in *Informations et correspondance ouvrières* ##106–107 (June–July 1971). Favorable review of Balazs's book, which has been translated into English as *Chinese Civilization and Bureaucracy*.

"Le Maoïsme à travers le Petit Livre rouge," *Informations et correspondance ouvrières* ##112–113 (December 1971–January 1972). Critique of Maoism and Mao's "Little Red Book."

"Le mouvement IVe Internationale en Indochine (1930–1939)," in *Cahiers Léon Trotsky* #40 (Grenoble, December 1989).

"Le mouvement IVe Internationale en Indochine (1940–1945)," in *Cahiers Léon Trotsky* #46 (Grenoble, July 1991). This lengthy two-part text (later largely incorporated into the *Vietnam 1920–1945* book) was translated into English by Harry Ratner as *Revolutionaries They Could Not Break: The Fight for the Fourth International in Indochina 1930–1945* (London: Index Books, 1995).

"Ngo Van aux Chroniques rebelles." Interview on Radio-Libertaire (November 18, 1995).

"Revolutionary witness: Vietnam's history of struggle against imperialism." Translation of a talk in London, published in *The International* #17 (London, January 1996).

"Pourquoi ce travail." Talk at a meeting of *Lutte Ouvrière* (May 26, 1996).

"Ngo Van se souvient." Interview about Nguyen An Ninh, published in *Cyclo, revue de l'association 10.000 printemps* (Autumn 1997).

"Rousseau et quelques figures de la lutte anticolonialiste et révolutionnaire au Viêt-nam," in *Études Jean-Jacques Rousseau* #10 (1998). Reprinted in *Au pays d'Héloïse*. On Rousseau's influence on early Vietnamese revolutionaries.

"Viêt-nam 1997." Two-part article in *Échanges* ##85–86 (1997–1998).

"Les révoltes de paysans dans le Nord," in *Échanges* #86 (March 1998). On peasant revolts in North Vietnam.

"La révolte paysanne de novembre 1956," in *Échanges* #86 (March 1998). On the peasant revolt of 1956.

"Le sort des paysans dans le Sud," in *Échanges* #87 (May 1998). On the condition of the peasants in South Vietnam.

"La nomenklatura," in *Échanges* #88 (Winter 1998–1999). On the Vietnam Communist Party's bureaucratic ranks and privileges.

"Les jauniers jaunes: la condition ouvrière sous le régime de 'l'économie de marché à orientation socialiste'," in *Échanges* #88 (Winter 1998–1999). On the condition of the workers under Vietnam's "market socialism."

"Les camps de 'rééducation'," in *Échanges* ##94–101 (2000–2002). Series of articles on the Vietnamese labor camps for political "reeducation." The material in the above-listed *Échanges* articles was largely incorporated into *Le Joueur de flûte et l'Oncle Hô: Viêtnam 1945–2005*.

"Utopie libertaire antique et guerre des paysans en Chine," in *Oiseau-Tempête* #8 (Summer 2001) and #11 (Summer 2004). Material later incorporated into the *Utopie antique* book.

"La preuve par Chirac." Leaflet on the Chirac–Le Pen presidential election by Hélène Fleury, Louis Janover, Monique Janover and Ngo Van (May 2002). Reprinted in *Le Monde Libertaire* and other publications.

"Introduction" to Phan Van Truong's *Une histoire de conspirateurs annamites à Paris* (L'Insomniaque, 2003).

"Hô Chi Minh 'dans la galerie des grands hommes'," in *La Quinzaine littéraire* #866 (December 1, 2003). Review of Pierre Brocheux's *Hô Chi Minh, du révolutionnaire à l'icône*.

"Quelques mots prononcés le 17 juin 2004 à la librairie Altaïr à Barcelona." Transcript of a talk in Barcelona, published in *Au pays d'Héloïse*.

* * *

Ngo Van wrote a number of articles in Vietnam during the 1930s about which we have little or no information. Probably a few of his later articles in France have also escaped our notice. Most of the above-mentioned articles can be found online at http://chatquipeche.free.fr/articles.html. The same website also presents other material by and about Ngo Van, including a large selection of his paintings.

INDEX

Vietnamese accents are omitted throughout this book. As in many other East Asian cultures, Vietnamese family names precede personal names. When consulting other sources, note that there are different ways of anglicizing Vietnamese place names. *Yen Bai,* for example, can also be found as Yen Bay, Yen bai, Yen bay, Yen-bai, Yen-bay, Yenbai and Yenbay. Note also that names of organizations are translated in a variety of ways. *Thanh Nien Cach Mang Dong Chi Hoi,* for example, can be found as Revolutionary Youth League, League of Young Revolutionary Comrades, Vietnamese Revolutionary Youth Association, Association of Revolutionary Vietnamese Youth, etc. In a few cases we have indicated common alternative versions to the ones used in this book, but it is often best to use the original Vietnamese names when searching the Web or consulting book indexes.

In order to help sort out the sometimes confusingly similar names of persons, groups and publications, brief parenthetical information is given for most entries. This information is intended only as a rough preliminary guide for readers who may be interested in following up some topic, and there are probably a few errors. In particular, the memberships and interrelations among the diverse Trotskyist groupings are not always clear. Some of the persons described simply as comrades or fellow prisoners were undoubtedly Trotskyists even if that is not specified in the book. "TR" means that a person is described as a Trotskyist but without any specific group membership being indicated. "LO" means that a person is described as belonging to a particular Left Opposition group or, more generally, simply to "the Left Opposition." But "Left Oppositionist" was an early synonym for "Trotskyist," and since many of the *La Lutte* members and all of the LIC members were more or less Trotskyist, many of them (along with others identified simply as "TR") were undoubtedly also Left Oppositionists during the earlier period when that label was more frequently used. And most of the LIC members had probably previously been *La Lutte* participants or supporters, and some may have remained so despite their differences (see Note 153 on the "October group").

This index covers the entire book except for the Bibliography. "N79" means Note 79, not page 79. Entries in **boldface** indicate biographies in Chapter 9.

Abbreviations:
CP: Communist Party
TR: Trotskyist
VF: Vietnamese radical who had spent time in France
AIP: member of Annamite Independence Party (1927–1929)
TN: member of Thanh Nien (1925–1930)
ICP: member of Indochinese Communist Party/Communist Party of Vietnam (1930–)
LO: member of one or more Left Opposition groups (ca. 1928–1934)
LL: member of *La Lutte* group (1933–1946)
LIC: member of League of Internationalist Communists (1935–1939; 1945–1946)
WM: member of Workers' Militia (1945–1946)
UOI: member of Union Ouvrière Internationale (France, 1948–1952)
CCG: member of Council Communist Group (Paris, 1954–1996)

Abelard, Peter [Pierre Abélard] (medieval philosopher), xv
action committees [*uy ban hanh dong*], 3, 12, 76–78, 91, 119, 125, 153, 155, 166, 170–171, 242, N77. *See also* **people's committees**
Agostini (Head Guard at Saigon Central Prison), 10, 12, 14–15, 69, 72–74, 82
anarchism; anarchists, viii–ix, xv, 2, 56, 197, 202, 237, Nviii, N2, N201, N211
Anderson, Andy: *Hungary '56,* N2
[*Anh* = "Brother"]
Anh Bay (Ngo Van's Brother Seven), 17–18, 20, 27, 29, 34, 36–39, 118, N20
Anh Duc [pseudonym of Ngo Van in WM], 137
Anh Gia [Dao Hung Long] (TN, ICP, LO), 52–53, 55, 86–87, 90–91, 93–94, 147, 153, 155, 167–168, **169–170**, 171–172
Anh Lo (Moi slave), 21–22
Anh Sau (radical restaurant owner), 110
Anh Tu (village magician), 19
Annam, L' (Saigon journal 1926–1928; successor to *La Cloche Fêlée*), Nviii
Annam Communist Party [*An Nam Cong San Dang*] (1929–1930), N170
Annamite Independence Party [*Parti Annamite d'Indépendance*] (1927–1929), 159, 163, 165
Anti-Imperialist League (1927–1935), 159, 165
Armstrong, Louis (jazz musician), 96
Arnoux, Louis (Sûreté Inspector in Cambodia), 100
Assassination Assault Committee (1945), 124
Ataturk, Mustafa Kemal (Turkish nationalist leader), N4
Aupick, Jacques (Baudelaire's stepfather), 43
"Auprès de ma blonde" (French popular song), 79, N79
Avant-garde, L' [The Vanguard] (ICP paper following 1937 split from *La Lutte*), 89, 92, 161, 242
Avrich, Paul: *Kronstadt 1921,* N2

Ba [Great-Lady] (guardian spirit), 17–19, 38
Ba Duong (Binh Xuyen pirate leader), 147.
Balazs, Étienne: *Chinese Civilization and Bureaucracy,* 202

Balzac, Honoré de (French novelist), 52
Ban Dan [The People's Friend] (Hanoi newspaper), 177
Bao Dai (puppet emperor of Vietnam 1926–1945 & 1949–1955), 107, 116, 169, 200, N116, N145
Bataille Internationale, La [The International Battle] (UOI bulletin), 199
Baudelaire, Charles (French poet), xiv, 40, 43, 78, 188, Nxiv, N40, N60, N67, N188
Bavaria (1918–1919 workers councils & "Council Republic"), 2, 197, N2
Bay Vien [Le Van Vien] (Binh Xuyen pirate leader), 147, 169
Bazin assassination (1929), 45, N45, N46
Bich Khe [Le Quang Luong] (radical poet), 90, **177–178**
Bilbao, Esteban (POUM, UOI), 199
Binh (TR in Cambodia), 95
Binh Xuyen river pirates, xviii, 124, 128–129, 147, 169, 194
Blum, Léon (French socialist politician; leader of Popular Front government), 65, 83, 90
Bo (nephew of Ngo Van), 132
Bolloten, Burnett: *The Spanish Civil War,* N2
Bolshevik Party; Bolsheviks; Bolshevism, 2, 85, 96, 197–198, 234, 237, N2, N77, N201. *See also* **Leninism**; **Trotskyism**; **Russian Communist Party**
Bolshevik-Leninist Group for the Construction of the Fourth International (Vietnam, 1936), 168, N153
Bon (Stalinist bureaucrat), 178
Bouin (Saigon prosecutor), 74, 76
Bouygues (personnel chief in Nanterre), 186
Brahma (Hindu god), 106
Brassens, Georges (French poet-singer), xix, 194, Nxix
Brévié, Jules (Governor-General of Indochina 1936–1939), 84, 92, 100, 161
Brinton, Maurice: *The Bolsheviks and Workers' Control: 1917–1921,* 234
Brocheton (Sûreté Inspector in Cambodia), 100
Buddha (Shakyamuni), 26–27, 29, 106
Buddhism, 26–27, 106, 114, 124
Buddhist Anchorites Group [*Tinh Do Cu Si*], 121
Bui Duy Tu (TR; comrade of Thai Van

Tam), 177

Bui Quang Chieu (leader of Constitutionalist Party), 41, N41

*Bulletin de la Ligue contre l'oppression
coloniale et l'impérialisme* [Bulletin of
the Anti-Imperialist League], 165

Cach Mang Thuong Truc [Permanent
Revolution] (LIC theoretical journal,
1935), 65, 74, 168

*Cahiers de discussion pour le Socialisme
des conseils* [Journal for Discussion of
Councilist Socialism] (CCG, 1962–1969),
218, 221

Cambodia, 95, 100, 102, 239, N50, N145

Camus, Albert (French writer), 169

Canh (TR friend), 103–105, 107

Cao Dai sect (1926–), 105–107, 117, 121–
122, 124, 128, 145–146, 245, N45

capitation tax, 27, 47, 92, 106–107, 239,
241, N27

Catholicism; Catholics, 30, 95, 134, 238

Céline, Louis-Ferdinand (French novelist),
xv–xvi, 79–80, N81

Center for Mutual Education (Saigon,
1933), 58, 81

CFDT [*Confédération Française
Démocratique du Travail*/French
Democratic Confederation of Labor]
(socialist-leaning national labor union),
207–213, 215, N207

CFTC [*Confédération Française
des Travailleurs Chrétiens*/French
Confederation of Christian Workers]
(Christian national labor union), 187

CGT [*Confédération Générale du Travail*/
General Confederation of Labor] (national
labor union dominated by French CP),
187, 204, 208–215, N208

Chanh [Thong Chanh] (assassin of Public
Prosecutor Jaboin, 1893), 109–110

Chanh Tri Tuan Bao [The Political Weekly]
(Tonkin TR paper, 1939; successor to *Thoi
Dam*), 177

Chau Van Giac (prisoner), 70

Cheng Bilan (Chinese TR; partner of Peng
Shuzi), 148–149

[*Chi* = "Sister"]

Chi Day. *See* **Nguyen Thi Dai**

Chi Muoi. *See* **Tran Thi Muoi**

Chi Nam Thin (ICP; Ngo Van's partner's

sister), 104, 114, 148–150

Chi Nguyet. *See* **Nguyen Trung Nyuget**

Chi Quy (WM nurse), 131

Chi Sau (Vo Buu Binh's partner), 94

Chiang Kai-shek [Jiang Jieshi] (military
dictator of China 1928–1948, then of the
"Republic of China" on Taiwan 1949–
1975), 235, 244

Chien Dau [Combat] (Tonkin TR bulletin),
120, 162, 178

Chin Ngoc (torturer), 6, 16, 109

China, ix–x, xv, xvii, 175–176, 200, 202,
220, 245, Nxvii, N4, N145, N155

—revolution of 1925–1927, 157, 175, 235

Chinese Communist Party, 149, 235

Chinh Phu Ngam [Lament of a Soldier's
Wife] (poem by Dang Tran Con), N179

Chirac, Jacques (French conservative
politician), N210

Christ, Jesus (Jewish religious innovator),
30, 106

Christianity, 106, 238. *See also* **Catholicism**

CIA, 244

Ciliga, Ante: *The Russian Enigma*, 234

Class Struggle, The (American TR journal,
1931–1937), 3

classes in French Indochina, 239–240

Cloche Fêlée, La [The Cracked Bell]
(Baudelaire poem, 1851), xiv, 78, Nxiv

Cloche Fêlée, La (Saigon journal edited by
Nguyen An Ninh, 1923–1926), xiv, 78,
158, 240

CNT [*Confederación Nacional del Trabajo*/
National Confederation of Labor]
(Spanish anarchist labor union), 193

Co Do [Red Flag] (Saigon ICP paper,
1929–), 47

Co Do [Red Flag] (Hanoi TR paper,
1944–1945), 120, 176

Co Giai Phong [Banner of Liberation]
(Hanoi ICP paper), 144

Co Vo San [Proletarian Flag] (ICP paper,
1930–), 50

Cognacq, Maurice (Governor of Cochinchina 1921–1926), 44

Cohn-Bendit, Daniel (May 1968 anarchist
spokesman), N211

Cold War (ca. 1945–1991), 200, 220

Colonial Council. *See* **elections**

Comintern. *See* **Third International**

Communist League [*Lien Minh Cong San*

Doan] (LO group within ICP, 1931–1932), 153, 167, 170

Communist League [full name: Communist League (Opposition)/*Ligue Communiste (Opposition)*] (French LO group, 1930–1934), 175. *See also* **Indochinese Group of the Communist League**

Communist League of China, 148

Communist Left Opposition (underground Vietnam group). *See* **Ta Doi Lap**

Communist Manifesto (Marx & Engels), 4, 52, 148, 164, N4

Communist parties, 57, 217–218, 220, 235–236, N77
—Chinese, 149, 233
—French, 64–65, 76, 82, 89, 159, 161, 173–175, 210–212, 221, 240, 242, N12, N208, N210, N221
—German, 233
—Russian/Soviet, 77, 89, 234, 236–237, N86. *See also* **Bolshevik Party**
—Spanish, N2
—Vietnamese. *See* **Indochinese Communist Party**
See also **Stalinism**

Confucianism, 106, N155

Confucius (ancient Chinese philosopher), 106

Constitutionalist Party [*Parti Constitutionaliste*], 41, 57, 90, 99, 107, 147, 156–157, 168, 171, 243, N41

Contre le Courant [Against the Current] (French LO paper), 159

Coulet, Georges: *Les Sociétés secrètes en terre d'Annam,* 130, 133

Council Communist Group [*Groupe Communiste de Conseils*] (Paris, 1954–1996), 203, N148

Craipeau, Yvan (French LO), 174

Cuong De (rebel prince), 152, 240, N155

Da (Ngo Van's younger son), xxiii, 148, 184, 193–194, N184

Daladier, Édouard (French prime minister 1938–1940), 99, 168

Dan Chung [The People] (ICP paper, ca. 1938–), 98–99, 126

Dang Van Long (LL; friend in France), 185, N185

Dao Hung Long. *See* **Anh Gia**

d'Argenlieu, Admiral Georges-Thierry

(High Commissioner of Indochina 1945–1947), 146

Dau (ICP peasant prisoner), 107

de Gaulle, Charles (leader of "Free French" forces in World War II; French president 1958–1969), 204, 221, 244, N221

De La Chevrotière, Henry Chavigny (editor of *L'Impartial*), 41, N41

De Leon, Daniel (American socialist leader), 202

Debord, Guy: *The Society of the Spectacle,* 237

Decoux, Jean (Governor-General of Indochina 1940–1945), 112, 116–117, N162

Delamarre, Émile (labor inspector), 240

Democratic Front (ICP electoral coalition, 1939), 98, 156–157

Dépêche d'Indochine, La [Indochina Dispatch] (Saigon newspaper), 12–13, 54, 58

Diem (puppet dictator). *See* **Ngo Dinh Diem**

Dien Tin (newspaper), 107

Diet (TR friend in Cambodia), 95–97

Do (Ngo Van's older son), xxiii, 148, 154, 184, N184

Do Ba The (friend of Ta Thu Thau), 162, 179

Doan Van Truong (TR), 93–94

Dolgoff, Sam: *The Anarchist Collectives,* N2

Dong (tortured prisoner), 60

Dong (WM), 131

Dong Vu [Ngo Van pseudonym], 199

Dormoy, Marx (French Minister of the Interior 1936–1938), 90

Dornier, Lambert (UOI, CCG), 199, 201, 203

Duc (ICP prisoner), 114

Duoc Nha Nam [The Torch of Annam] (Saigon Constitutionalist paper), 90, 171

Duoc Vo San [The Torch of the Proletariat] (paper of the Indochinese Group of the Communist League), 175

Duong Bach Mai (VF, ICP, LL; organizer of Vietminh secret police in Cochinchina), 59, 65, 99, 115, 122, 124, 127, 144, 156–158, 165

Duong Van Tu (imprisoned worker), 94

Duong Van Tuong (TR), 94

Duy Tan (Vietnamese emperor 1907–1916; exiled for plotting against the French), 107–108

Dzu (radical lawyer), 140

Eastern Study Movement [*Dong Du*]
(1905–1909), N155
Échanges et Mouvement, N203
Eisner, Kurt (German independent socialist
leader), N2
elections, N56
—Saigon City Council (1933), 56–58, 81,
160, 163, 165, 167, 242
—Saigon City Council (1935), 59, 163, 165
—Saigon City Council (1937), 86, 161
—Cochinchina Colonial Council (1939),
98–99, 156–157, 161, 163–164, 166, 175,
243
Engels, Friedrich (revolutionary theorist),
164, 189, N4
Estonia (failed 1924 coup), 157, 235
Étoile Nord-Africaine [North African
Star] (Algerian nationalist organization
1926–1937), 90

fascism, 82, 235
Fernández, Jaime (POUM, UOI), 199
Ferry, Jules (French prime minister
1880–1885), 238
"Five Dragons," 240
Flambeau d'Annam, Le [The Torch of
Annam] (Saigon Constitutionalist paper),
90–91, 115, 147
Fourth International (1938–), 87, 90, 93,
95, 98, 144, 148, 156, 161, 166, 169,
174–175, 177–178, 237
France:
—Enlightenment (18th century), 241, N155
—Revolution (1789–1794), 210–211, 241
—revolution of 1830, N9
—revolution of 1848, 43, 208
—Paris Commune (1871), 204, 210, 238,
241, N210
—Popular Front (1936–1938). See **Popular Front**
—Vichy regime (1940–1944), 112, 236,
243, N112, N116, N148
—May 1968 revolt, 204, 207–216
Franco, Francisco (Spanish fascist general;
dictator 1939–1975), 193, 243, N2
Frank, Pierre (French LO), 167, 179
French Communist Party, 64–65, 76, 82, 89,
159, 161, 173–175, 210–212, 221, 240,
242, N12, N208, N210, N221
French Confederation of Business Enter-
prises [*Conseil National du Patronat*

Français], N210
French Socialist Party, 82, N12. *See also*
Popular Front

Gaido (foreman in Nanterre), 187, 191–192
Gallienne, Jacques (UOI), 199
Gandhi, Mohandas (Indian anticolonial
leader), 106
Ganofsky, Edgar (LL), 172, **176–177**
Garros, Georges: *Forceries humaines,* 4, N4
Gélot (torturer), 5, 16, 72
General Confederation of Labor [a.k.a.
Workers for National Salvation] (Vietminh
national labor union), 130, 178
General Workers Federation. *See* **Saigon-Cholon Workers Federation**
Geneva Conference (1954), N145
Gentizon, Paul: *Mustapha Kémal ou
l'Orient en marche,* 4, N4
German Communist Party, 235
Germany, 157, 200, 235
—Nazis; Nazi regime (1933–1945), 235–
236, 243, N112
See also **Bavaria**
Gide, André (French writer), 90, 177, N90
Gitton, Marcel (French CP leader), 89
Go Vap streetcar workers' action committee,
119. *See also* **Workers' Militia**
Gómez, Paco (POUM; Spanish emigrant
friend in France), 192–193
Gontarbert, Sania (UOI, CCG), 197–199,
201
Gracey, Douglas (commander of Allied
forces in Indochina 1945–1946), 126–127,
131, 244
Great-Lady [*Ba*] (guardian spirit), 17–19, 38
Grenelle Accords (May 1968), 210–211,
213, 215, N210
Guérin, Daniel (French libertarian socialist),
159, 163
Guillaume (fellow worker in Nanterre), 186
Guomindang [Kuomintang] (Chinese
Nationalist Party), 235, N4
Guyon (boss in Saigon), 54
Guyot (worker friend in France), 194

Han Thuyen (Tonkin journal of historical
analysis), 178
Hegel, Georg Wilhelm Friedrich (German
philosopher), 202
Héloïse (lover of Peter Abelard), xv

Hémery, Daniel (historian), 144

Hien (Hongai-Campha workers council delegate), 143

Hieu, Lady (generous lady memorialized by banyan tree), 30–31, N30

Histoire de la Résistance, Saigon-Cholon-Giadinh 1945–1975 (Stalinist history), 125

Hitler, Adolf (dictator of Nazi Germany 1933–1945), 236, 244, N2

Hitler-Stalin Pact (German-Soviet Non-aggression Pact, 1939–1941), 101, 236, 243

Ho Chi Minh [Nguyen Ai Quoc] (VF; leader of TN, ICP & Vietminh; president of North Vietnam 1945–1969), vii, x, xvi–xviii, 1, 68, 120, 143–145, 162–163, 179, 198–201, 219–221, 236, 240–245

Ho Huu Tuong (VF, LO, LL, LIC; leading figure of "October" tendency), 8, 11, 15, 52, 55, 59, 61, 64, 86–88, 115, 153, 156, **167–169**, 170–172, N153

Ho Van Duc (WM), 131

Ho Van Nga (VF; founder of National Party for the Independence of Vietnam & of National United Front), 144

Hoa Hao sect (1939–), 114, 117, 121–122, 124, 144–145, 245

Hoang Van Dao: *Viet Nam Quoc Dan Dang: A Contemporary History of a National Struggle, 1927–1954*, N45

Hon (Marseilles smuggler), 63

Hongai-Campha workers-councils "Commune" (August–November 1945), viii, 120–121, 143, 147, 244, N2

Hugo, Victor (French writer), 9, 52, 106, N9, N101

Humanité, L' (French CP paper), 159

"Hundred Flowers" movement (China, 1956–1957), xvii, Nxvii

Hungary (1956 revolution), xvii, 2, 197, N2

Huong (TR in Cambodia), 95

Huot (assassinated dignitary), 48

Huynh Phu So. *See* **Mad Monk**

Huynh Van Dam (alleged assassin of an informer), 54

Huynh Van Phuong (VF, AIP, LO, LL), 56, 159, 164

ICO [*Informations et Correspondance Ouvrières*/Workers' News and Letters] (French ultraleftist paper & group), 203, 216, N203

ICP. *See* **Indochinese Communist Party**

Impartial, L' (Saigon right-wing colonial paper), 41

India, 217

Indochina, French conquest of, 238–239

Indochina War (1945–1954), vii, 145, 183, 199–200, N116, N145

Indochinese Communism group [*Dong Duong Cong San*] (TR group, 1931–1932), 153, 160

Indochinese Communist Party [ICP] (1930–1945; later renamed Vietnam Workers Party, then Communist Party of Vietnam), vii, x, xiv, 1, 50, 52, 54–56, 64–65, 70, 87, 99–100, 104, 126, 143–144, 153, 167, 170, 175, 198, 240–243, N50, N169. *See also* **Vietminh**

Indochinese Communist Party (1929–1930: one of the early groups that merged into the above-mentioned party), 169, N169

Indochinese Congress movement [*Dai Hoi Dong Duong*] (1936–1937), 76–78, 153, 166, 173, 177, 242, Nviii, N77

Indochinese Group of the Communist League [*Groupe Indochinois de la Ligue Communiste*] (LO group in France, ca. 1930–1934), 117, 156, 167, 172–175

Indochinese Left Opposition group (in France). *See* **Indochinese Group of the Communist League**

Indochinese Mutual Aid Association (Paris), 165, 173

Indochinese Section for the Fourth International (1935), 175

Informations et Correspondance Ouvrières. *See* **ICO**

Insomniaque, L' (Ngo Van's publishers in Paris), ix, xv

Intellectuals' Group [*Groupe des Intellectuels*], 121

International Antiwar Congress (Amsterdam, 1932), 173

International War Crimes Tribunal (1966–1967), N220

"Internationale" (revolutionary song), 123, 136, 215

Internationalist Communist Party [*Parti Communiste Internationaliste*] (French TR party), 174, 199

Internationalist Workers (anticonscription group in Gia Dinh, 1939), 152

Isaacs, Harold: *The Tragedy of the Chinese Revolution,* vii, x, 149, 176, 235

IWW [Industrial Workers of the World] (anarcho-syndicalist union), 202

Jaboin (assassinated public prosecutor), 110

JAG [*Jeunesse d'Avant-Garde/Thanh Nien Tien Phong*/Vanguard Youth] (1945), 117–118, 121–124, 128, 130

Japan, 99, 240, N155

—occupation of Indochina (1940–1945), 116–119, 236, 243–244, N116

Jeune Annam [Young Annam] (1920s nationalist group), 41, 158, Nviii

Jeunesse d'Avant-Garde. *See* **JAG**

Jeunesse Patriotes [Patriotic Youth] (French fascistic group), 159

Johnson, Lyndon Baines (US president 1963–1969), 220

Journal des Étudiants Annamites [Annamite Students' Newspaper] (France, ca. 1927–1929), 163–165

Justice (Saigon socialist paper), 141

Kamenev, Lev (Bolshevik), 77

Kha (imprisoned school principal), 101

Khai Dinh (puppet emperor of Vietnam 1916–1925), 107–108

Khanh (prison guard), 107

Khrushchev, Nikita (USSR head of state 1953–1964), N86

Kierkegaard, Soren (Danish philosopher), 201

Kim Van Kieu [The Tale of Kieu] (epic poem by Nguyen Du), 161

Kinh An Do (ICP workmate), 122, 126

Korsch, Karl (revolutionary Marxist theorist), 237

Kronstadt revolt (Russia, 1921), 2, 197, 234, N2

La Lutte [Struggle] (newspaper & group; included both Stalinists & Trotskyists 1933–1937, then only Trotskyists 1937–1946), 56–57, 64–65, 69–70, 74, 77, 84–86, 89, 92, 95, 97–99, 123, 127, 129, 131, 136–138, 144, 148, 156–158, 160–168, 172, 175–177, 242, Nviii, N11, N57, N153

La Van Rot (VF, LO), 167, 172

Lacombe (Sûreté Chief), 58

Lam Thanh Thi (Saigon friend), 112

Lan (Hongai-Campha workers council delegate), 143

Landauer, Gustav (German anarchist), N2

Lao Cong [The Worker] (LO paper, 1932), 170

Lao Dong (official Vietnam labor union paper), 178

Lao Tzu (ancient Chinese sage), 106

Laos, 239, N50, N145

Larousse Élémentaire (French dictionary), 33

Lascaux (lawyer), 96

Laval, Pierre (French prime minister 1935–1936), 64

Laval-Stalin Pact (Franco-Soviet Mutual Assistance Pact, 1935), 64–65, 81, 174, 242

Lavau (Saigon judge), 74

Le (Hongai-Campha workers council delegate), 143

Le Ky (WM), 137

Le Ngoc (LIC, WM), 119, 130–131, 137

Le Petit, Claude (French poet), xv

Le Quang Luong. *See* **Bich Khe**

Le Thanh Long (LL), 144

Le Thi Dinh (woman prisoner), 68

Le Van Hoach (puppet president of "Republic of Cochinchina" 1946–1947), 146

Le Van Huong (WM), 131

Le Van Kim (lawyer), 7, 76

Le Van Oanh (TR), 94, **153–154**

Le Van Phat [a.k.a. My] (TN; Rue Barbier victim), 67

Le Van Sanh [Léon Sanh] (student accused of Bazin assassination), 45

Le Van Thu (VF, LL), 56, 157

Le Van Vung (LL), 129

League for the Rights of Man, 41

League of Internationalist Communists for the Construction of the Fourth International [*Chanh Doan Cong San Quoc Te Chu Nghia—Phai Tan Thanh De Tu Quoc Te*] (TR group 1935–1939), 11, 64–66, 74–75, 81, 111, 151–153, 168, 171, 237, 242, N11, N153

League of Internationalist Communists (revival of the above, 1945–1946), 117, 119, 123, 125–127, 130, 171, 173–174,

176, 244–245, N153
Leclerc, Jacques-Philippe (commander of French forces in Indochina 1945–1947), 133, 137, 145
Left Opposition, 170, 175, 236, 241, 250
—French, 159
—Russian, 175, 236
—Spanish, 192
—Vietnamese, 56, 58, 70, 153–154, 164, 167, 170, 242. *See also* **Ta Doi Lap**; **Indochinese Group of the Communist League**
See also **Trotskyism**
Legrand (Sûreté Inspector), 50–51
Lenin, Vladimir Ilyich (Bolshevik leader), 86, 168, 234, 237, N86
Leninism, 2, 173, 197, 237, N201
Lien minh cong san doan [Communist League] (LO group within ICP, 1931–1932), 153, 167, 170
Life magazine, N18
Liu Jialiang (Chinese TR), 149, 174, **175–176**
Liu Khanh Thinh (LIC, WM), 119, 142–143, 148–149, 174
Lo (peasant prisoner), 72
Loye (lawyer), 76
Lu Sanh Hanh [a.k.a. Lucien/Luc] (ICP, LO, LIC, UOI), 3, 5, 11, 15, 58, 64, 74–76, 82, 87, 96, 116–117, 119, 127, 142, 149, 153, 155, 168, **170–172**, 184, 199, 242, N11
Luc Van Tien (epic poem by Nguyen Dinh Chieu), 20, 39, 71
Luong Duc Thiep (TR), 120, 162, **178–179**
Lutte, La. See **La Lutte**
Luxemburg, Rosa (Marxist revolutionary), 237
Ly Thai Bach (poet), 106
Ly Tu Trong [a.k.a. Nguyen Huy] (alleged killer of Inspector Legrand), 51

Mad Monk [*le Bonze Fou*] (Huynh Phu So, founder of Hoa Hao sect), 113–114, 117, 124, 145
Malaquais, Jean (radical French writer), 148, N148
Malraux, André (French novelist) 79
Mandel, Georges (French Colonial Minister 1938–1940), 161
Mangano, Romeo (UOI), 199

Manifesto (by LIC, 1945), 171
Manifesto (by Nguyen Te My, Tonkin 1945), 120
Manifesto of Annamite Students (by Tran Van Thach, 1928), 165
Mao Zedong [Mao Tse-tung] (Chinese CP leader & dictator), xvii, 148, N204
Maoism; Maoists, x, 204, Nxvii, N204
March 22nd Movement (France 1968), 211–212, N211
Marr, David: *Vietnamese Anticolonialism 1885–1925*, N155
Marx, Karl (revolutionary theorist), 2, 4, 51, 156, 160, 189, 197, 201–202, 237, N2, N4, N189, N201
Marxism; Marxists, ix, 201–202, 237, N201
Marxist Cultural Group [*Groupe Culturel Marxiste*] (French group in Saigon, 1945–1950), 141
May 1968 revolt (France), 204, 207–216
Mendès-France, Pierre (French moderate socialist politician), 212
Mett, Ida: *The Kronstadt Uprising* [a.k.a. *The Kronstadt Commune*], N2
Michel, Louise (French anarchist), xv
Militant, Le (Saigon TR paper, 1936–1937), 86, 90, 168, N153
Minh ["The Swimmer"] (TR of Ta Thu Thau group), 138
Minh Mang (emperor of Vietnam 1820–1841), 105
Minoda Fujio (Japanese Governor of Cochinchina, 1945), 117
Moen, Sophie (UOI, CCG; Ngo Van's partner in France), xiv, 199, 201, 203–204, and painting facing p. 169
Mohammed (founder of Islam), 106
Moi tribespeople, 21, 58
Molinier, Raymond (French LO), 156, 167, 174
Montaigut (Provincial Administrator), 110
Montesquieu, Baron de (18th-century French political philosopher), N155
Moscow Trials (1936–1938), 1, 77, 85, 90–91, 96, 103, 144, 157, 166, 168, 198, 243, N77
Moutet, Marius (French socialist; Colonial Minister 1936–1938), 72, 78, 83
Mühsam, Erich (German anarchist), N2
Munis, Manuel [Manuel Fernández Grandizo y Martínez, a.k.a. G. Munis]

(UOI), 199

Muoi Tri (Binh Xuyen pirate leader), 147

Mussolini, Benito (Fascist dictator of Italy 1922–1945), N2

My, Michel ("The Tiger of Cho Lach"; father of Nguyen Van Nam), 142, 172

Nadaillat (assassinated colonial judge), 45

Nadeau, Maurice (LO), 175

Nagy, Imre (Hungarian reformist politician), N2

Nam Bo Provisional Executive Committee (Vietminh self-appointed government in Cochinchina 1945–1946), 122–123, 126–127, 162, 244

Nam Ha (Binh Xuyen pirate leader), 147

Nam Lua [Fifth Fire] (guerrilla gang & Hoa Hao leader), 113, 145

Nam Nu Gioi Chung (Saigon bourgeois journal), 52

Napoleon III [Louis-Napoléon Bonaparte] (French emperor 1852–1870), 238

National Party for the Independence of Vietnam [*Viet Nam Quoc Gia Doc Lap Dang*] (1945), 117, 121

National Party of Vietnam. *See* **VNQDD**

National United Front [*Mat Tran Quoc Gia Thong Nhut*] (August 1945), 121–122, 144, 147

NATO, N221

Naville, Pierre (French LO), 156, 167, 174, N174

Nay (prisoner sentenced to death), 10

Nazis; Nazi Germany, 235–236, 243, N112

Nehru, Jawaharlal (prime minister of India 1947–1964), 169

Nghe-Tinh soviets [peasant soviets of Nghe An & Ha Tinh provinces, 1930–1931], viii, 48–49, 167, 169, 200, 241

Nghi (WM), 137, 139

Ngo Chinh Phen (LIC), 5, 75–76, 147, **152**

Ngo Dinh Diem (American puppet president of South Vietnam 1955–1963), 169, 194, N116, N145

Ngo Thiem (TN; Rue Barbier assassin), 51

Ngo Van's relations:

—mother, 3–4, 17–22, 24, 26, 29–32, 34–36, 38, 42, 76, 87, 109, 111, 118–119, 130, 132, 179, 183

—father, 18, 20–22, 25–26, 29, 32–33, 39

—Sister Two, 140–141, N20

—Sister Five (living near Saigon), 18, 34, 37, 87, 111, N20

—Brother Seven [Anh Bay], 17–18, 20, 27, 29, 34, 36–39, 118, N20

—Brother Ten, 20, 132, N20

—Brother Twelve, 20, 38, 132, 140, N20

—Great Aunt, 29

—Great Uncle, 21

—Uncle Four, 29

—female cousin (living near Saigon), 35

—female cousin (living in Saigon), 40, 42

—male cousin (generous), 29

—male cousin (sons massacred), 118

—Bo (nephew), 132

—Xung (nephew), 132

—nephew (seen in 1997), xviii

—partner (in Vietnam), 108, N184

—Aunt Two (partner's mother), 107

—Chi Nam Thin (ICP; partner's sister), 104, 114, 148–150

—Do (older son), xxiii, 148, 154, 184, N184

—Oanh (daughter), xxiii, 148, N184

—Da (younger son), xxiii, 148, 184, 193–194, N184

Ngo Van's writings:

—*Au pays de la Cloche fêlée* (2000), ix, xiv, xviii

—*Au pays d'Héloïse* (2005), ix, xv

—*Avec Maximilien Rubel, une amitié, une lutte 1954–1996* (1997), N201

—*Bien Ca Chieu Hom* (poem, ca. 1931), 51

—*Contes d'autrefois du Vietnam* (2001), N30

—*Divination, magie et politique dans la Chine ancienne* (1976), xv

—*Le Joueur de flûte et l'Oncle Hô: Vietnam 1945–2005* (2005), ix, xvi–xvii

—"Prolétaires et paysans, retournez vos fusils!" (1951 article), 199

—*Revolutionaries They Could Not Break* (1995), 238

—"Ta Thu Thau and Bolshevik-Leninist Politics" (1939 article), 97

—*Utopie antique et guerre des paysans en Chine* (2004), xv

—*Vietnam 1920–1945: révolution et contre-révolution sous la domination coloniale* (1995), ix, xiv–xv, 1, 238, Nviii, N45

—*Vu an Moscou* (1937 pamphlet on the Moscow Trials), 91

See also Bibliography, pp. 246–249.

Ngo Van Xuyet [full name of Ngo Van], 76
Ngon (Arsenal worker), 138, 157
Nguyen Ai Quoc. *See* **Ho Chi Minh**
Nguyen An Ninh (VF, LL; one of the "Five
    Dragons"), xiv, 40–42, 44–45, 56–57, 60,
    77–79, 81–82, 107, 155–156, 158, 163,
    165, 201, 240, Nviii, N45
"Nguyen An Ninh Secret Society" [*Hoi Kin
    Nguyen An Ninh*] (probably nonexistant
    movement, 1928–1929), 45, N45
Nguyen Binh [Nguyen Phuong Thao] (ICP;
    Vietminh commander), 143, 147
Nguyen Binh Khiem (poet), 106
Nguyen Dinh Chieu [a.k.a. Do Chieu]
    (anticolonialist poet), 39
Nguyen Hoa Hiep (VNQDD member &
    "Third Division" leader), N124
Nguyen Hue Minh (LO; partner of Ho Huu
    Tuong, sister of Nguyen Trung Nguyet),
    153, 167
Nguyen Huu Dung [a.k.a. Ba De] (Tonkin
    TR), 121
Nguyen Huu The (prisoner), 70
Nguyen Kim Luong (TR), 87
Nguyen Ngoc Dien (Cao Dai leader),
    105–107
Nguyen Ngoc Suong (executed woman
    doctor), 138
Nguyen Ngoc Tot (woman prisoner), 68
Nguyen Te My (Tonkin TR), 120
Nguyen Thai Hoc (VNQDD leader), N46
Nguyen The Truyen (VF; founder of AIP;
    one of the "Five Dragons"), 159, 240
Nguyen Thi Ba (woman prisoner), 68
Nguyen Thi Dai ["Chi Day"] (woman
    prisoner), 67–68
Nguyen Thi Loi (LL), 129
Nguyen Thi My. *See* **Vo Thi Bang**
Nguyen Thi Nam (woman prisoner), 69
Nguyen Thi Nho (woman prisoner), 68
Nguyen Thi Sau (woman prisoner), 68
Nguyen Ton Hoan (Tonkin TR student), 120
Nguyen Trung Nguyet ["Chi Nguyet," a.k.a.
    Bao Lan] (TN; Rue Barbier accomplice),
    51, 67–69, 153
Nguyen Uyen Diem (TR; comrade of Thai
    Van Tam), 177
Nguyen Van Be (tortured prisoner), 60
Nguyen Van Chuyen (LIC, WM), 127, 144
Nguyen Van Cu (VF, LO), 167
Nguyen Van Dai (LO; partner of Tran Thi
    Chin), 153
Nguyen Van Dut (prisoner), 70, 73
Nguyen Van Hoang (LO; tortured prisoner),
    60
Nguyen Van Huong (WM), 137
Nguyen Van Kim (TR), 87
Nguyen Van Linh [a.k.a. René] (VF, LO,
    LIC, WM), 116, 119, 128–132, 139–142,
    149, 155, 167, 172, **173–174**, N174
Nguyen Van Man (imprisoned worker), 94
Nguyen Van Nam [a.k.a. Antony] (VF, LO,
    LL, LIC), 119, 128, 130, 132, 142, 149,
    155, 167, **172–173**, 197
Nguyen Van Nguyen (ICP, LL), 59
Nguyen Van Nhi (VF, LO), 167
Nguyen Van Nho (imprisoned worker), 94
Nguyen Van Nu (prisoner, author of
    Memories of Poulo Condore), 71
Nguyen Van Sam (Constitutionalist editor of
    Le Flambeau d'Annam), 90, 147
Nguyen Van Sang (peasant prisoner), 11,
    72–73
Nguyen Van So (VF, LL), 138, 157, **163**
Nguyen Van Soi (TR), 93–94
Nguyen Van Tam ("The Tiger of Cai Lay"),
    146
Nguyen Van Tao (VF, ICP, LL; head of
    Vietminh police in Cochinchina; later Ho
    Chi Minh's Minister of Labor), 56–59, 65,
    77–78, 82, 86, 89, 99–100, 119, 122, 126,
    156, 161, 165
Nguyen Van Thieu (American puppet presi-
    dent of South Vietnam 1965–1975), 169
Nguyen Van Thinh (TN; Rue Barbier
    assassin), 51
Nguyen Van Thinh [Dr. Thinh] (puppet
    president of "Republic of Cochinchina,"
    1946), 146
Nguyen Van Thuong (LO, WM), 55, 60, 176
Nguyen Van Tien (LL), 94, 138, 157,
    166–167
Nguyen Van Trong (TR), 94
Nguyen Van Trong (ICP; provincial
    Vietminh chief), 133–135, 137
Nguyen Van Vang (LIC), 131, 144
Nietzsche, Friedrich (German philosopher),
    201, Nviii
NLF [National Liberation Front, a.k.a.
    Vietcong] (successor of the Vietminh,
    1960–1975), xviii, 220–221, N145, N219
North Africa, 90, 174

Notre Voix [Our Voice] (Hanoi ICP paper), 243

Oanh (Ngo Van's daughter), xxiii, 148, N184
"October" group (LO group associated with *Thang Muoi*), 153, N153
"On the March" [*Len Dang*] (patriotic song), 117, 123, 136
Ong Thiet (district school teacher), 31
opium, 97
Orwell, George (radical English writer), vii, 2, Nxiii, N2
OSS [American Office of Strategic Services], 120, 244
Ouvrard (Sûreté Inspector in Cambodia), 100

Pagès, Pierre-André (Governor of Cochinchina 1934–1939), 86, 92
Pannekoek, Anton (theorist of workers councils), 237, N2
Paris Commune (1871), 204, 210, 238, 241, N210
Pascal, Blaise (17th-century French philosopher), 1, N1
Paz, Abel (anarchist historian), xviii
Paz, Maurice (French LO), 159
peasant revolts:
—1908, 41, 49
—1916, 18, 106
—1930–1931, 4, 47–50, 56, 165, 169, 241. *See also* **Nghe-Tinh soviets**
—1938, 96
—1940, 108, 111, 243
—1945, 126, 143
Pellico, Silvio: *My Prisons,* 4, N4
Pennetier, Marcel (UOI), 199
Peng Shuzi (Chinese TR), 148
people's committees, viii, 121, 123, 125, 127, 131, 144, 171, 173, 177, 244. *See also* **action committees**
"Père Duchêne" (radical song), xv
Péret (boss in Saigon), 54
Péret, Benjamin (surrealist poet; UOI), 199
Perrard, Guy (CCG), 201, 203
Perroche (head torturer), 6, 16, 75
Pesch, Edgar (UOI, CCG), 199, 201
Pétain, Philippe (Vichy France head of state 1940–1944), 111–112, N112
Pham Ngoc Thach (doctor & anticolonialist;

founder of JAG), 112, 117, 122
Pham Thi Loi (TN; Rue Barbier participant), 68
Pham Van Dong (LO), 55
Pham Van Dong (ICP; prime minister of Vietnam 1955–1987), 68
Pham Van Kinh ["An Do"] (ICP prisoner), 70, 115
Pham Van Muoi (LIC), 76, **152**
Phan Boi Chau (pioneer anticolonial leader), 155, 240, Nviii, N155
Phan Chau Trinh [a.k.a. Phan Chu Trinh] (VF; one of the "Five Dragons"), 41–43, 172, 240, N155
Phan Khanh Van (worker & writer friend), 52
Phan Thanh Hoa (Tonkin TR student), 120
Phan Van Chanh (VF, AIP, LO, LL), 55–56, 138, 157, 159, **163–164**
Phan Van Hai (TR), 53
Phan Van Hum (VF, LO, LL), 44–45, 58–59, 78, 88, 99, 144, **155–158**, 166–167
Phan Van Kim (assassin of Judge Nadaillat), 45
Phan Van Truong (VF; one of the "Five Dragons"), 7, 43–44, 240, N44
Phnong tribespeople, 58
Phuc (UOI), 184, 199
Phung (timorous roommate in Saigon), 44–46
Phung (helpful contact in My Tho), 108
Phuong Lan (friend of Ta Thu Thau), 161, 179
Piatakov, Georgy (Bolshevik), 85
Plato (ancient Greek philosopher), 4
Plutarch (ancient Greek biographer), 4
Politzer, Georges: *Elementary Principles of Philosophy,* 163
Pompidou, Georges (French prime minister 1962–1968; president 1969–1974), 215
Popular Front (France 1936–1938), 65, 76–77, 82–84, 87, 89–90, 161, 168, 170, 173, 177, 235–236, 242–243, N12, N77, N210
Popular Front (Spain 1936–1939), 235, N2
Porte des Lilas (1957 film by René Clair), 194
Poulo Condore (penal colony), N18
POUM [*Partido Obrero de Unificación Marxista*/Workers Party for Marxist Unification] (Spanish revolutionary Marxist party), 2, 192, 197, 243, N2

Quan Thuong Hao (Tonkin TR), 179
Quatrième Internationale [Fourth International] (French TR journal), 171–172
quoc ngu (Vietnamese writing system), 238
Quoc Te IV [Fourth International] (TR monthly in Paris), 173–174

Radek, Karl (Bolshevik), 85
Radical Party [*Parti Radical*] (French centrist party), 82
Ravachol (French anarchist), xv
Reed, John: *Ten Days That Shook the World*, 4, N4
Remarque, Erich Maria: *All Quiet on the Western Front*, 4, N4
Résurrection, La (AIP paper, 1928–1929), 159
Revolutionary Workers Party [*Dang Tho Thuyen Cach Mang*] (TR party, 1945), 166
Revolutionary Youth League. *See* **Thanh Nien**
Riazanov, David (Bolshevik Marx scholar), 4, N4
Richepin, Jean (French poet) 43, N43
Rivoal, Henri-Georges (Acting Governor of Cochinchina, 1936), 78
Rodríguez, Agustín (POUM, UOI, CCG), 199, 201, 203
Rosmer, Alfred (French LO), 159
Rossi, Tino (popular French singer), 96
Roubaud, Louis: *Vietnam: la tragédie indochinoise*, 4, 46–47, N4
Rousseau, Jean-Jacques (18th-century French writer), 4, 43, Nviii, N43, N155
Rousset, David (French LO), 174, N174
Rubel, Maximilien (CCG; radical Marx scholar), 2, 197, 201–203, 237, N201
Rue Barbier affair (1928–1930), 44, 50–51, 67–68, 153
Russell, Bertrand (British philosopher), 220, N220
Russia [USSR/Soviet Union], vii, xvii, 1–2, 57, 65, 85, 89–90, 157, 160, 174–175, 197–198, 200, 220, 234–237, 242–244, N2, N4, N77, N90
—1905 revolution, N2
—1917 revolution (February & October), 1, 107, 198, 200, 234, N2, N4, N77, N201
See also **Moscow Trials**
Russian Communist Party [Communist

Party of the USSR], 77, 89, 234, 236–237, N86. *See also* **Bolshevik Party**
Russo-Japanese war (1904–1905), N155

Saigon (newspaper), 162
Saigon City Council. *See* **elections**
Saigon-Cholon Workers Federation [General Workers Federation/Syndicalist Workers Federation] [*Lien Doan Tho Thuyen/Lien Uy Tho Thuyen*] (1937), 86–87, 93, 154
Saigon-Shanghai-Osaka [*Saigon–Thuong hai–Hoanh tan*] (travel account), 60
Sartre, Jean-Paul (French writer), 220, N220
Second International (1889–), 235
Sedov, Leon [Lèv] (Trotsky's son), 177
Séguy, Georges (CGT leader), 211–212, 215, N210
Serge, Victor: *Memoirs of a Revolutionary*, vii, 234
Sino-Japanese war (1937–1945), 176
Situationist International (innovative revolutionary group, 1957–1972), 237
Social Studies Circle (Paris, 1934), 173
Socialisme ou Barbarie [Socialism or Barbarism] (French ultraleftist journal & group, 1948–1965), 237, N203
socialist parties, 235
Socialist Workers Party of North Vietnam [*Dang Tho Thuyen Xa Hoi Viet Bac*] (TR party, 1945), 178
Souvarine, Boris: *Stalin: A Critical Survey of Bolshevism*, 234
soviets, N2. *See also* **workers councils; Nghe-Tinh soviets**
Spain (civil war & revolution, 1936–1939), vii–viii, 2, 90, 130, 157, 192–193, 197, 199, N2
Spanish Communist Party, N2
Spinoza, Baruch (17th-century philosopher), 202
Staël, Madame de (French writer), 52
Stalin, Josef (USSR dictator 1927–1953), xvii, 1, 57, 64, 71, 77, 85–86, 89, 101, 168, 198, 234–237, N77, N86
Stalinism; Stalinists, ix, xvii, 2, 198, 234–237, N201
—Chinese, x, N145
—French. *See* **French Communist Party**
—Russian, 1, 91, 232–233, 235, N86
—Spanish, 192, N2
—Vietnamese, vii–viii, 56–57, 64, 77, 82,

85, 87, 89–92, 98–100, 115, 119–123, 126–130, 136, 138, 144, 152, 156–157, 160–162, 164–171, 173–174, 177–178, 197, 236, 240, 242–245, etc. *See also* **Indochinese Communist Party**; **Vietminh**

See also **Communist parties**

State Employees Federation [*Fédération des Fonctionnaires*], 121–122

strikes:

—1930–1931, 50, 54, 65

—1936–1937, 83–84, 86, 92–94, 153–154, 242

—1938, 96

Sun Tzu: *The Art of War,* 85

Sun Yat-sen (Chinese nationalist leader), 4, 106, N4

Sung (Saigon housemate & comrade), 4

Suu (Saigon friend), 141

Suzanne (wife of Paco Gómez), 193–194

Swift, Jonathan (17th-century satirist), xv

Syndicalist Workers Federation. *See* **Saigon-Cholon Workers Federation**

Ta Doi Lap [Communist Left Opposition] (1931–ca. 1935), 52, 54–55, 154, 160, 164, 167. *See also* **Left Opposition (Vietnamese)**

Ta Khac Triem (TR), 87, 93–94, **154**

Ta Thu Thau (VF, AIP, LO, LL), 55–58, 60, 65, 77–78, 81–82, 86, 89, 97–100, 105, 127, 138, 148, 156–157, **158–163**, 164–167, 175, 179

Tai, Hue-Tam Ho: *Radicalism and the Origins of the Vietnamese Revolution,* Nviii, N45

Tan Lo [Ngo Van pseudonym], 97

Tan Viet [*Tan Viet Cach Mang Dang*/New Vietnam Revolutionary Party] (1925–1929), 51

Taoism; Taoists, xv, 106

Tay (prison guard), 8

Terauchi Hisaichi (Japanese general), 126

Tet Offensive (1968), 219, N219

Thai Van Tam (Tonkin TR), **177**

Than Chung (newspaper), 155, 158

Thang Muoi [October] (theoretical journal of Ta Doi Lap, 1931–1932; revived 1938–1939), 52, 95, 167, 169, 172, N153

Thanh Nien [*Thanh Nien Cach Mang Dong Chi Hoi*/Revolutionary Youth League]

(1925–1930; precursor of ICP), 44, 50–51, 67–68, 169, 241, N170

[*Thay* = "Teacher"]

Thay Giao Dong (village school teacher), 22

Thay Giao Nai (district school teacher), 31

Thay Ung (district school teacher), 31

Thay Tho [Wage and Salary Workers] (TR bulletin, 1938), 169–170, N153

Thi Nhut [Tran Thi Nhut; some other sources give "Tran Thu Thuy"] (TN; "femme fatale" in Rue Barbier affair), 68

Thien (WM), 131

Thiet (schoolmaster), 34–35

Thieu (puppet dictator). *See* **Nguyen Van Thieu**

Thinh, Dr. *See* **Nguyen Van Thinh**

"Third Division" [*De Tam Su Doan*] (independent nationalist anticolonialist army, 1945–1946), 124, 131–133, 137, 142, N46, N124

Third International [Comintern] (1919–1943), 1, 90, 144, 160, 198, 234–236, 241, N50

Third World anticolonial struggles, ix–x, xiii, 217–218

Tho Thuyen Tranh Dau [Workers' Struggle] (paper of Bolshevik-Leninist Group, 1936), 168

Thoi Dam [Chronicles] (paper of Tonkin *Tia Sang* group, 1938), 177

Thorez, Maurice (French CP leader 1930–1964), N210

Thu (LL), 136

Tia Sang [The Spark] (Saigon TR paper, 1939), 97, 170–172, 177, N153

Tia Sang [The Spark] (Tonkin TR paper & group, ca. 1938–1939), 177

Tien Dao [Vanguard] (newsletter of LIC), 4, 65, 74, 76, 242

Tien Quan [Vanguard] (LO broadsheet, Brussels, 1930), 156, 167

Tieng Tho [Workers' Voice] (TR paper in postwar France), 199

To Hoai (writer), 179

Toller, Ernst (radical German writer), N2

Ton Duc Thang (TN, ICP; instigator of Rue Barbier murder; Vietnam president 1969–1980), 51, 68

Ton Thanh Nien ["Ton the Young"] (prisoner), 71

Tong (ICP prisoner; later Vietminh police

agent), 114

Tran Chanh (Sûreté Inspector), 108

Tran Dang (journalist), 178

Tran Dinh Minh [a.k.a. Nguyen Hai Au] (Tonkin writer; LIC, WM), 120–121, 130, 142, **176**

Tran Huu Do (fellow exile in Mekong Delta), 110

Tran Nguon Phieu (resistance fighter), 158

Tran Quang Vinh (Cao Dai leader), 145

Tran Quoc Kieu (WM), 131

Tran Thi Chin (TN, ICP, LO; sister of Tran Thi Muoi), **153**

Tran Thi Day (woman prisoner), 69

Tran Thi Hanh (woman prisoner), 69

Tran Thi Muoi ["Chi Muoi"] (ICP, LO, LIC; partner of Anh Gia), 55, **152–153**

Tran Tien Chinh (Tonkin LO), 121

Tran Trong Kim (prime minister of Japanese puppet government in Vietnam, 1945), 116

Tran Truong (TN; Rue Barbier assassin), 51

Tran Van An (independent anticolonial-ist, later a leader of the National United Front), 57

Tran Van Giau (VF, ICP, Vietminh; head of Nam Bo Provisional Executive Commit-tee), 65, 70–71, 82, 115, 122–127, 129, 133, 142, 144–145, 162, 164, 166, 171, 244

Tran Van Si (VF, LO, LL), 167, 172–173, **174–175**

Tran Van Thach (VF, AIP, LL), 56–59, 65, 92, 99, 115, 123, 138, 156–157, 163, **164–166**, N138

Tran Van Thanh (WM), 131

Tran Van Ty (judge), 8–9, 15–16, 146

Tran Van Vi (ICP prisoner), 70, 85

Tranh Dau [Struggle] (Vietnamese-language paper of *La Lutte* group), 95, 98–99, 148, 156, 166

Traven, B. [Ret Marut] (anarchist novelist), xv, N2

Tricoire (prison chaplain), 125

Trinh Dinh Thao (lawyer), 76

Trinh Hung Ngau (VF, LL; anarchist), 56, Nviii

Trinh Van Lau (LIC), 64, 75–76, 111, 122, **152**, 242, N11

Trotsky, Leon (Bolshevik leader), 1, 4, 71, 77, 85, 103, 105, 168, 175, 177, 198,

234–237, 241, N4, N77, N86

Trotskyism; Trotskyists, ix, 2, 197–198, 234–237, 242–243

—Chinese, 176

—French, 199, N174

—Russian, 57, 85, 235

—Vietnamese, vii–viii, 56–57, 64, 85–87, 89–90, 92–93, 98–100, 121, 131, 144, 149–179, 199–200, 234, 242–245, N11, etc.

See also **Left Opposition**

Trum Nhut (impoverished neighbor), 32

Truong Minh Hai (imprisoned teacher), 158

Tsuchihashi Yuichi (Japanese Governor-General of Indochina, March–August 1945), 116

Tu Cao (Marseilles barber), 63

Tu Duc (emperor of Vietnam 1847–1883), 238

Tu Ty (Binh Xuyen pirate leader), 147

Tu Van Hon (TR typographer-journalist in Cambodia), 95, 100–101

Tuan (village school inspector), 26

Tuan (Tonkin TR student), 120

Ty (sailor friend), 60–61

Typographers Trade Union Federation (Hanoi), 178

UNEF [*Union Nationale des Étudiants de France*/French National Student Union], 211–212, N211

Ung Hoa (LL), 157

United States of America (in Vietnam War), vii, xvi–xvii, 120, 219–221, N18, N145, N219

UOI [*Union Oùvrière Internationale*/ International Workers' Association] (France-based ultraleftist group, 1948–1952), 199, 201

USSR. *See* **Russia**

Van Tien [nickname of blind prisoner], 71, 73

Van Van Ba (LIC), 76, **152**

Van Van Ky (LIC), 15, 75–76, 122, **151**

Vandenstein (worker friend in France), 194

Vanguard Women (female counterpart of Vanguard Youth), 118

Vanguard Youth. *See* **JAG**

Varenne, Alexandre (French socialist; Governor-General of Indochina 1925–

1928), N155
Vérité, La [The Truth] (French Communist League paper), 160
Vichy France (1940–1944), 112, 236, 243, N112, N116, N148
Viet Nam Quoc Dan Dang. *See* **VNQDD**
Vietcong [National Liberation Front/NLF] (successor of Vietminh, 1960–1975), xviii, 220–221, N145, N219
Vietminh [*Viet Nam Doc Lap Dong Minh Ho*/Front for the Independence of Vietnam] (ICP front group, 1941–1950s), 114, 119–123, 126–128, 130–137, 140, 142–147, 149–150, 157, 162–163, 166–167, 169, 173–174, 176, 179, 200, 243–245, N124.
Vietnam Modernization Society [a.k.a. Vietnam Reformation Society/*Viet Nam Duy Tan Hoi*] (1904–1912), 240, N155
Vietnam Restoration Society [*Viet Nam Quang Phuc Hoi*] (1912–1920s), 240, N155
Vietnam War (1960–1975), vii, xvi–xvii, 219–221, N18, N145, N219
Vietnamese Communist Party. *See* **Indochinese Communist Party**
Vishinsky, Andrey (prosecutor in Moscow Trials), 77, 82
Vishnu (Hindu god), 106
VNQDD [*Viet Nam Quoc Dan Dang*/ National Party of Vietnam, a.k.a. Vietnamese Nationalist Party] (1927–1930), 44, 51, 241, N45, N46, N124
Vo Buu Binh (LO), 87, 93–94, **154**
Vo Nguyen Giap (ICP; Vietminh military leader), 120

Vo Thi Bang [a.k.a. Nguyen Thi My] (LO), 60, **153**
Vo Thi Van (ICP, LO, LIC; partner of Lu Sanh Hanh), 87, **153**
Vo Van Don (LIC; coolie workmate), 4, 64, 75–76, 85, 122, **151–152**
Voix Libre, La [The Free Voice] (Saigon paper 1923–1932), 176
Voline: *The Unknown Revolution,* vii, 234

Waldeck-Rochet (French CP leader), 210, 221, N210
Wilde, Oscar (British writer), xv
women rebels, viii, 47, 67–69, 92
workers councils, viii, 2, 120, 143, 173, 177, 197, 200, 244, N2
Workers for National Salvation [*Cong Nhan Cuu Quoc*] (Vietminh national labor union), 130
Workers' Militia [*Doan Cong Binh*] (formed by Go Vap streetcar workers, 1945–1946), viii, 130–134, 137, 142, 144, 174, 176, 245
Workers' Slate (*So lao dong*), 57–59, 160
World War I (1914–1918), 17, 219–220, 234–235, N2
World War II (1939–1945), 101, 116, 118, 185, 219–220, 236, 243–244, N185

Xung (nephew of Ngo Van), 132

Yen Bai revolt (1930), 46–47, 50, 155–156, 160, 163, 165, 167, 241, N46

Zinoviev, Grigory (Bolshevik), 77